£20. BPNA. Jan 1993

CLINICS IN DEVELOPMENTAL MEDICINE NO. 110
HANDEDNESS AND DEVELOPMENTAL DISORDER

Clinics in Developmental Medicine No. 110

HANDEDNESS AND DEVELOPMENTAL DISORDER

D. V. M. BISHOP

Department of Psychology
University of Manchester

1990
Mac Keith Press
OXFORD: Blackwell Scientific Publications Ltd.
PHILADELPHIA: J. B. Lippincott Co.

© 1990 Mac Keith Press
5a Netherhall Gardens, London NW3 5RN

All rights reserved. No part of this publication may be reproduced, stored in a retrieval system, or transmitted in any form or by any means, electronic, mechanical, photocopying, recording or otherwise, without the prior permission of the publishers

First published 1990

British Library Cataloguing in Publication Data

Bishop, Dorothy V. M.
  Handedness and developmental disorder.
  1. Man. Left-handedness and right-handedness
  I. Title
  152.335

ISBN (UK) 0 632 02842 4
    (USA) 0 397 48019 9

Printed in Great Britain at The Lavenham Press Ltd., Lavenham, Suffolk
Mac Keith Press is supported by **The Spastics Society, London, England**

To Patrick Rabbitt

AUTHOR'S APPOINTMENTS

DOROTHY VERA MARGARET BISHOP, M.A., M.Phil., D.Phil.   MRC Senior Research Fellow, Department of Psychology, University of Manchester.

CONTENTS

ACKNOWLEDGEMENTS	page viii
FOREWORD *Paul Satz*	ix
1. WHY HANDEDNESS?	1
2. HANDEDNESS AND CEREBRAL LATERALIZATION	18
3. THE GENETICS OF HANDEDNESS	32
4. THE DEVELOPMENT OF HANDEDNESS	53
5. THE DEFINITION AND MEASUREMENT OF HANDEDNESS	69
6. COGNITIVE CORRELATES OF HANDEDNESS	82
7. EARLY BRAIN DAMAGE AND PATHOLOGICAL LEFT-HANDEDNESS	90
8. EPILEPSY	101
9. MENTAL IMPAIRMENT	104
10. AUTISM AND RETT SYNDROME	110
11. SPECIFIC READING RETARDATION (DEVELOPMENTAL DYSLEXIA)	117
12. SPECIFIC DEVELOPMENTAL DISORDERS OF SPEECH AND LANGUAGE	130
13. STUTTERING	140
14. HANDEDNESS, HORMONES AND DEVELOPMENTAL DISORDERS	146
15. CONCLUSIONS AND CLINICAL IMPLICATIONS	163
APPENDIX—A Selection of Assessment Procedures	169
REFERENCES	179
AUTHOR INDEX	199
SUBJECT INDEX	204

ACKNOWLEDGEMENTS

The impetus for writing a book on handedness came in 1988, when I was invited by Christopher Gillberg to give a series of seminars on developmental disorders, including one on handedness, to a group of Swedish paediatricians and psychologists. I was delighted when a common interest in the topic of handedness first introduced me to Christopher some 10 years ago, and I am pleased now to be able to record my thanks to him for providing, albeit unwittingly, the stimulus for this book.

I felt a book was needed because of what I perceived as the theoretical stagnation of research in this area, in my view largely due to widespread reliance on inventories for the measurement of handedness. Having said that, I would like to note one striking exception to this trend. My early interest in this topic as an undergraduate was stimulated by reading the work of Marian Annett, who was never satisfied with simply recording superficial aspects of handedness behaviour but tried to find ways of getting at the underlying causes of such behaviour. I would like to take this opportunity to thank her for opening my eyes to fresh approaches. Although we sometimes find ourselves on different sides of a theoretical fence, I know research on handedness would be impoverished without her contribution.

It is fitting that this book should be published by the Mac Keith Press, as it was Dr Martin Bax and his editorial team who published my first research paper on this topic in the journal *Developmental Medicine and Child Neurology* in 1980. I would like to extend especial thanks to Dr Pamela Davies who encouraged me at all stages of the work, and to Mr Pat Chappelle, for his meticulous and sensitive work at the copy-editing stage.

FOREWORD

I am delighted to have been asked to write this foreword to Dorothy Bishop's volume on *Handedness and Developmental Disorder*. In 15 tightly packed chapters she has managed to address most of the substantive issues on this lively and controversial topic. Her appraisal of these issues is presented in her usual clear, incisive manner, such that the reader is enabled to distinguish fact from myth.

It is unfortunate that this subject has engendered so much controversy and confusion over the years. Bias regarding left-handedness dates at least from the Old Testament and has persisted throughout antiquity to the present day. As Hardyck and Petrinovitch[1] noted in an earlier review:

> Among the contemporary ideological descendants of the Biblical scribe who, along with their ancestor, would be eager to consign the left-handed to burn in hell forever, would be found a good many neurologists, neurosurgeons, and neuropsychologists, sharing among themselves the frustrations of seeing their theories of cerebral function unable to account for the bilateral cerebral organization found in many of the left-handed.

Indeed, these theoretical frustrations led one observer to lament that left-handers 'seem to have been created on purpose to upset all the different conceptions which have prevailed during the last century in connection with the pathology and physiology of the two hemispheres.'[2]

In the past two decades, Dorothy Bishop has been one of the foremost thinkers on the topic of handedness and development disorder. The present volume, which integrates much of her earlier and current work, as well as the world literature on the subject, represents one of her finest contributions to date.

She opens her concluding remarks by noting that, 'There is almost no pattern of cerebral lateralization or handedness that has not at some time been mooted as the cause or correlate of one kind of developmental disorder', and goes on to recommend three ways in which some of this confusion could be resolved: '(1) by being aware of methodological problems that bedevil handedness research and lead to spurious associations; (2) by adopting a theoretical perspective that distinguishes different reasons why handedness and disorder might be linked; and (3) by using assessment procedures that can distinguish between theories' (p. 163).

Bishop buttresses each of these recommendations with a critical appraisal of the strengths and weaknesses of apposite studies. A major theme that carries across each of the chapters, in particular that on developmental disorders, is the concern for type I error in published reports. Bishop notes a traditional disrespect for the null hypothesis—a position which my colleagues and I share.[3] She suggests that this attitude may in part be shaped by publication bias in journals which favour reports of significant rather than null results. For example, if for every published report noting significant findings 19 null reports go unpublished, then in meta-analysis studies combining results from the literature the reporting bias inevitably will be increased.

Bishop offers numerous examples of how flaws in methodology, theory and/or assessment may lead to premature or misleading conclusions. Nowhere is this more evident than on the topic of cognitive impairment in left-handers, including speech and reading disorders. Bishop shows that if one accepts study reports without regard to methodological merit, then one will find those which strengthen traditional myths and fears concerning left-handedness. However, her penetrating critique of the literature shows that the evidence for a link between handedness and disorder (including cognitive impairment) is inconclusive. If one examines the better controlled population as well as clinic studies, left-handers do not, on the average differ from right-handers. Nor has a link between left-handedness and speech or reading disorder been clearly demonstrated.

With respect to research on stuttering, Bishop cites Bloodstein's humerous remark that, 'It has been a notable and constant feature of the cerebral dominance theory of stuttering for nearly fifty years that every time it is given up for dead it twitches.'[4] She notes that the putative links between handedness and stuttering rest largely on studies conducted in earlier decades using less rigorous designs. In the last decade, most studies have obtained null results. Nevertheless, the hope that such a link will be proved persists, prompting Bishop to warn that such optimism 'seems incautious given the multitude of cherished theories that have been broken on the rack of stuttering research' (p. 145).

Her chapter on handedness, hormones and developmental disorders represents the most comprehensive and perhaps the most incisive contribution to the volume. She notes that the hormonal theory of Geschwind and Galaburda[5] is extremely compelling, with broad explanatory attempts to integrate concepts of laterality and developmental disorder with prenatal alterations in brain organization. The theory has attracted widespread and often uncritical acceptance in the scientific literature. However, Bishop asks whether it deserves the attention it has received. After a critical appraisal of the evidence, she concludes that this attention may have been ill-deserved. Although the theory represents a bold and perhaps creative attempt to integrate data on handedness, developmental disorder (reading and speech) and autoimmune disorder, evidence associating left-handedness with dyslexia—a critical link in the theory—remains lacking. Indeed, Bishop contends that the report by Geschwind and Behan[6] of an increased rate of dyslexia in left-handers 'is so discrepant with other studies that it does more to cast doubt on the validity of their study than to convince one that an association exists' (p. 162).

While a link between dyslexia and autoimmune disorder has some weak support, the explanation for this association remains obscure. Another problem with the hormonal theory is that it is difficult to determine what would constitute disproof. Bishop captures the essence of the problem as follows:

We have seen that the theory has been used to predict that left-handers will have both inferior and superior verbal abilities. Because the precise outcome depends on testosterone levels, sensitivity of target issues to testosterone, timing and duration of hormonal influences, duration of pregnancy and age at puberty, almost any pattern of cognitive abilities can be explained in terms of the theory. (p. 162)

In summary, Bishop has critiqued magnificently the major issues on handedness and developmental disorder. The volume is informative in style and content, and is appropriate for students, educators, clinicians and researchers.

PAUL SATZ, PH.D.,
PROFESSOR OF MEDICAL PSYCHOLOGY,
CHIEF OF NEUROPSYCHOLOGY,
UNIVERSITY OF CALIFORNIA,
LOS ANGELES.

REFERENCES

1. Hardyck, C., Petrinovitch, C. F. (1977) 'Left-handedness.' *Psychological Bulletin*, **84**, 385–404.
2. Subirana, A. (1969) 'Handedness and cerebral dominance.' *In:* Vinken, P. J., Bruyn, G. W. (Eds.) *Handbook of Clinical Neurology*, Amsterdam: North Holland. (p. 248)
3. Soper, H., Cicchetti, D., Satz, P., Light, R., Orsini, D. L. (1988) 'Null hypothesis disrespect in neuropsychology: dangers of alpha and beta errors.' *Journal of Clinical and Experimental Neuropsychology*, **10**, 225–270.
4. Bloodstein, O. (1981) *A Handbook on Stuttering. 3rd Edn.* Chicago: National Easter Seal Society. (p. 139).
5. Geschwind, N., Galaburda, A. M. (1985) 'Cerebral lateralization. Biological mechanisms, associations and pathology.' *Archives of Neurology*, **42**, 428–459 (Part I); 521–552 (Part II); 634–654 (Part III).
6. Geschwind, N., Behan, P. (1982) 'Left-handedness: association with immune disease, migraine, and developmental learning disorder.' *Proceedings of the National Academy of Sciences*, **79**, 5097–5100.

1
WHY HANDEDNESS?

We have many paired organs that are structurally symmetrical, but in most cases they are also functionally symmetrical. Human handedness is an intriguing exception. The main focus of interest in this book is the neuropsychological significance of individual variation in handedness. However, before we can address this issue, we need to know something about the nature and origins of human handedness. The question 'why handedness?' can be dissected into two distinct components. First, why do we show a preference for one side rather than developing equal skill with both hands? In other words, why aren't people ambidextrous? Second, given that hand preference exists, why is there such a preponderance of right-handers, instead of equal numbers of people preferring the left and the right?

Why aren't people ambidextrous?
Imagine a world in which, instead of showing hand preference, people had an equal ability to do skilled tasks with either hand. One can see that this would have certain advantages in making human beings more adaptable. A traveller wedged up against the window in an aeroplane would be able to write or eat with the unrestricted hand, whichever this may be. A mechanic crawling beneath a car would be able to use a screwdriver with the hand nearest the component. A broken arm would not prevent one from writing.

If ambidexterity makes people more able to adapt to a changing environment, then why do humans show handedness? There are two possibilities. Either handedness does have advantages over ambidexterity, leading to its evolution by natural selection, or handedness is a non-adaptive by-product of some other adaptive human characteristic.

The notion that handedness is advantageous has been popular for many years but is usually stated as a self-evident truth (*e.g.* Hildreth 1949*a*). To evaluate this explanation more critically, two sources of evidence are relevant: studies of human handedness for different activities, and data on hand preference in other species.

Degree of human hand preference shown for different activities
Two related hypotheses can be formulated concerning the adaptive advantages of handedness. The first may be termed the *motor learning* hypothesis. In the early stages of learning a motor skill, performance is slow, different muscle groups are poorly coordinated, and feedback is monitored so that corrective adjustments can be made. As the movement pattern is learned, a motor programme is developed that specifies the sequence of coordinated movements of different muscles, so enabling the action to be executed as a stereotyped, pre-programmed whole, without using feedback systems (Keele 1982). It makes sense to suppose that the

more stereotyped the movement pattern, the more advantageous it would be to concentrate learning on one side.

If this is correct, then we would expect handedness to be most apparent in highly skilled, stereotyped, pre-programmed movements. Stereotypy of a movement will to some extent depend on the amount of practice an individual has had in executing that movement, but it will also be affected by the speed and precision involved in the action, and on how far the movement involves adaptation to changing external circumstances. Instantaneous, ballistic movements, such as throwing a dart, provide no opportunity for utilizing corrective feedback, so have to be pre-programmed to be performed accurately. It follows, then, that frequency of carrying out an action and stereotypy can to some extent be dissociated, and some very frequent actions, such as carrying a dish of food, may be less stereotyped than relatively infrequent activities, such as throwing a cricket ball.

A further factor that is likely to be important is bilaterality of movement. Corballis and Beale (1976) suggested that handedness will be particularly beneficial in bimanual tasks, where the two hands perform complementary functions. Rather than both hands learning to perform either role, division of labour would enable each to acquire a specialized skill.

The second hypothesis may be termed the *interference* hypothesis. There is some evidence that learning a motor movement with one hand facilitates performance of mirror-image movements with the other hand. Young children carrying out an effortful motor action with one hand frequently produce associated movements of the other side (Connolly and Stratton 1968, Lazarus and Todor 1987). More rarely, individuals have been observed who produce mirror-writing when using the non-preferred hand (Fig. 1.1)*. The neurophysiological basis of such phenomenona is not understood. One view is that mirror movements are a consequence of the tonic function of ipsilaterally projecting pyramidal tracts. As the child develops, a callosally mediated inhibitory system matures, suppressing activity of the ipsilateral pathway (Dennis 1976, Nass 1985).

If learning a set of movements with one hand facilitates mirror movements of the other side, then handedness should be particularly adaptive when learning non-mirror-reversible tasks. For activities such as handwriting or operating a corkscrew there may be a functional advantage in restricting learning to one hand, because if one attempted to switch between hands there could be interference between the different sets of movements learned by each hand, rather than any positive transfer. In contrast, there should be no interference for activities that can be performed by enantiomorphic movements of the two hands (*i.e.* movements that are mirror-image counterparts). Brushing the teeth is an example of such a movement: the task may be performed by holding the toothbrush in the right hand and moving it up and down going from the left side of the mouth to the right, or by holding the brush in the left hand and starting from the right side of the mouth and going to the left. The left hand movement observed in a mirror is indistinguishable

---

*Many reported cases of mirror-writing occur when children are copying, and so could reflect perceptual confusion. Examples of spontaneous mirror-writing, such as that shown here, are harder to find.

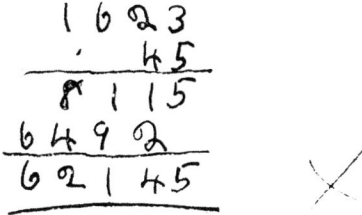

Fig. 1.1. *(a)* Ordinary writing of right-handed 11-year-old girl.

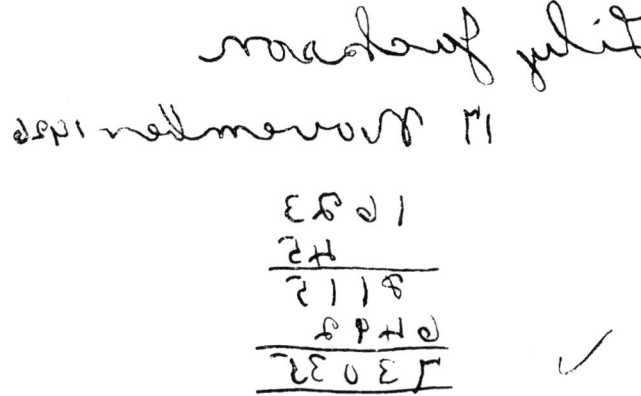

Fig. 1.1. *(b)* Spontaneous mirror-writing by same girl, written with left hand while right hand temporarily incapacitated. (Reprinted from Burt 1937, p. 343.)

from the unreflected right hand movement. In many cases, whether or not an action is mirror-reversible is determined by the design of implements: corkscrews, screwdrivers and wall can-openers are examples of devices that can be operated in one direction only. However, in other instances it is not the design of the implement but the product of the action that constrains direction of movement. Drawing with a pencil is mirror-reversible, writing is not. Thus an artist drawing a face may move the pencil in a clockwise direction, but could produce the same result using an anticlockwise movement of the other hand. However, when using a pencil to write one must proceed from left to right, so whereas the left-hander

TABLE 1.I
Percentage of children using the same hand in four trials (two sessions separated by two-week interval) (Bruml 1972)

Task	Group (age range)		
	Kindergarten (5:4–6:5) N = 60	Grade 2 (7:4–9:7) N = 60	Grade 4 (9:5–11:9) N = 60
Draw	100	100	100
Eat	87	80	100
Clasp hands	97	100	97
Snap fingers	97	100	97
Point	53	83	93
Clap adult's palm	87	83	93
Throw ball	80	97	93
Clap hand and knee	80	87	87
Reach high	87	79	83
Pick up ball	90	80	80
Touch nose	60	60	77
Build tower	57	60	67
Place beads in bottle	40	67	47

pushes the pencil towards and beyond the midline of the body, the right-hander pulls the pencil from the midline towards the side.

To test the predictions of these two hypotheses, we need to know to what extent people show handedness for different types of activities. Data on this question are sparser than one might have imagined. Although there have been numerous studies assessing hand preference for a wide range of activities, relatively few provide information about the extent to which an individual *consistently* prefers one side over a series of occasions. Buxton (1937) observed college freshmen carrying out the same unimanual action on 10 trials and computed the odd–even reliability for each activity. There was high, though by no means perfect, consistency in hand used from trial to trial for placing pegs in a pegboard and throwing; moderate consistency for reaching for an object; and very low consistency for the action of brushing imaginary lint from the clothing. Bruml (1972) reported the proportions of children who used the same hand on four different trials for a range of activities (Table 1.I). This study, like that of Buxton, illustrated variability from one task to another but did not include sufficient tasks to identify characteristics associated with stable preferences. For this information we have only questionnaire studies to rely on. Figure 1.2 shows data from a study by Provins *et al.* (1982), who asked students to rate 75 activities on a seven-point scale ranging from –3 (always performed with left hand) through 0 (no hand preference) to +3 (always performed with right hand).

Can we identify common properties of those tasks which give consistent hand preferences? To investigate this question, I rated each of the activities in Figure 1.2 on six dimensions: the extent to which it involved (1) strength, (2) precision and (3) speed, (4) whether or not it was instantaneous, and whether (5) mirror-reversible movements or (6) bilateral coordination were involved. Finally, I made a rough

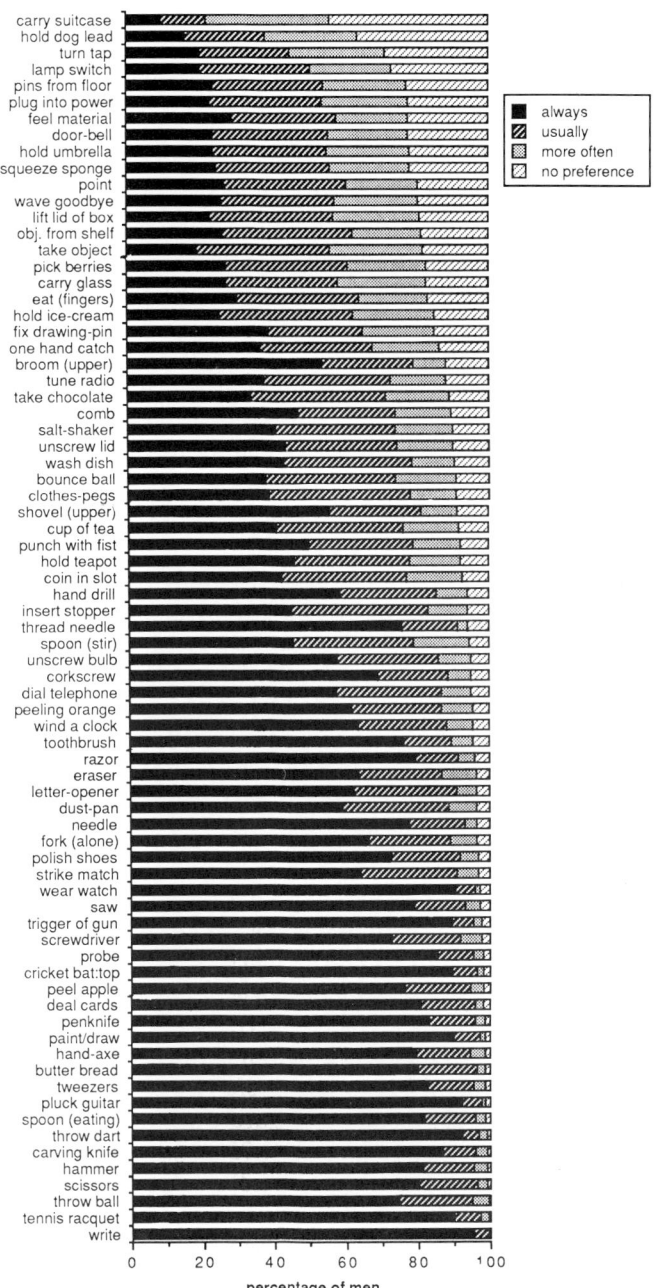

Fig. 1.2. Percentages of men responding ±3 (always R or always L), ±2 (usually R or usually L), ±1 (more often R or more often L) or 0 (no preference) to different items on a handedness questionnaire. (Data from Provins *et al.* 1982; sample comprised 934 male students.)

guess of the number of times the action would be carried out by an average man every year. (This latter variable was converted to a log to normalize data.) These data were entered into a multiple regression analysis to see which best predicted the frequency with which individuals showed a consistent hand preference. Precision of movement emerged as the strongest predictor, closely followed by bilaterality. The only other significant predictor was whether or not the movement was instantaneous. Thus the extent to which individuals show a consistent hand preference was greatest for precise movements, especially those which involve complementary actions of the two hands, and those requiring an instantaneous, pre-programmed movement (such as throwing). Virtually all activities that involved holding a tool in a precision (pincer) grip (Fig. 1.3) gave strong hand preferences. The one exception was holding a comb, where it would be physically awkward to reach the side of the head with the opposite hand. Grasping objects in a power (palmar) grip in order to pick them up or carry them was not an activity for which strong hand preferences were evident. The frequency of carrying out the movement was unrelated to hand preference (note, for instance, the relatively weak hand preference shown for turning on a tap compared to throwing a ball). These results, then, agreed well with predictions from the motor learning hypothesis. However, no support was obtained for the interference hypothesis. Contrary to expectation, whether or not a movement was mirror-reversible was not significantly related to consistency of hand preference. This informal analysis should not be regarded as definitive, in view of the fact that ratings of predictor variables were made by a single individual without external validation. It does suggest, however, that it would be worthwhile designing a set of items specifically to investigate the role of different characteristics in determining handedness for activities. A recent study of this kind was reported by Steenhuis and Bryden (1989), and lent support to the conclusion that precision of motor skill involved in an action is a major determinant of how far people show consistent hand preference for that activity.

Comparative studies of handedness
If handedness is more adaptive than ambidexterity because it leads to improved motor skill, then this should apply equally to non-human species, and so one might expect to observe handedness (or pawedness) in other animals. Warren's (1980) comprehensive and influential review of animal handedness came to the conclusion that, in general, non-human species are ambidextrous. Some studies, including several by Warren and his colleagues, had found consistent paw preferences in individual animals such as cats, monkeys and rats, but the distributions obtained were quite unlike those for human hand preferences, with a high proportion of animals showing inconsistent preferences, and the remainder equally distributed between left- and right-handedness. In short, he concluded, handedness is a specifically human phenomenon. This would seem to contradict the view that handedness can be explained in evolutionary terms.

A bold attack on Warren's conclusions was launched by MacNeilage *et al.* (1987). They suggested that our failure to detect lateral preferences in non-human primates arose from too simplistic an approach to animal handedness. Reanalysing

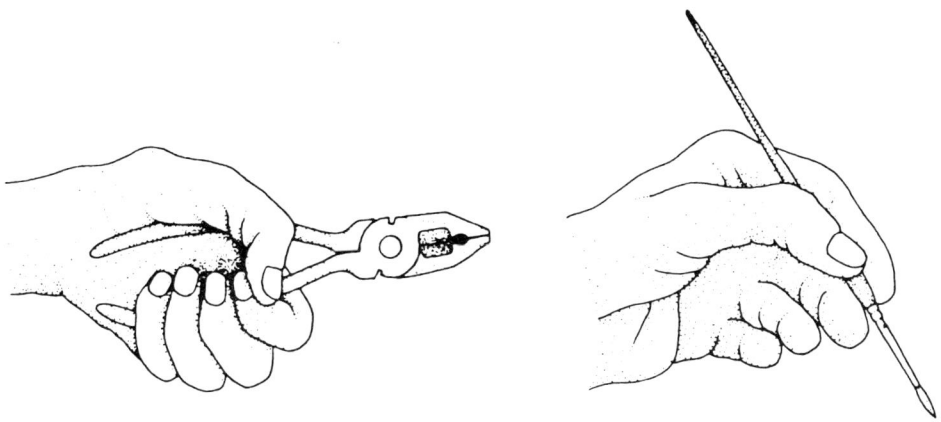

Fig. 1.3. Power grip (*left*), and precision grip (*right*). (Reprinted from McFarland 1981, p. 578.)

studies from the literature they proposed that, at least in Old World monkeys, there was evidence for consistent hand preferences which had been overlooked because, while the animals tended to show a left hand preference for reaching for food, they showed a right hand preference for manipulative skills. Thus, they argued, evidence for animal handedness had been obscured because on average the two tendencies cancelled out. The paper presenting this case was published together with commentaries from a wide range of specialists in the field, and it is evident that few contemporaries of MacNeilage *et al.* were swayed by their arguments. The data they used as support were criticized as scanty, weak, and inappropriately analysed. Furthermore, some commentators reported new data relevant to the debate, but in no case did these offer any support for the position of MacNeilage *et al.* (Deuel and Schaffer 1987, Lehman 1987, Steklis and Marchant 1987, Vauclair and Fagot 1987).

Nevertheless, it does seem that Warren's conclusions about the lack of handedness in animals need some qualification, and the debate raised by MacNeilage *et al.* highlighted the need to distinguish three questions about animal handedness: (1) Is there any tendency for all members of a species to show a consistent bias in direction of hand preference on a particular task? For instance, if we count the percentage of times individual monkeys use the right hand to pick up raisins, will the average value for a group of monkeys deviate significantly from 50 per cent? (2) How consistent are individual animals in hand preference from one task to another? If we record the percentage of occasions that a monkey uses the right hand for picking up raisins, grooming, or manipulating a stick, will there be significant positive correlations between these three measures? (3) To what extent do individual animals show consistent hand preferences (significantly different from chance) on a particular task? If monkeys are observed picking up raisins, how many of them show a significant tendency to use the same hand on repeated observations?

In considering possible advantages of handedness over ambidexterity for motor skill learning, only question (3) is relevant. A substantial part of Warren's argument against animal handedness was concerned with handedness consistency between individuals within a species (question 1), and consistency of individuals across tasks (question 2). Most experts would agree that monkeys and apes do not in general show handedness in these senses. However, as far as question (3) is concerned, opinion is more divided. Warren accepted that individual animals might show consistent hand preferences, but only in artificial situations when they were trained for prolonged periods in experimental apparatus. However, some recent studies have reported that individuals of certain species do show significant hand preferences, not just in the laboratory, but also when observed in natural settings (*e.g.* Brooker *et al.* 1981; see also Lehman 1987).

Furthermore, Warren's description of hand preferences as 'artefactual' consequences of training implies that the observations have no relevance for human handedness. Yet it could be argued that it is precisely for highly trained, practised activities that handedness confers adaptive advantages. The tasks of reaching for an object or picking up food, widely used in observational and experimental studies of primates, are ones for which humans typically report relatively weak hand preferences (see Fig. 1.2). No study has, to my knowledge, directly compared human and non-human primates on hand preference for comparable tasks. There are obvious reasons for this: the sorts of skilled activities that are assessed when rating human handedness are in general not appropriate for other primates. Quite apart from differences in social behaviour, cognitive ability, cooperativeness and motivation, apes and monkeys do not have the precise control of individual digits possessed by humans (Napier 1980). Prosimians and New World monkeys are capable of only one prehensile pattern, opening and closing the hand. Old World monkeys and apes have a differentiated prehensile grip, but not all of them have good manipulative skills. The gorilla has good ability for thumb–finger opposition, but it is not a tool-user and it perversely ignores alien objects placed in its environment by those wishing to test its laterality (Schaller 1963).

Could it be, then, that failure to find highly consistent hand preferences in individual animals is simply a consequence of the tasks employed? If so, then we would expect to find more evidence of handedness if we considered highly skilled activities involving precise use of tools or bimanual coordination. The best-known example of a highly skilled motor activity observed in the wild is termite-fishing by chimpanzees (Goodall 1965, 1986). Individual animals may, over a period of years, develop considerable proficiency in probing termite nests with stalks, using a precision grip and achieving a level of expertise that humans have difficulty in matching (Teleki 1974). This, then, is an activity where the precision of the motor action and the amount of practice needed to accomplish it approach that seen in human tool use. Yet chimpanzees are absolutely ambidextrous in this activity (Goodall, *personal communication*). It would be premature on the basis of this one piece of evidence to reject the idea that handedness for skilled activities has an adaptive advantage. The lack of preference observed for termite-fishing could reflect the fact that the environment constrains the movement: the optimal hand to

Fig. 1.4. Chimpanzee using stereotyped bimanual action to peel grapefruit. (Reprinted from Albrecht and Dunnett 1977, p. 65.)

use will depend on the animal's position relative to the heap and the direction of the tunnel into the nest. Furthermore, there are some observations of chimpanzees showing handedness for highly practised actions involving bimanual coordination. Goodall (*personal communication*) mentioned a small unpublished study that indicated that individual chimpanzees did show consistent hand preferences when cracking open fruits. Albrecht and Dunnett (1971) found that when wild chimpanzees were given a liberal supply of grapefruit they often developed stereotyped actions for peeling them, and individual animals were highly consistent in the hand used to do the peeling, although there was no population preference for left or right (Fig. 1.4). Finally, Bolser *et al.* (1988) reported experimental data from a small study in which three language-trained chimpanzees were given a handedness inventory covering a range of actions. Gross ballistic tasks yielded no consistent hand preference, while fine motor sequential tasks revealed consistent preferences within animals, although these could be for either right or left.

Overall, the data on animals do not give a convincing answer to the question of whether handedness has adaptive advantages for motor learning. What is clear is that we need to concentrate on looking for evidence of hand preferences in tasks that resemble those for which human hand preferences are strong, namely those that involve high precision or complementary bimanual actions.

Why aren't there equal numbers of left- and right-handers?
Right-handedness as a species-specific trait
A major reason for favouring the view that handedness is an adventitious rather than an adaptive characteristic is the population bias to right-handedness. Even if we could prove that hand preference facilitated motor skill learning, we would still be left with the problem of why most humans prefer the right hand. This does seem to be a specifically human trait. Although there are interesting cases of lateral bias in other species (*e.g.* left-footedness in parrots—Rogers 1980, Harris 1989), the only non-human primate for whom a population tendency to right-handedness has been claimed is the gorilla. Schaller (1963) found that when picking up pieces of food, wild mountain gorillas showed no hand preference and would reach out with whichever hand was nearest to the source of food. However, he did report that in 90 out of 110 chest-beating displays that were observed, it was the right hand that led. Although the chest-beating display serves the function of intimidating rather than aggressing, it does culminate in the uprooting of small trees and swiping at nearby vegetation (and human observers, if present), so one may be forgiven for querying the level of accuracy of these observations, particularly since the rate of alternation of beating of the two hands is extremely rapid. The only other evidence for right-handedness in gorillas comes from detailed observations of very small samples of animals. Le Gros Clark (1928) described a celebrated tame gorilla called John Daniels II who 'was evidently right-handed, though sometimes when told to shake hands, did so with his left hand'. A slight bias in favour of the right side was reported for a gorilla observed by Yerkes (1928) and two animals studied by Riess *et al.* (1949), but these were not consistent enough to be regarded as showing hand preference. In contrast, Fischer *et al.* (1982) observed four captive lowland gorillas picking up apple wedges and reported that over all observations for all animals, the right hand was used on 96 per cent of occasions. Note, however, that this is inconsistent with Schaller's observation of wild mountain gorillas. Warren (1977) cited a study conducted in Antwerp Zoo, which found no hand preference in three lowland gorillas or in three out of five mountain gorillas. The remaining two mountain gorillas were *left*-handed. Recently, Fagot and Vauclair (1988) reported an equal number of left- and right-handers in a group of 10 captive lowland gorillas observed reaching for food.

The suggestion of right-handedness in gorillas is provocative, but the evidence is weak, sample sizes are invariably small, and, as gorillas do not manipulate objects or use tools, the behaviours for which handedness has been observed bear little relationship to those for which humans show hand preference. Fagot and Vauclair argued that the task used to assess handedness was of crucial importance, but in so far as they did find hand preferences in their subjects (on a novel spatial task requiring precise alignment of two openings) the trend was for the group to be left- rather than right-handed.

We must ask, then, what factor applies to humans but not to other species and leads to the phenomenon of right-handedness.

Warfare shield theory
The Victorians, inspired no doubt by Darwin's recently published theory of evolution, considered that right-handedness might confer some survival value on the human species. The 'warfare shield theory' is commonly attributed to Thomas Carlyle, although Harris (1980) uncovered a possibly earlier source:

If a hundred of our ambidextrous ancestors made the step in civilization of inventing a shield, we may suppose that half would carry it on the right arm and fight with the left, the other half on the left and fight with the right. The latter would certainly, in the long run, escape mortal wounds better than the former, and thus a race of men who fought with the right hand would gradually be developed by a process of natural selection. (Pye-Smith 1871, p. 145—cited by Harris 1980, p. 40).

This theory is ingenious but not very plausible. The sword has only been in use since Bronze Age times, so any advantage conferred by right-handedness would have to be substantial to have resulted in the preponderance of right-handers we see today. The position of the heart is only slightly biased to the left side of the body, and it is hard to see how a right-handed grip on the sword could significantly improve one's chance of surviving a battle, particularly as most swords were designed as instruments for slashing at the enemy, rather than stabbing. There is no evidence that the prevalence of right-handedness has increased since the introduction of the sword.

Cultural pressures
Perhaps the simplest theory is that which regards right-handedness as a learned behaviour. Corballis and Beale (1976) noted that while non-human species inhabit an environment where left and right are largely irrelevant, this is not so for humans. Social organization forces us to take heed of left and right: this enables us to share implements specialized for one hand, and to develop social customs based on conventional use of one side, such as shaking hands. How far, then, can social custom and specific training account for the phenomenon of right-handedness? Earlier this century it was popular to regard social and cultural forces as the sole explanation for human right-handedness. Blau (1946) talked of dextrality as a 'cultural law'.

A major problem for this learning hypothesis is that it cannot explain how the bias towards right-handedness in human cultures originated. If there were no underlying biological predisposition to prefer one side, we must suppose that primitive man was ambidextrous. One must then assume that, when tools were first invented, they were designed to be used with the hand preferred by the person who made them. Others using the tool would have difficulty unless they used the same hand too. This might lead to better developed overall skill of one hand in that society, so that future tools would also be specialized for that side. Thus an initial chance bias to the right side might result in widespread preference for right-handedness in skilled activities (Hildreth 1949*a*). According to this explanation, we might expect to find evidence of less right-handedness in primitive societies. There are obvious problems in estimating the relative frequencies of right- and left-handedness in ancient civilizations. Biblical records occasionally make reference to handedness, and when they do they imply that left-handedness was relatively rare (*e.g.* Judges 20:15–16). This impression is supported by analyses of representational art. Coren and Porac (1977) investigated works of art from different historical periods showing people engaged in unimanual activities: the persons so depicted were predominantly right-handed, with the proportion of left-handers showing no significant change from ancient to contemporary times. Evidence from prehistoric tools is more difficult to assess and has been used both to support and to refute the notion that primitive humans were ambidextrous, although recent studies using up-to-date methods generally concur that Stone Age man was biased towards right-handedness. Spennemann (1984) found a preponderance of right-handed use of bone implements from Neolithic sites, as judged by the pattern of grinding striations. Although there was variation in the frequency of right-handedness from site to site, there was no evidence for an historical trend towards increasing right-handedness.

As Broca pointed out in 1865, if handedness were solely a consequence of cultural pressures, then we would expect geographical as well as historical variability in its manifestation, especially for isoated communities. A marked preponderance of right- over left-handers is found in such geographically diverse peoples as Alaskan Eskimos, Australian Aborigines, the Temne of Sierra Leone, Hong Kong Chinese peoples (Dawson 1974), Japanese schoolchildren (Komai and Fukuoka 1934), North American Indians (Downey 1927), Congolese children (Verhaegen and Ntumba 1964) and Nigerian children (Bakare 1974). No culture has yet been described in which there are equal numbers of left and right-handers or a preponderance of left-handers. The highest proportion of left-handedness that I could discover from a reliable source was for the Kwakiutl Indians of British Columbia, 17 to 22 per cent of whom were left-handed or ambidextrous for writing (Marrion 1986).*

A further argument against an explanation solely in terms of social learning is that right-handedness is found for many activities that are not culturally sanctioned, as well as for those that are. Westerners are trained to write and hold a knife using the right hand, but parents are unlikely to be concerned which hand is used for activities such as tooth-brushing and hammering, yet these too are typically

---

*Marrion reported that no fewer than 6 per cent of Kwakiutl Indians could write with either hand. However, there is no tradition of written language in this culture, and many adults do not write after leaving school. Marrion (*personal communication*) noted that many treat writing their name as an activity akin to drawing.

performed with the right side. Those favouring a learning explanation might counter this argument by proposing that untrained activities are affected by generalization of a trained preference, or are learned by imitation. However, neither of these processes can explain why individuals who manifest a natural left-hand preference for writing or eating, but who are then forced by cultural pressure to use the right hand, persist in preferring the left hand for other activities (Teng *et al.* 1976).

Although the human bias to right-handedness cannot be explained purely in terms of learning and cultural pressures, it would be misleading to suggest that overt and covert cultural pressures play no part. A relaxation of attitudes towards handedness in Western cultures provides a plausible explanation for the secular increase in left-handedness (Brackenridge 1981), although this may not be the whole story. (Another possibility is that modern writing implements make it much easier to write left-handed.)

In many non-Western societies, cultural laws may be more important than man-made artefacts in determining attitudes. It is common to find that the right side symbolizes what is good, strong and masculine, whereas the left stands for evil, weakness and femininity. Children are trained to use the right hand for activities such as eating and the left for unclean activities such as bottom-wiping. Needham (1973) assembled a collection of essays on the significance of right and left in different cultures, showing that there is considerable variation from one society to another in how deviations from social rules are tolerated. In some cases, such as the Toradja of Celebes (Sulawesi) and the Gogo of central Tanzania, left-handedness is regarded as a harmless eccentricity, provided that the individual has a consistent hand preference and does not confuse the hand used for clean and unclean activities. Evans-Pritchard (1953) noted that the Nuer of the Upper Nile attached considerable importance to left and right in their ceremonies, but did not regard handedness of individuals as important: it was simply said of a left-handed man that his left hand was his right hand. In other societies, however, individuals who reverse the cultural rule are not tolerated: among the Temne of Sierra Leone children are punished if they use the left hand for a right-handed activity, and the natives of the Netherlands Indies would bind the left arm of children who showed signs of left-handedness. Kidd, writing in 1906, described how the Kafir people of South Africa would deliberately scald the hand of a child who seemed to be naturally left-handed. Bakare (1974) noted that in traditional Nigerian families a gift would be withdrawn if the child proffered the left hand to receive it.

Dawson (1972, 1974) has pointed out that hunting and fishing cultures, such as Eskimo and Australian Aborigine peoples, tend to show higher rates of left-handedness than agricultural communities, such as the Temne and the Chinese Hakka, and he suggested that this may be accounted for by the emphasis on independent values and the relatively low degree of conformity found in nomadic groups. Agricultural groups living in static villages have been shown to be much less permissive, with strong pressures on children to conform, a social pattern which may have survival value in this type of environment. Dawson put forward a similar explanation for sex differences in handedness. Most surveys find that left-

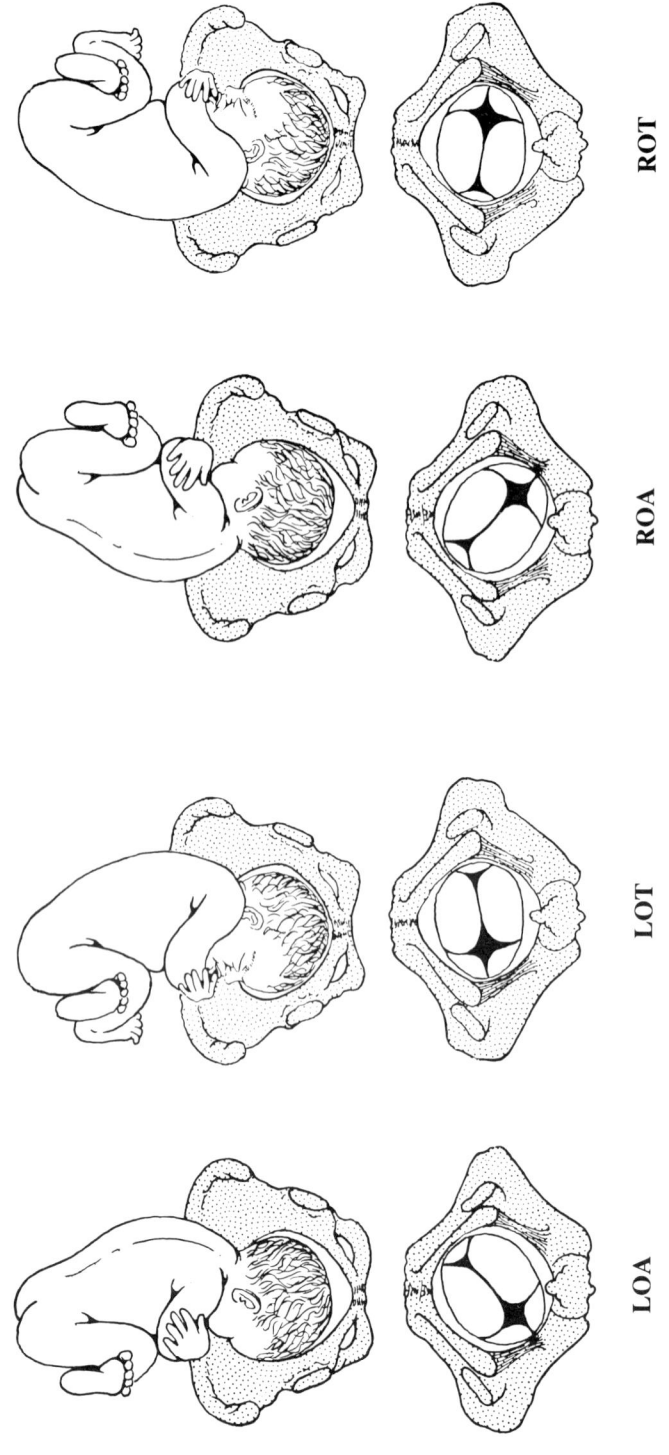

Fig. 1.5. Birth positions for vertex delivery. The left occiput anterior (LOA) and temporal (LOT) positions are slighty more common than the corresponding positions on the right. (Adapted from Benson 1983, p. 150.)

TABLE 1.II
Handedness (for ball throwing) at 2 years in relation to birth position (Churchill *et al.* 1962)

Birth position	Left-handed N	(%)	Mixed N	(%)	Right-handed N	(%)
Neither parent left-handed						
Left occiput anterior	28	(5.3)	71	(13.3)	433	(81.4)
Right occiput anterior	46	(10.3)	72	(16.1)	329	(73.6)
One or both parents left-handed						
Left occiput anterior	7	(10.0)	17	(24.2)	46	(65.7)
Right occiput anterior	12	(22.6)	13	(24.5)	28	(52.8)

handedness is slightly more frequent in males than females. This could be because in most societies there is more pressure for girls to conform to cultural norms than for boys (see also Hildreth 1949b, Porac *et al.* 1986). Dawson's conclusion seems a reasonable one: social pressure is not the sole determinant of handedness, but it interacts with biological factors to determine the rate of left-handedness observed in a culture.

Birth position
Lateral bias in human populations is evident even at the moment of birth. The vertex presentation is the most common birth position, and the left occiput is more often anterior than the right (Fig. 1.5). Harris (1980) researched the origins of the view that positioning of the infant *in utero* or at birth can determine handedness. He traced this theory back to an early 19th century paper by Comte, who proposed that birth position gave an indication of intrauterine position, and that the majority of babies *in utero* would have the left arm against the mother's back, with less opportunity for movement than the right. However, he produced only anecdotal evidence that birth position bore any relationship to later handedness. Harris discovered subsequent and apparently independent formulations of this theory, but no scientific test of its predictions, until a study by Overstreet in 1938 demonstrated not only that there was no relationship between birth position and subsequent laterality, but also that birth position was a poor indicator of prenatal position.

However, more recent reports have revived interest in this theory. Churchill *et al.* (1962) investigated hand preference in over 1000 2-year-olds whose birth position had been recorded as left or right occiput anterior. They found a small but significant association between handedness and position at birth (Table 1.II). Handedness was also related to parental hand preference, but the association between child handedness and birth position remained significant even after excluding those with left-handed parents. A weak trend for a link between head position at birth and handedness at 7 years was confirmed for boys but not girls in the Collaborative Perinatal Project (Ehrlichman *et al.* 1982). Churchill *et al.* considered a range of explanations for this association, noting that asymmetrical damage to the brain during delivery may be more important than asymmetrical position *in utero*.

TABLE 1.III
Distribution of supine head position preferences of newborn infants (Michel and Goodwin 1979)

Birth position	Supine head position preference		
	Significantly right	*No preference*	*Significantly left*
Left occiput anterior / Left occiput transverse	35	21	2
Right occiput anterior / Right occiput transverse	12	31	8

Although the underlying causal mechanism is not understood, there is evidence that birth position is related to the newborn supine head position (Michel and Goodwin 1979) (Table I.III), and there is a significant, though weak, relationship between newborn head position and subsequent hand preference (see Chapter 4). Asymmetrical head posture is found just as frequently in children born by caesarian section (Turkewitz 1977, Ehrlichman *et al.* 1982), indicating that lateralized brain trauma during the process of birth is not a plausible explanation for this phenomenon.

Overall, there is evidence that position before and during birth can influence handedness. However, the relationships are too weak for this to be an adequate explanation for the human bias to right-handedness.

How mothers hold their babies
Another early theory discussed by Harris (1980) maintained that mothers carry their babies on their right arm, leaving the infant's right arm a freer field of motion than the left, and so encouraging its use. The facts do not support this: irrespective of maternal handedness, the most popular position for mothers to hold babies is in their left arm (Salk 1973), with the infant's right arm having little opportunity for movement, a lateral bias which, according to Burt (1937), is reflected in pictures of the Madonna and Child (Fig. 1.6). The reason for this bias is unclear. Right-handed mothers told Salk that they held the baby in the left arm so as to leave the preferred right hand free, whereas left-handed mothers claimed that they held the baby in the left arm because they were left-handed. Salk's preferred explanation was that the baby is better able to hear the maternal heartbeat when held in the left arm, and that this soothes the infant and strengthens the bond between mother and child.

Biological asymmetries
The universality of right-handedness in diverse cultures and its specificity to humans has led to the conclusion that there must be some biologically based explanation for the phenomenon. Early theorists concentrated on asymmetries in the position of body organs or in the circulation of the blood, but these received no empirical support (see Harris 1980). More recent investigations of asymmetries in pyramidal decussation have not confirmed any link with handedness in individuals (Kertesz and Geschwind 1971).

Fig. 1.6. The most common position for mothers to carry their babies, irrespective of maternal handedness. (Hugo Van Der Goes: *Virgin and Child*.)

One major difference between man and other animals is our ability to speak. Could handedness be a secondary consequence of cerebral lateralization for language? Annett (1975) has put the case succinctly:

The main difference betwen human and non-human species in forelimb preferences is that the human distribution is shifted in favour of the right hand. Of all possible agents for this shift the first candidate for consideration must be some factor linked with the human capacity for speech. The fact that most people depend on the left hemisphere for speech suggests the presence of some feature of left hemisphere organisation which makes it especially suited to this role. Could not this same feature also give an advantage to the right hand such that a slight weight in favour of that hand operates on the accidental distribution of differences to produce a dextral shift in the distribution? (p. 307)

This topic is sufficiently complex to merit a chapter to itself.

2
HANDEDNESS AND CEREBRAL LATERALIZATION

On superficial examination, the two cerebral hemispheres appear symmetrical, yet we now know that in functional terms they are quite different. In the middle of the 19th century Dax and Broca independently discovered that loss of articulate speech ('aphemia') was almost always caused by a lesion of the left cerebral hemisphere in the region of the third frontal convolution (see Berker *et al.* 1986). This association was subsequently confirmed in numerous series of patients with focal brain damage, and was extended to encompass a link between more posterior lesions of the left hemisphere and receptive aphasia. Originally it was assumed that the right side of the brain was less important for mental processes, but it is now recognized that in most people the right hemisphere is specialized for non-verbal, visuospatial functions. This change in emphasis was accompanied by a change in terminology. In the past, it was usual to speak of 'cerebral dominance', with the implication that the hemisphere controlling language was all-important. Nowadays it is more common to refer to cerebral lateralization or cerebral asymmetry, emphasizing that the relationship between the hemispheres is complementary.

Studies of aphasia after focal brain damage
Broca was quick to realize that handedness might be linked to cerebral lateralization. The major pathways from the motor cortex to the musculature are crossed, so the function of the right hand is largely controlled by the left hemisphere, and vice versa. Broca was impressed by evidence that the convolutions of the left cerebral hemisphere develop before those of the right, and he suggested that this leads both to more precocious development of motor control of the right hand, and to left hemisphere control of the execution and coordination of articulation. He raised the question of whether the hemisphere that is specialized for language functions would also be dominant for motor functions, in which case we would expect left-handedness to go with right hemisphere language. It was subsequently discovered that this was not the case, and that left hemisphere lesions frequently caused aphasia in left-handers (Goodglass and Quadfasel 1954, Ettlinger *et al.* 1956). As Subirana (1969) remarked: 'left-handers . . . seem to have been created on purpose to upset all the different conceptions which have prevailed during the last century in connection with the pathology and physiology of the two hemispheres' (p. 248).

However, handedness and cerebral lateralization are not totally unrelated. Data from several sources indicate that although most left-handers, like right-handers, have left hemisphere language representation, the frequency of atypical cerebral lateralization is much higher in left-handers than right-handers. Alekoum-

TABLE 2.I
Estimates of the percentages of cerebral lateralization types by handedness (Alekoumbides 1978)

Laterality of lesion that will cause aphasia	Capability of intact hemisphere to compensate	Non-right-handers %	Impure right-handers* %	Pure right-handers %
Left only	None	12	11	99.5
	Partial	26	37	0
	Total	13	48	0
Either	Total	36	0	0
Right only	None, partial or total	13	4	0.5

*Family history of left-handedness or slight tendency to left-handedness.

bides (1978) used data from 29 reported series of cases to derive estimates of the proportions of right-handers and non-right-handers* who had language represented in the left only (L), right only (R), or both (B) cerebral hemispheres. These estimates were made as follows: for each handedness group, the observed percentage of those who become aphasic after a left hemisphere lesion will be the sum of groups L and B, and the observed percentage who become aphasic after a right hemisphere lesion will be the sum of groups R and B. On the assumption that R, L and B represent all possible types of brain organization, R+L+B must equal 100, and the frequency of each group can be calculated by simple algebra. Alekoumbides' conclusions are summarized in Table 2.I. A striking feature of these data is the difference in frequency of right hemisphere language representation in right- and non-right-handers. Note, nonetheless, that most non-right-handed aphasics have left hemisphere lesions.

Alekoumbides went on to consider the available data on recovery from aphasia and concluded, in agreement with the views of Conrad (1949), Subirana (1958, 1969) and Luria (1970), that aphasia is relatively milder in non-right-handers. Alekoumbides took recovery from aphasia as an indication that the uninjured hemisphere was able to mediate language to some extent and he argued from these data that the representation of language in the two hemispheres varies over a continuous spectrum from strict left hemisphere language representation, through various degrees of bilateral representation, to exclusively right hemisphere mediation.

Satz (1979) independently carried out an analysis of published data sets with the same aim: to achieve a model of hemispheric speech lateralization in the left- and right-handed. Like Alekoumbides, he concluded that the data could only be accounted for by assuming that a substantial proportion of left-handers (estimated at 70 per cent) had some degree of bilateral language representation.

---

*Definitions of handedness varied from study to study, with some authors classifying by writing hand and others taking into consideration handedness for a range of activities. For analysis purposes, Alekoumbides grouped together as 'non-right-handed' all those who showed any departure from consistent right-handedness. The question of handedness assessment is treated at greater length in Chapter 5.

TABLE 2.II
Patterns of cerebral organization in right- and left-handers*

Visuospatial function	Language function		
	Left hemisphere %	Bilateral %	Right hemisphere %
Right-handers			
Left hemisphere	26.7	0	4.7
Right hemisphere	60.5	0	8.0
Left-handers			
Left hemisphere	24.8	6.4	5.3
Bilateral	6.8	4.4	2.4
Right hemisphere	30.3	11.8	7.8

*Based on Bryden *et al.* (1983), collapsing across sex and familial sinistrality.

In order to arrive at such estimates, investigators have to rely on data sets that are often poorly described and ambiguous. One particular source of concern is that where information is collated retrospectively from clinical records, assessment of handedness may not have been independent of the patient's status. Physicians are more likely to look for evidence of left-handedness in an aphasic patient with a right hemisphere lesion than in non-aphasic patients or in aphasics with left hemisphere lesions, and this could lead to inflated estimates of aphasia in left-handers (Kimura 1983). Provided one's criteria are lax enough, some signs of left-handedness can be uncovered in almost anyone. Consider, for instance, the idiosyncratic list of items used by Luria (1970) as evidence for 'left-handed tendencies' which included: a large left hand, well-developed venous system on the back of the left hand, a wide finger-nail on the fifth finger of the left hand, highly developed musculature on the right side of the face, facility with the left hand in spontaneous untaught activities, left thumb on top when clasping the hands, and overestimation of the size of a sphere held in the right hand relative to one held in the left. Few of these tests have been validated, and some, such as hand-clasping, are known to be unrelated to other aspects of laterality. It would be interesting to know how many unselected patients would show left-handed tendencies on at least one of these indices.

A study that overcame these problems was conducted at the University of Vienna by I. and K. Gloning and associates (Gloning *et al.* 1969, Gloning 1977). An investigation was made of all non-right-handed neurological patients seen between 1950 and 1965 who had a brain lesion that was eventually verified by autopsy. This group of 57 patients was compared with 57 strictly right-handed patients who were individually matched with the non-right-handers in terms of size, location and type of cerebral lesion. Aphasia was overall more frequent in non-right-handers than in right-handers, the excess being due to non-right-handers who became aphasic after right hemisphere lesions. No such cases were observed in the right-handers. Transient aphasias were also more common in the non-right-handed group, especially after right hemisphere lesions.

Kimura (1983) also found that when aphasia occurred, it was less severe in left-handers than in right-handers. However, in her study of a consecutive series of 412 patients with unilateral lesions, she did not find that aphasia was more common in left-handers. She suggested that discrepancies with the Glonings' study might reflect different aetiologies in the patients who were studied. A further point to note is that, unlike those authors, she did not match left- and right-handers in terms of location and extent of lesion.

It is commonly assumed that lateralization of visuospatial functions will be complementary to that for language. However, an analysis of aphasia and spatial disorder in 270 patients with unilateral lesions (Bryden *et al.* 1983) showed that language and spatial functions are statistically independent (Table 2.II). Although these figures are imprecise estimates, they make the point that the same hemisphere may control both language and visuospatial functions.

Anaesthetizing one hemisphere: the Wada test
Intractable epilepsy can often be relieved by surgical removal of diseased brain tissue, but it is important to ensure that the surgery does not encroach upon areas crucial for language functions. The Wada test (Wada and Rasmussen 1960) is a procedure for assessing cerebral lateralization in such cases. Sodium amytal is injected into the arterial system of one side of the brain prior to surgery, with right and left sides being injected on different days so that the two sides can be compared with respect to their participation in language functions. Immediately after injection, functions dependent upon the injected hemisphere are disrupted for five to 10 minutes, with loss of motor control and sensory function on the contralateral side. Simple tests of language (*e.g.* naming pictures, saying the days of the week) are administered during this interval to discover whether the non-anaesthetized hemisphere is capable of carrying out these activities. The usual finding is that when the left hemisphere is injected, the patient becomes mute, and then as speech returns there are dysphasic errors, with perseveration, substitution, sequencing errors and occasional jargon. In contrast, injection of the right hemisphere usually produces only a very brief disruption of speech immediately after injection.

The population to whom the Wada test is given is not a normal one. All patients suffer from epilepsy, and many neurological centres restrict the use of the test to cases where non-right-handedness, an unusual neuropsychological profile and/or history of early left hemisphere damage give grounds for suspecting atypical language representation.

Nevertheless, results obtained with the Wada test have been of considerable interest for our understanding of links between handedness and cerebral lateralization, and, provided one excludes patients who suffered injury to the left hemisphere early in life, the relationships between handedness and cerebral lateralization that have been reported are consistent with those from studies of aphasia in patients with focal brain lesions. Table 2.III shows data from a study by Rasmussen and Milner (1977), in which the patient population is divided into those whose epilepsy was associated with brain damage sustained before the age of 6 years and those with later onset. For those patients in whom handedness, and

TABLE 2.III
Language lateralization in 262 patients as determined by the Wada test*

Handedness	Left N	(%)	Language representation Bilateral N	(%)	Right N	(%)
Patients without clinical evidence of early left hemisphere lesion						
Right (N = 140)	134	(96)	0	—	6	(4)
Left or mixed (N = 122)	86	(70)	18	(15)	18	(15)
Patients with clinical evidence of early left hemisphere lesion						
Right (N = 42)	34	(81)	3	(7)	5	(12)
Left or mixed (N = 92)	26	(28)	17	(19)	49	(53)

*After Rasmussen and Milner (1977).

presumably cerebral lateralization, were well established prior to onset of disease, there is a clear link between left-handedness and atypical (either bilateral or right hemisphere) language representation. It is also evident that cerebral lateralization and handedness can be influenced by early brain damage. An early left hemisphere lesion raises the probability that the patient will have bilateral or right hemisphere language representation in association with left-handedness. Similar results were reported by Rey *et al.* (1988).

Use of the Wada test confirmed what had previously been suggested by studies of focal brain injuries, namely that cerebral representation of language need not be exclusively in one hemisphere. In some patients, both hemispheres participate in language functions. Milner *et al.* (1966) described 18 patients (17 of whom were left-handed or ambidextrous) in whom some dysphasia was produced by injection of either hemisphere. In six of these patients speech was not arrested after injection of the left or right side, although there was some dysphasia. Furthermore, in nine patients there was a dissociation between deficits on a naming task and impairments in serial speech (saying the days of the week and counting forwards and backwards): left hemisphere injection disrupted one of these functions and right hemisphere injection the other.

Unilateral electroconvulsive therapy
Electroconvulsive therapy (ECT), a standard treatment for severe depressive illness, involves administering an electric current to the scalp of an anaesthetized patient via two elecrodes, causing a convulsion. To minimize the side-effect of memory disturbances, it has become standard practice to administer the treatment unilaterally, with electrodes placed over the non-dominant hemisphere. Warrington and Pratt (1973) and Fleminger and Bunce (1975) confirmed that, in right-handers, verbal memory impairment was least when treatment was administered to the right side of the brain, whereas in left-handers, the effect of laterality of treatment was much less clear-cut. Despite the differences in populations (depressed vs. epileptic patients), ECT studies yield information about cerebral lateralization in left- and right-handers that agrees well with that obtained using the Wada test.

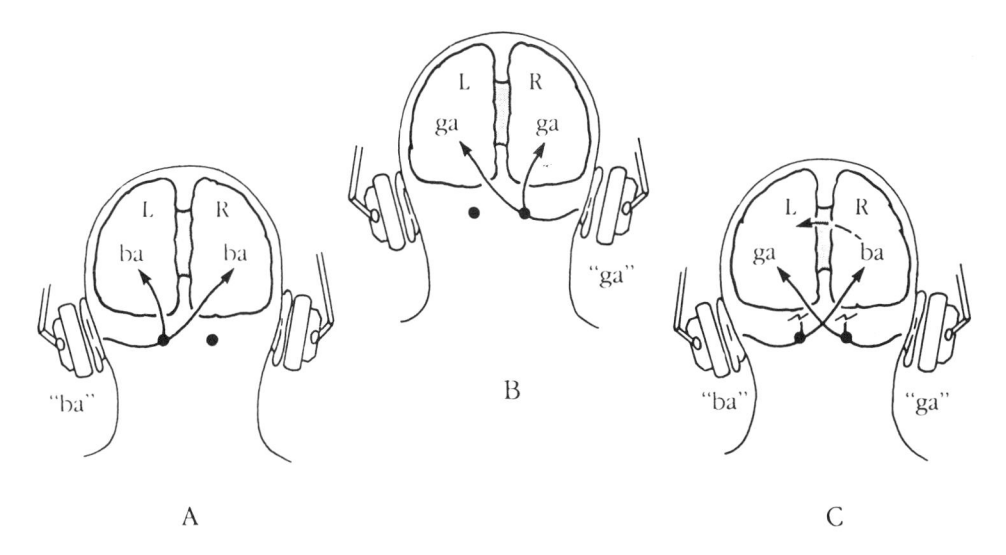

Fig. 2.1. Kimura's model of dichotic listening. Each ear projects to both hemispheres, so with monaural presentation, stimuli presented to either ear can be processed directly in the left hemisphere. When competing stimuli arrive at the two ears, the weaker ipsilateral pathway is suppressed, so the only direct route from ear to auditory cortex is via the stronger contralateral pathway. Stimuli delivered to the right ear are processed directly in the left hemisphere, but those from the left ear are accessible to the left hemisphere only via the cerebral commissures. (Reprinted from Springer and Deutsch 1981, p. 68.)

Functional asymmetries in left- and right-handers

Another source of evidence for links between handedness and cerebral lateralization comes from studies of functional cerebral asymmetries in normal, healthy individuals. The earliest of these studies was by Kimura (1961b), who used a dichotic listening task in which a person is presented with competing auditory messages to the two ears. For instance, 'one–seven–three' might be heard in the left ear, and 'nine–two–eight' in the right ear. The subject is asked to report as much as possible from both messages. In a study of epileptic patients, Kimura noticed most subjects recalled slightly more stimuli presented to the right than to the left ear. However, patients with right hemisphere speech (as confirmed by the Wada test) showed the opposite pattern. Thus, recall of dichotic stimuli was better in the ear contralateral to the hemisphere that mediated language. If stimuli were alternated between the two ears, rather than being presented simultaneously, no consistent ear advantage was found (Kimura 1961a). Kimura proposed the following physiological explanation for these findings. Both ears project to both cerebral hemispheres, but the crossed pathway to the contralateral hemisphere is the stronger. When the left hemisphere receives competing stimuli from the left and right ears, the weaker ipsilateral pathway from the left ear will be suppressed (Fig. 2.1). In the majority of people the right hemisphere does not process verbal stimuli, so the only way a message from the left ear can be interpreted is by transmission of the information to the left hemisphere via the corpus callosum, which links the two hemispheres. Thus, although the left hemisphere language processor receives input from both ears, the right ear message is received directly, whereas input from the left ear arrives by a more indirect route via the corpus callosum. This is thought to be responsible for the disadvantage for left ear stimuli relative to those from the right ear.

The right ear advantage for verbal stimuli in dichotic listening is a reliable finding which has been replicated in many studies with different stimuli and various modifications of the technique. It can, for instance, be demonstrated even when the person is not required to remember the stimuli, but merely to monitor an incoming stream of speech for a particular word (Geffen and Caudrey 1981). Furthermore, the right ear advantage is specific to *verbal* stimuli. Other types of auditory input, such as environmental sounds and music, do not give a right ear advantage and may indeed show a bias in favour of the left ear (and right cerebral hemisphere) (Kimura 1964, Knox and Kimura 1970).

An analogous functional asymmetry has been demonstrated for visual stimuli. As shown in Figure 2.2, each eye projects to both cerebral hemispheres, with the left half of the visual field projecting to the right hemisphere and vice versa. If a person fixates a central point, then visual stimuli presented in the left half of the visual field will be projected to the right hemisphere and those presented in the right half will be projected to the left hemisphere. Although the two hemipheres can communicate via the corpus callosum, the pathway from eye to brain is more direct for the contralateral visual field. Studies in which literate subjects are asked to report briefly presented verbal materials, such as letters, reliably find a right visual field advantage, analogous to the right ear advantage obtained with dichotic listening (Kimura 1966). Non-verbal visual stimuli such as faces or dot patterns, in contrast, do not reveal such a bias and may give a left visual field advantage. A detailed review of the application of these techniques for assessing functional asymmetry is given by Hiscock (1988).

One clear prediction, following from the evidence from neurological patients, is that the right ear advantage in dichotic listening, and the right visual field advantage in half-field studies, should be less pronounced in left-handed groups. In general, this prediction has been supported, the usual finding being that left-handers have reduced asymmetry rather than a reversal of asymmetry (Bryden 1965; Satz *et al.* 1965, 1967; Curry 1967; Curry and Rutherford 1967), although Knox and Boone (1970) reported a left ear (right hemisphere) advantage when strongly left-handed subjects were given a difficult dichotic listening task.

Use of dichotic and visual half-field tests to assess cerebral lateralization
Because functional lateral asymmetries on tasks such as dichotic listening are significantly related to cerebral lateralization, investigators have been attracted to the use of dichotic ear asymmetry as a non-invasive means of establishing direction and degree of cerebral lateralization in individuals. Unfortunately, things are not so simple. According to Berlin (1977): 'Using dichotic listening to infer the magnitude of left hemisphere superiority is like using noise-level measurements to infer the speed of an automobile' (p. 303). The relationship between cerebral lateralization

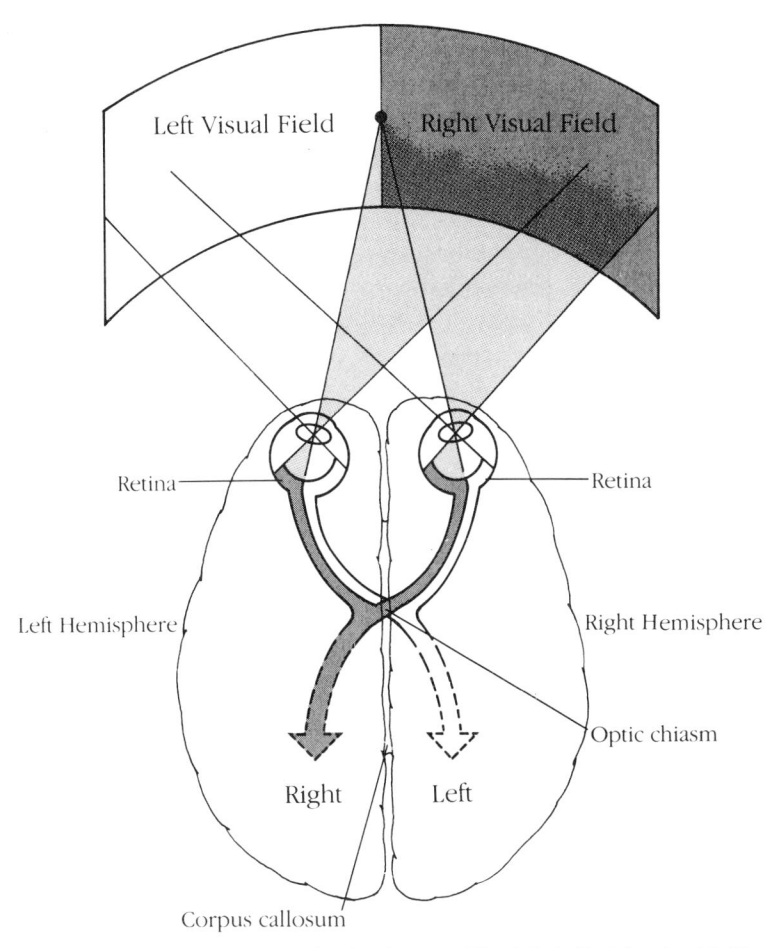

Fig. 2.2. Neural pathways from the eyes to the visual cortex. The right half of the visual field projects to the left occipital cortex, and the left half of the visual field to the right occipital cortex. Lateralized presentation is achieved by flashing stimuli briefly in one half-field as the subject fixates centrally. (Reprinted from Springer and Deutsch 1981, p. 32.)

and dichotic ear asymmetry, while significant, is far from perfect, and the proportion of right-handers who show a left ear advantage for verbal stimuli (suggestive of right hemisphere processing) is around 20 per cent, far greater than the estimates based on neurological data of the proportion of right-handers with right hemisphere speech (Satz 1977).

The agreement between dichotic and visual measures of laterality is also far from perfect (Zurif and Bryden 1969); furthermore, although a right ear advantage for verbal materials is a very reliable finding in normal *groups*, the stability of individual scores may not be high enough to give confidence that the size or direction of a person's score will be the same when assessed on different occasions. In fact, many individuals reverse ear advantage on retesting (Blumstein *et al.* 1975,

Berlin 1977, Geffen and Caudrey 1981). Variation may arise in part because factors such as task demands, acoustic characteristics and attentional bias can affect size of ear advantage. Even where reliability is acceptable, results of a dichotic test may not agree with those from visual half-field testing (Fennell *et al.* 1977). A further question concerns how to compute an index of lateral asymmetry: some indices, such as difference scores, do not take into account overall level of performance, whereas others, such as proportions, do. Choice of one index rather than another can lead to different interpretations concerning extent of lateral asymmetry and there is no consensus as to which index is most appropriate (Colbourn 1981). This problem arises not just when interpreting ear or visual field advantages for individuals, but also when comparing two groups with different levels of overall accuracy. If one group has high verbal ability and the other is impaired, then should one correct for overall level of accuracy before comparing groups? While this may seem sensible, it could be argued that one reason for low verbal attainment might be weak lateralization, in which case correcting for level of performance before comparing laterality will remove exactly the effect of interest.

Lateralization of motor control
Aphasia is not the only neurological symptom that is specifically associated with left hemisphere lesions. Liepmann, around the turn of the century, noted that patients with a right hemiplegia showed impaired purposive movements of the unaffected left side, as indicated by difficulty in imitating skilled movements and demonstrating the use of objects, a disorder known as apraxia (see Geschwind 1975, for an account of this work). Heilman (1979) reviewed the more recent literature on this topic and confirmed Liepmann's original observations, showing that in right-handed patients almost all cases of apraxia are due to lesions of the left cerebral hemisphere.

The question immediately arises as to whether, as Liepmann suggested, the preferred hand is the one controlled by the hemisphere specialized for motor learning. Alas, the brain is not so simple. In one of the largest studies to be conducted on this topic, Kimura (1983) administered an apraxia test to 351 patients with unilateral cerebral lesions. The test involved copying meaningless arm movements with the side ipsilateral to the lesion. Severe apraxia was observed in 30 per cent of right-handers with left-sided lesions, but in only 3 per cent of those with right-sided lesions. In left-handers, however, apraxia was unrelated to side of lesion, being observed in around 9 per cent of all patients.

The parallels with data on language lateralization are striking: right-handers show strong lateralization to the left hemisphere, whereas left-handers show little, if any, bias. Furthermore, this pattern is sustained in studies of motor functions in neurologically intact individuals. Kimura (1973*a,b*) found that spontaneous gestures while speaking were made predominantly with the right hand by right-handers, whereas left-handers were equally likely to gesture with the right or left hand.

There has been some debate in the literature over how far apraxia is specifically a disorder of executing meaningful movements. A study by Kimura and

Archibald (1974) demonstrated that the disorder of manual movement observed after left-hemisphere damage is not restricted to symbolic gestures, but also affects the ability to copy meaningless movements of the hands and arms, although the ability to imitate static postures is unimpaired.

Similarities between patterns of lateralization observed for motor actions and language have led to speculation as to whether both sets of observations arise from a common biological basis. One obvious question is whether handedness for other actions is simply a secondary consequence of right-handedness for writing, a motor activity where left hemisphere control is to be expected, given that language is involved. This is an attractively simple theory, but it cannot be sustained in the light of evidence demonstrating a bias towards right-handedness in illiterate as well as literate societies (Ardila *et al.* 1989).

Another possibility is that all motor control is lateralized, and speech is just one aspect of motor activity that happens to have been extensively studied. The problem with this argument is that it fails to specify why humans should be unique in having motor functions lateralized. Brain (1945) suggested a resolution, arguing that the bilateral synchronization of precise articulations involved in speech necessitates control by a single, lateralized centre. Once a motor speech centre is established in the left hemisphere, he argued, this leads to hand dominance and lateralization of control of purposeful manipulations. Note that on this view, it is not complementary bimanual actions that provide the impetus for laterality, but the need for fine control of bilateral symmetrical movements (cf. Chapter 1).

Physical asymmetries of the brain in left- and right-handers
Awareness of physical differences between the two halves of the brain dates back nearly a century (see review by Rubens 1977), but for many years this work was forgotten, and it was assumed that there were no consistent asymmetries in brain morphology. Interest in this topic grew following a study by Geschwind and Levitsky (1968), who confirmed the presence of physical asymmetries between the two sides and linked these to functional asymmetries in language processing. Morphological asymmetries can be studied from post-mortem material, or, in living patients, by using imaging techniques such as CT scan and angiography.

Studies of the parietal and temporal lobes have shown that areas of the left hemisphere known to be involved in language comprehension are typically larger than the corresponding regions on the right. An early observation was that the Sylvian fissure is of greater length on the left than the right and usually ends at a higher position on the left. The region of the temporal lobe known as the planum temporale (Fig. 2.3), which is part of Wernicke's area, is significantly larger on the left side than the right in about 70 per cent of people, and if one averages across all individuals, the left planum temporale is 40 per cent larger than the right. Furthermore, the same type of asymmetry has been shown in radiographic examination of the skulls of primitive man. Asymmetry of the planum temporale has been found in fetal brains and this has been used as evidence that the left hemisphere specialization is present before birth.

Another type of morphological asymmetry is left occipital petalia, *i.e.* a more

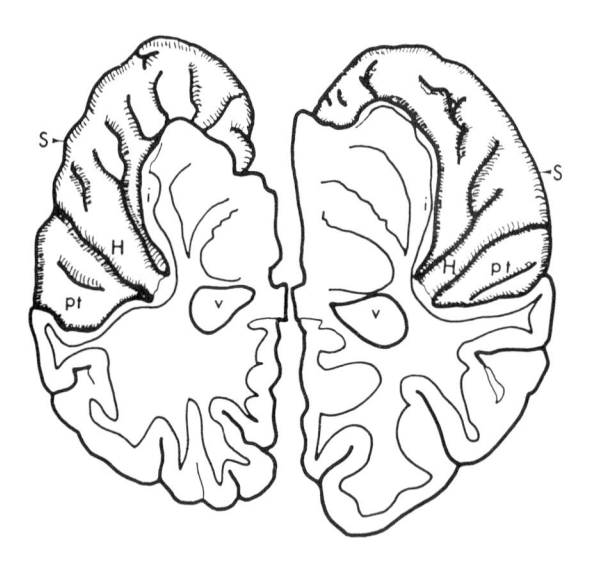

Fig. 2.3. Typical asymmetry of the planum temporale (pt), the roughly triangular region lying posterior (inferior in the diagram) to the transverse auditory gyrus of Heschl (H) and bound laterally by the Sylvian fissure (S). This pattern of asymmetry is seen in approximately two-thirds of normal human brains. (Reprinted from Geschwind and Galaburda 1987, p. 30.)

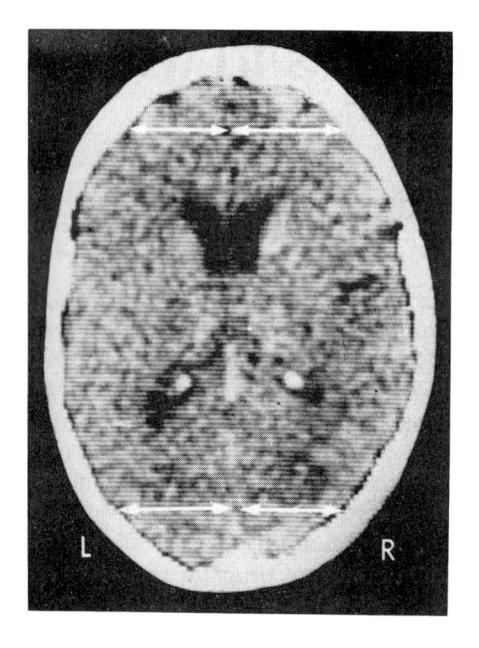

Fig. 2.4. Computerized axial tomogram of brain showing usual pattern of asymmetry: note wider left occipital lobe (lower arrows) and wider right frontal lobe (upper arrows). (Reprinted from LeMay 1982, p. 275.)

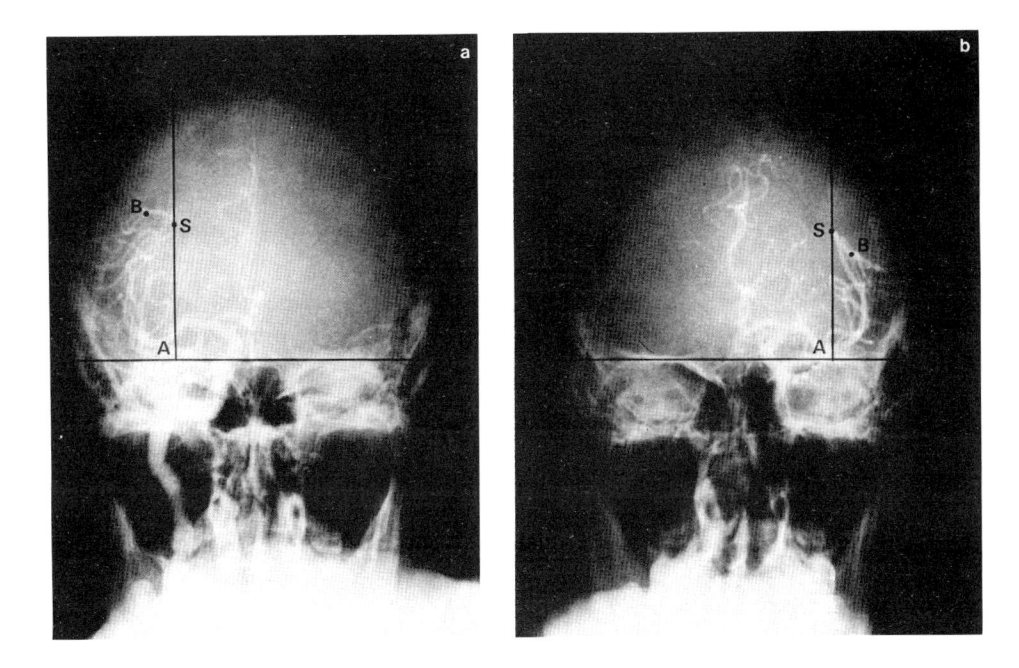

Fig. 2.5. Right and left carotid angiograms of a patient with left hemiphere speech representation showing typical Sylvian arch asymmetry. (Reprinted from Ratcliff *et al.* 1980, p. 91.)

marked indentation of the skull that results from greater protrusion of the left occipital lobe (Fig. 2.4).

It would, of course, be dangerous to assume that physical measurements indicate the amount of brain power available for a given function. In many areas of the brain it is the right side that is better developed than the left. The right frontal lobe generally protrudes more than the left, and Broca's area in the left frontal lobe appears smaller than the homologous area in the right hemisphere (although the measurements could give a misleading impression of brain surface area because of the different gyral patterns in the two hemispheres—Falzi *et al.* 1982). Could it be merely coincidence that the left hemisphere is larger than the right in those posterior brain areas involved in language? In her review of this area, Witelson (1980) argued that the answer appears to be no, because there is some direct evidence linking physical measurements of the brain with both handedness and language representation.

Ratcliff *et al.* (1980) measured the asymmetry of the posterior Sylvian branches of the middle cerebral artery (Fig. 2.5) from carotid angiograms of 59 patients in whom the lateralization of language had been established using the Wada test. Their results are reproduced in Figure 2.6. The usual asymmetry of the vessels was found in those with left hemisphere language, but not in those with atypical functional lateralization. The latter subgroup did not show a reversal of

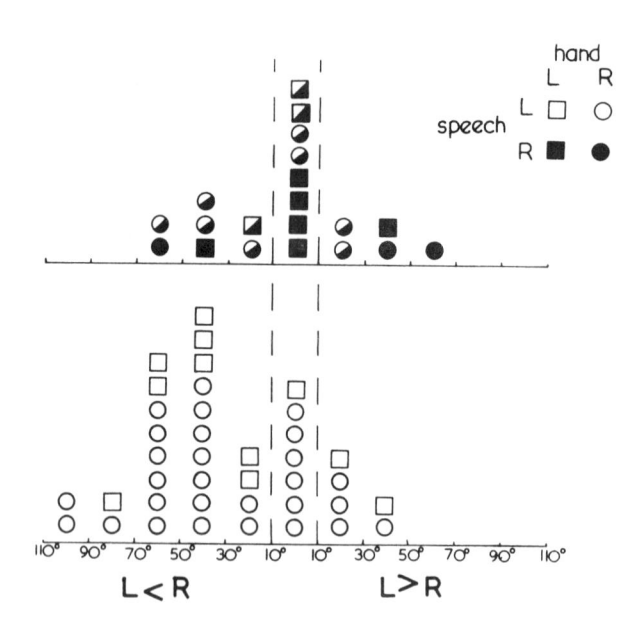

Fig. 2.6. Distribution of Sylvian arch asymmetry in patients with left, bilateral or right hemisphere language representation. (Reprinted from Ratcliff *et al.* 1980, p. 92).

morphological asymmetry so much as a lack of asymmetry. Asymmetries in the frontal and occipital regions appear also to be related to handedness, but the association is weak, and only reaches significance when large samples including many left-handers are studied. LeMay (1977) studied 120 right-handers and 121 left-handers and found that 61 per cent of right-handers and 40 per cent of left-handers showed a wider frontal expanse on the right side, whereas 19 per cent of right-handers and 27 per cent of left-handers showed a wider frontal expanse on the left side. Deuel and Moran (1980), using a sample of 94 children including 15 non-right-handers, found no significant link between frontal and occipital morphological asymmetries and handedness, and concluded that one should not infer functional cerebral asymmetry of the individual on the basis of such measures. Chui and Damasio (1980) cautioned that petalias could be affected by infant head-position (see Chapter 4), and hence might reflect the consequences rather than the underlying cause of asymmetrical function.

There is one remaining problem for those who regard morphological asymmetries as the basis for functional asymmetries in language representation. Morphological asymmetries similar to those found in humans have been reported in some species of ape and monkey (LeMay and Geschwind 1975, Yeni-Komshian and Benson 1976, LeMay *et al.* 1982, Falk *et al.* 1986, Heilbroner and Holloway 1988). In certain cases, such asymmetries are evident in the area corresponding to Broca's area in humans. Non-human primates do not talk and are not in general right-handed: the one species for whom there is any suggestion of right-handedness, the gorilla (see Chapter 1), shows the least marked morphological brain asymmetries (LeMay and Geschwind 1975). The only way one can account for this sort of finding is by arguing that the development of lateralized language functions capitalized on a pre-existing bias in primates towards greater physical development of the left temporal lobe. Indeed, although right-handedness is not a characteristic of sub-human species, there is plentiful evidence of asymmetrical brain function in other animals (Denenberg 1988). Of particular interest is a set of studies by a group of workers in the USA which has been used to claim that there is a non-human analogue to lateralized specialization for language comprehension. There is evidence that the Japanese macaque (*Macaca fuscata*) has specialized neural apparatus for processing communicative vocalizations: these monkeys readily learn to discriminate calls made by conspecifics, but have much greater difficulty with acoustically similar but meaningless noises, whereas species other than Japanese macaques find the two classes of sound equally difficult (Zoloth *et al.* 1979). What is particularly interesting about this research is that lesion studies and experiments using lateralized presentation of materials indicate that perception of communicative vocalizations by macaques appears to be mediated by the left superior temporal gyrus (Beecher *et al.* 1979, Heffner and Heffner 1984, Petersen *et al.* 1984). Much more work needs to be done in this area: in particular, it would be interesting to see whether functional lateralization relates to morphological asymmetries in the same species. If this link between lateralization in human and non-human species is confirmed, it would indicate that the original basis for cerebral specialization might have arisen through differentiation in mechanisms for auditory comprehension, rather than in speech output.

3
THE GENETICS OF HANDEDNESS

Every child is even and either handed till some grown fool interferes with it.
Charles Reade (1878—cited in Harris 1980)

Although right-handedness is the norm, a substantial minority of people are left-handed and a few are ambidextrous. What factors are responsible for this individual variation in handedness?

The notion of a genetic basis for handedness has waxed and waned in popularity. Hildreth (1949c) concluded a review of the literature thus:

People are right- or left-handed because they have learned to be, not because they were born that way. Handedness is habitual behavior influenced by circumstances operating throughout the growth period . . Acquiring handedness follows the laws of learning and habit formation just as any other behavior that results from practice and exercise . . (p. 264)

The sources Hildreth reviewed were characterized more by opinion than evidence, and where evidence was available it was likely to be misinterpreted. A common fallacy was to assume that because handedness was not observed in young infants, it must be learned. This is wrong on two counts. First, the logic is faulty. One has only to consider the example of Huntington's chorea to recognize that a genetically determined condition may not become evident until late in life. Second, the facts are questionable. Although handedness is not an obvious feature of young infants, other lateral preferences are reliably found, and these have been linked to later handedness (see Chapter 4). Theories that attribute handedness solely to cultural pressures or explicit training find it difficult to account for such evidence. Of course, appearance of a characteristic early in life does not prove genetic inheritance any more than late appearance disproves it. As Turkewitz (1977) stressed, a behaviour present from birth need not be inherited: experience *in utero* or in the perinatal period could be a determining factor.

Segregation in families
An obvious first step in investigating a genetic basis for handedness is to look at segregation in families. Very few of the early investigators did this, an exception being Ramaley (1913), who studied handedness in 305 families and concluded that left-handedness was inherited as a Mendelian recessive character. However, his data did not provide strong support for this view. The proportion of left-handed children who had two right-handed parents was 45.6 per cent, much higher than his theory would predict. In the two families where both parents were left-handed some right-handed children were born: if left-handedness were a recessive characteristic, then all offspring of two left-handers should be left-handed. A larger study was conducted in 1928 by Chamberlain, whose data have been criticized as internally inconsistent (Levy and Nagylaki 1972). We may take pity on

TABLE 3.I
Handedness data from Chamberlain's (1928) family study

Handedness of parents (father : mother)	Number of families	Number of offspring Total	Left-handed N	(%)
R : R	2031	7225	307	(3.9)
R : L	55	196	27	(13.8)
L : R	82	268	26	(9.7)
L : L	33	63	26	(46.0)

Chamberlain, who, working as he did in a pre-computer age, was somewhat overwhelmed by the data he collected, stating despondently, 'There are too many variables in a problem of this kind for the human mind to cope with.' In fact, the internal inconsistencies in his report are not particularly serious, and he did convincingly demonstrate an increase in left-handedness among offspring of left-handed parents, consistent with a genetic influence (Table 3.I). Rife (1940) confirmed this result, reporting figures of 92.4 per cent, 80.5 per cent, and 45.4 per cent right-handedness for offspring of right–right, right–left, and left–left matings respectively. However, as with Ramaley's study, the data did not fit any simple Mendelian pattern. Families with two left-handed parents frequently had right-handed children, and, conversely, many left-handed children were born to two right-handed parents.

Although the data cannot be fitted by a Mendelian model with one-to-one correspondence between genotype and hand preference, Trankel (1955) showed that the data sets of Ramaley, Chamberlain and Rife could be accounted for by a simple genetic model if one assumed that the manifestation of a recessive allele were affected by enviromental factors, and perhaps also by other genes. Thus, he argued, there was a dominant gene for right-handedness and those lacking this gene would tend to become left-handed. However, some of them would become right-handed through environmental influences.

However, before accepting a genetic explanation, one needs to consider an alternative account in terms of environmental influence. The fact that handedness of children is positively correlated with that of parents could also be accounted for in terms of cultural rather than genetic inheritance. Left-handed parents could influence their children by adopting a more tolerant attitude towards non-right-handedness, or by providing a left-handed model for the child to imitate. However, these sorts of explanation cannot explain results such as those of Liederman and Kinsbourne (1980a), who demonstrated that the lateral bias of head-turning in newborn babies was related to parental handedness. Those with two right-handed parents were significantly more likely to turn their heads to the right than to the left, but this bias was not seen in offspring of left-handed parents. Furthermore, the relationship was similar, regardless of which parent was left-handed, so one cannot explain the link in terms of maternal factors affecting the prenatal or neonatal environment.

Adoption studies

Another way of assessing the relative importance of cultural and genetic inheritance is to study children growing up with step-parents or adoptive parents. Studies by Hicks and Kinsbourne (1976) and Longstreth (1980) showed that handedness of students was unrelated to that of step-parents but was related to biological parents. However, in both studies many step-parents only joined the family after the child's handedness was already established, so this cannot be regarded as adequate disproof of a role of imitation in determining hand preference.

Much more impressive evidence comes from a study by Carter-Saltzman (1980) in which handedness was investigated in a group of children, all of whom had been adopted in infancy (Table 3.II). The first point noted by Carter-Saltzman was that non-right-handedness was not uncommon in biological or adoptive children of two strongly right-handed parents. This is incompatible with the notion that imitation of parents is the main explanation of non-right-handedness. A second point was that the proportion of right-handedness in children was similar whether one or both adoptive parents were non-right-handed or both were strongly right-handed. The only result that was discrepant with this pattern was the significant decrease in right-handedness in children whose adoptive mother was non-right-handed. However, there were few children in this category and it seems likely that this was a spurious association, given that no decrease in child right-handedness was found when both adoptive parents were non-right-handed. Overall, the Carter-Saltzman study indicated that non-biological parents have little or no influence on a child's handedness.

In contrast, there were significant relationships between the handedness of children and that of their biological parents. Furthermore, the proportions of non-right-handers were similar for those with a non-right-handed mother and those with a non-right-handed father. This rules out explanations in terms of very early non-genetic maternal influences, such as maternal carrying or feeding practices or prenatal environment of the fetus. The finding that biological relationships are more important than postnatal experiences points towards a genetic explanation.

Twin studies

The twin study is the classical method for evaluating genetic contributions to behavioural characteristics. Monozygotic (MZ) twins are genetically identical, whereas dizygotic (DZ) twins have, on average, 50 per cent of their genes in common, so by comparing concordance rates in these two types of twin pair we can estimate how far genetic constitution plays a role in determining a given behaviour. When we do so, we find that twin pairs who are discordant for handedness (one right-handed and one left-handed) are not uncommon, and there is little difference in concordance rates between MZ and DZ twins. Carter-Saltzman *et al.* (1976) summed data from early studies to give rates of 22.5 per cent discordance for MZ twins and 19.3 per cent for DZ twins. Their own study of 187 MZ and 176 DZ same-sex twin pairs gave discordance rates of 24.6 per cent and 30.7 per cent respectively, figures that agree closely with those reported by Boklage (1981).

TABLE 3.II
Handedness data from Carter-Saltzman's (1980) adoption study

Handedness of parents (father : mother)	Biological children N	Right-handed %	Adopted children N	Right-handed %
Handedness classified as left or right				
R : R	340	89	355	86
R : L	38	76	16	75
L : R	22	73	37	95
L : L*	—	—	—	—
Handedness classified as strongly right-handed or non-right-handed				
R : R	194	53	228	54
R : non-R	69	49	54	37
non-R : R	101	46	91	53
non-R : non-R	39	28	42	55

*Too rare to give adequate sample.

More recent studies yielded similar results (Springer and Searleman 1980, Neale 1988). Such findings have been used to argue that handedness cannot be genetically determined (Collins 1970, Tambs *et al.* 1986).

However, it can be argued that the twin data do not provide grounds for rejecting genetic accounts. We shall consider below some models which postulate genes that lead to chance determination of hand preference and which therefore predict imperfect concordance for MZ twins.

Levy and Nagylaki (1972) have argued that twin data are in any case inappropriate for evaluating genetic theories because the rate of non-right-handedness is significantly higher than in singletons, indicating that idiosyncratic factors operate to determine handedness in twins. The evidence for an excess of left-handedness in twins was reviewed by Springer and Searleman (1980), who concluded that both MZ and DZ twins had rates of left-handedness above population values, this increase reflecting the contribution of discordant pairs rather than a raised frequency of pairs concordant for left-handedness. McManus (1980*a*), however, has questioned whether twinning and left-handedness are associated, noting that very few studies compared twins and singletons on the same handedness assessment. A recent population survey by Ellis *et al.* (1988) which made such a comparison found only a non-significant trend for twins to be more left-handed than singletons.

The available evidence is inadequate to come to any firm conclusions about whether twins are more likely to be left-handed than singletons. If we suspend disbelief and accept that there may be an increased prevalence of left-handedness in twins, we then need to consider why this should be so. Five explanations have been offered.

Pathological left-handedness in twins
It has been suggested that the increased perinatal risks undergone by twins lead to

an unusually high rate of pathological left-handedness (see Chapter 7). This could account for an increase in left-handedness in both MZ and DZ twins. If this is the correct explanation, one would predict that left-handed twins would have more evidence of perinatal hazards, would be more likely to be clumsy with the non-preferred hand than right-handed twins, and should be inferior on intellectual abilities. Available data on this point are sparse and inconclusive. Gordon (1920), who was one of the first to note that many twins were discordant for handedness, argued that the left-handed twin was often the smaller and was more likely to be mentally handicapped, but his sample was not large and it was unclear how cases were collected. Two contemporary studies on this topic obtained conflicting results (Carter-Saltzman *et al.* 1976, Springer and Searleman 1980), but neither supported the view that the left-handed member of a discordant pair was intellectually inferior. Boklage (1981) found a higher rate of left-handedness in second-born twins and argued that their birth risk was greater than that of first-borns, but Christian *et al.* (1980) found exactly the opposite, with a substantial excess of first-born children among the left-handed members of discordant MZ pairs.

Teng *et al.* (1976) pointed out that cases of pathological left-handedness will constitute a higher proportion of the population of all left-handers in countries such as China where there is strong social pressure to be right-handed. They found that twinning was associated with both decreased right-handedness and reduced college entrance in a large Taiwanese population, which is consistent with the view that there is an excess of left-handedness among twins due to the influence of pathological factors. This suggests that if we could find some independent way of discriminating between pathological and natural left-handers in Western cultures (see p. 95), we might be able to obtain clearer evidence for different distributions of handedness in twins and singletons. However, against this view is Annett's (1985) finding of a significant excess of left-handers among twins as compared to singletons even when probable pathological left-handers (those scoring more than two standard deviations below the mean on a test of manual dexterity) were excluded from consideration.

Mirror imaging
Newman (1928) argued that concordance for handedness in MZ twins would depend on the stage of development at which the embryo split into two. The axis of symmetry is established during gastrulation, so the suggestion was that when splitting was delayed until after this stage, the resulting twins would be mirror-image pairs, who would be discordant for handedness. Some indirect support for this view was obtained by Hay and Howie (1980), who noted that substantial differences in birthweight between MZ twins were indicative of the fetofetal transfusion syndrome, which occurs when twins split more than four or five days after conception and hence are monochorionic. They found that discordant handedness in MZ but not DZ twins was associated with substantial birthweight differences between members of the twin pair. One might argue that the transfusion syndrome would heighten the risk of pathological left-handedness, and that it is brain damage rather than mirror-imaging which explains this finding.

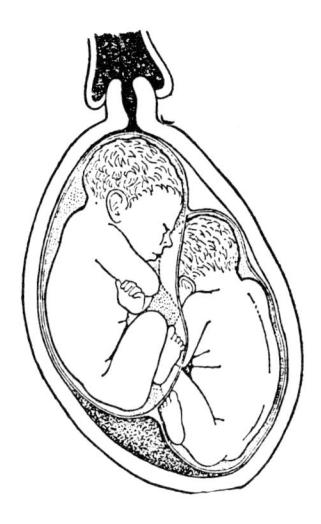

Fig. 3.1. Crowding *in utero* affects position of the fetuses in twin pregnancies. (Reprinted from Bailey 1972, p. 304.)

However, Hay and Howie found that the heavier twin was as likely as the lighter to be the left-hander.

The concept of mirror-imaging in twins appears to be be enjoying a resurgence in popularity. Nevertheless, it appears to be a rare phenomenon (in the study by Carter-Saltzman *et al.* only four out of 46 discordant MZ pairs were thought on physical appearance to be mirror images) and, as Rife (1939) pointed out, this theory cannot explain why there is an increase in frequency of left-handedness in DZ as well as in MZ twins. Rife (1940) further noted that Newman's theory predicted that mirror reversal of the viscera (situs inversus) should be observed in one member when MZ pairs were discordant for handedness, but this is not generally found.

Fetal position
In Chapter 1 the possibility was raised that position of the fetus could influence subsequent handedness (see pp. 15–16). Rife (1940) suggested that deviations from usual fetal position (Fig. 3.1) could result in an excess of left-handers. Now that we have good imaging techniques that make it possible to observe the fetus *in utero*, it would be worthwhile conducting a systematic study to evaluate this interesting hypothesis.

Delayed fetal maturation
Annett (1985, 1987) also implicated prenatal crowding as a factor affecting handedness in twins, but the mechanism she proposed was maturational. She suggested that crowding in late fetal life may retard development, slowing the appearance of differences between the cerebral hemispheres at some critical phase of brain growth, leading to an increased frequency of left-handedness in both MZ and DZ twins. Indeed, there is evidence that at 19 to 32 weeks gestation the development of various sulci and gyri is delayed by two to three weeks in twins

compared to singletons (Gilles *et al.* 1983). Annett noted that language development is often delayed in twins and she argued that this too was an indication of delayed maturation. It would be interesting to see whether a raised frequency of left-handedness is particularly striking among twins who are late to talk.

Left-handedness and predisposition to produce twin offspring
Boklage (1981) argued that non-right-handed parents are more likely than right-handed parents to produce twins. He asked parents of twins to specify the handedness of themselves, their twins and other family members. A singleton control group was not used, but the rate of left-handedness reported in twins (around 20 per cent for both MZ and DZ) was higher than in studies assessing singletons by comparable means. Furthermore, the rate of left-handedness in first-degree relatives was not significantly different from that in twins (18 per cent in brothers, sisters and fathers, and 13 per cent in mothers). Much lower rates of left-handedness were reported in *second*-degree relatives of twins.

In agreement with Rife (1939), Boklage noted that there was a relationship between parental handedness and twin handedness, *i.e.* left-handed twins tend to have left-handed relatives. He concluded that we need not assume any additional factors over and above normal genetic mechanisms to account for the raised frequency of left-handedness in twins. Boklage's findings are tantalizing, but must be greeted with some scepticism. First, the difference in left-handedness that he reported for first- and second-degree relatives of twins could simply reflect the fact that people's responses about handedness of other family members who do not live with them will be less reliable than their reports of the handedness of themselves, their spouses and children. Second, when Boklage (1977) reanalysed Rife's (1940) data he found a *deficit* of left-handers in non-twin first-degree relatives of MZ twins compared to all singleton families. Furthermore, to account for Boklage's data, there would have to be some factor that predisposed non-right-handed parents to produce twins, and this effect would have to apply to both MZ and DZ twinning, even though these arise at different stages of development and for different reasons. Boklage's findings need to be replicated on a fresh sample using direct assessment of hand preference, rather than self-classification, and including a singleton control group. If reliable, they pose an intriguing puzzle for theories concerning the origins of twinning.

Genetic models of handedness
We have seen that handedness data from family pedigrees do not fit any simple Mendelian model that postulates genotypes with a direct correspondence to left- and right-handed phenotypes. More complex genetic models are needed to explain the data.

Levy and Nagylaki's two gene model
Levy and Nagylaki (1972) proposed a genetic model that accounted for both handedness and cerebral lateralization for language. Two genes were postulated. The first gene, with two alleles, L and l, determined which hemisphere was

TABLE 3.III
Possible genotypes: Levy–Nagylaki two-gene model

Genotype	Language laterality	Handedness	%*
LLCC	L	R non-inverted	33.7
LLCc	L	R non-inverted	21.9
LLcc	L	L inverted	3.5
LlCC	L	R non-inverted	20.2
LlCc	L	R non-inverted	13.1
Llcc	L	L inverted	2.1
llCC	R	L non-inverted	3.0
llCc	R	L non-inverted	2.0
llcc	R	R inverted	0.3

*Based on Levy and Nagylaki's (1972) estimates of gene frequency (fit A).

language dominant. The second, with alleles C and c, determined whether hand control was ipsilateral or contralateral to this hemisphere. Complete penetrance was assumed. The possible genotypes derived from this model are shown in Table 3.III.

It was further suggested that writing posture might be a phenotypic indicator of genotype, those with inverted writing posture (Fig. 3.2) having motor control exerted via ipsilateral pathways, whereas the non-inverted posture would correspond to control by the contralateral hemisphere. Levy and Nagylaki claimed that the frequencies of inverted (60 per cent) and non-inverted (40 per cent) left-handed writers were consistent with the view that the former have left hemisphere language representation and the latter right hemisphere language representation. Those rare individuals with the genotype llcc would be right-handers who adopt an inverted writing posture (Dr Nagylaki being an example of such an individual).

There are several difficulties for this model. Levy and Nagylaki proposed that the degree of cerebral lateralization associated with the LL genotype was stronger than that for the Ll genotype and that Ll individuals would be more likely to make a full recovery from aphasia after a left hemisphere lesion than those who are LL, because the heterozygote could use the right hemisphere for language, whereas the homozygote could not. It was predicted that individuals who are ll would not become aphasic after a left hemisphere lesion because their language is mediated by the right hemisphere. A review of reported cases of left-handed aphasic patients did not support the model: of 15 patients with aphasia and presumed right hemisphere injury, 14 made a full recovery from the aphasia. In the face of such data, the Levy–Nagylaki model could only be rescued by adding a new postulate that the degree of cerebral specialization associated with the ll genotype is extremely weak (Levy 1976).

Furthermore, the use of writing posture as a behavioural marker of underlying genotype has been shown to be unrealistic. Although initial behavioural studies looked promising (Levy and Reid 1976, 1978; Moscovitch and Smith 1979), later

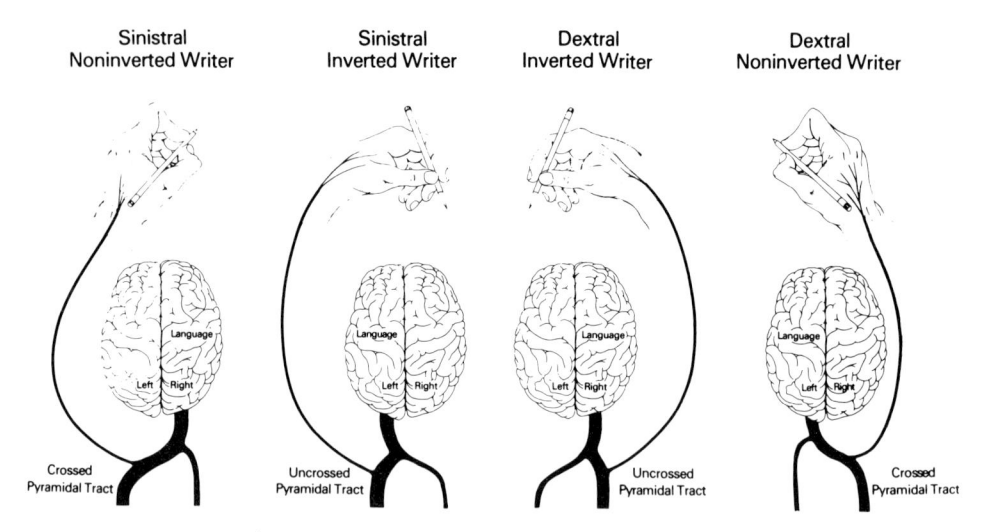

Fig. 3.2. Postulated relationships between handedness, cerebral dominance and writing posture. (Reprinted from Levy and Reid 1978, p. 122.)

investigations using such methods as dichotic listening have failed to find differences in functional lateralization between those with inverted and non-inverted handwriting postures (Peters and McGrory 1987). A small-scale study by Volpe *et al.* (1981) showed that for four left-handers investigated using the Wada test, side of language representation was the opposite to that predicted by the Levy–Nagylaki model. This was followed by a report by Ajersch and Milner (1983), who found no relation between speech lateralization and writing posture in 131 patients given the Wada test. Furthermore, inverted posture was observed in left-handers with right-sided weakness, whose hand function was almost certainly controlled by contralateral pathways. Finally, many left-handers can readily write using either inverted or non-inverted posture. Most researchers now agree that writing posture is probably largely determined by educational experience, and is not an important variable.

The final problem for the two gene theory concerns its ability to handle family pedigree data. Levy and Nagylaki obtained a reasonable fit of their model to family data reported by Rife (1940). However, Hudson (1975) subsequently showed that the fit to other data sets, including some gathered by Annett, was poor. Levy (1976, 1977*a*) has argued that the criterion of left-handedness used will affect the fit obtained: writing hand is unsatisfactory because it is subject to cultural pressures. However, a subsequent reanalysis by Annett (1978) using a different criterion of left-handedness showed that this did not improve the fit of the Levy–Nagylaki model.

Annett's right shift theory
Annett (1975) proposed a radically different approach to the genetics of handed-

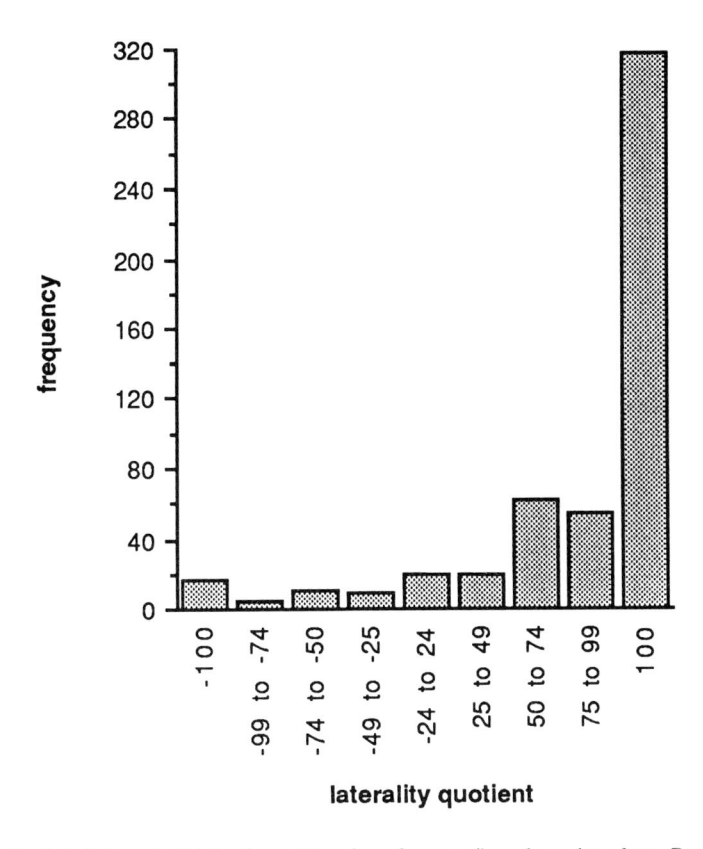

Fig. 3.3. Typical J-shaped distribution of hand preference (based on data from Peters and Durding 1978). (For definition of 'laterality quotient', see p. 70.)

ness. All previous theories had taken as their starting point the assumption that what was inherited was a bias either to the right or to the left. Annett, in contrast, proposed that the genotype determines whether there is a bias to the right, or no bias to either side. She arrived at this model by contrasting handedness in human and non-human species, noting that in animal populations one could observe consistent hand preferences in individuals, but these were equally likely to be for the left or right, and there was no evidence that heredity played any part in their determination. Thus, in non-human species, it seemed that handedness was determined entirely by chance environmental factors that resulted in one side being slightly more proficient than the other. Annett proposed that for animals other than humans the distribution of relative proficiency of the two sides was normal with a mean at zero.

Annett then considered human handedness. Human hand-preference data form a J-shaped distribution (Fig. 3.3), yet when relative proficiency of the two hands is the measure, a near-normal distribution is usually obtained, with the mean not at zero but shifted towards the right-hand end of the scale. Annett therefore argued that non-human and human species did not differ in the shape of the distribution of relative skill of the two sides, but only in its location: in effect the human distribution is like the non-human distribution with a constant added (Fig. 3.4). She postulated that in humans, as in other animals, chance plays a substantial role in determining handedness, but that superimposed on chance effects there is a *right shift factor* that gives a selective advantage to the right hand. Hand preference, she argued, is a function of relative skill of the two hands. In general, those with better right hand skill will be right-handed, and those with better left hand skill will be left-handed, with strength of hand preference being determined by the size of difference in skill between the hands. Cultural pressures will serve to make right-handedness more likely than left-handedness among those with little difference in skill between the two sides.

Is this 'right shift factor' constant in all humans? If so, we would expect left hemisphere language to be universal; however, we know that this is not so, and a substantial minority of people have language mediated bilaterally or by the right hemisphere (see Chapter 2). Furthermore, if handedness were determined the same way in all individuals, by the combined effect of chance influences and the right shift factor, then we would not expect to find any similarities in handedness between members of the same family (except for those similarities that could be accounted for by shared environment, imitation and training). Annett proposed that the right shift factor is inherited, with two alleles, rs+ and rs−, determining the extent to which an individual shows the bias to the right hand. Individuals homozygous for the rs− allele lack the right shift factor, and so their handedness is determined by chance, whereas those who have the rs+ allele either in single or double dose (rs+− or rs++) will be biased to the right.

The initial motivation for formulating the right shift theory was the observation that for both humans and other animals the distribution of L–R differences in hand skill is approximately normal. However, the genetic part of the theory treats the population as a mixture of individuals, some with no right shift factor (rs− −) and others with the factor in moderate (rs+−) or large (rs++) dose. According to this conceptualization, the population distribution of relative hand skill should show some departure from normality. This apparent contradiction is less of a problem than it may appear. Except where there is substantial separation between the means, a mixture of normal distributions with different means is very similar in shape to a single normal distribution, especially if there is a substantial discrepancy in the size of the distributions (Fig. 3.5).

One can predict the nature of the distribution of relative hand proficiency scores in the population, depending on the degree of dominance of the rs+ allele. If rs+ is completely dominant, the rs++ and rs+− genotypes will be phenotypically indistinguishable. Alternatively, there may be additivity, so that the phenotype for rs+− is intermediate between that of rs++ or rs− −. Annett and Kilshaw (1983) showed that data on hand differences in a peg-moving task could be fitted best by an additive model. Thus, the observed distribution of relative hand skill in humans is conceptualized as a mixture of three underlying distributions (Fig. 3.6). Note that there is no one-to-one correspondence between hand preference and genotype: a

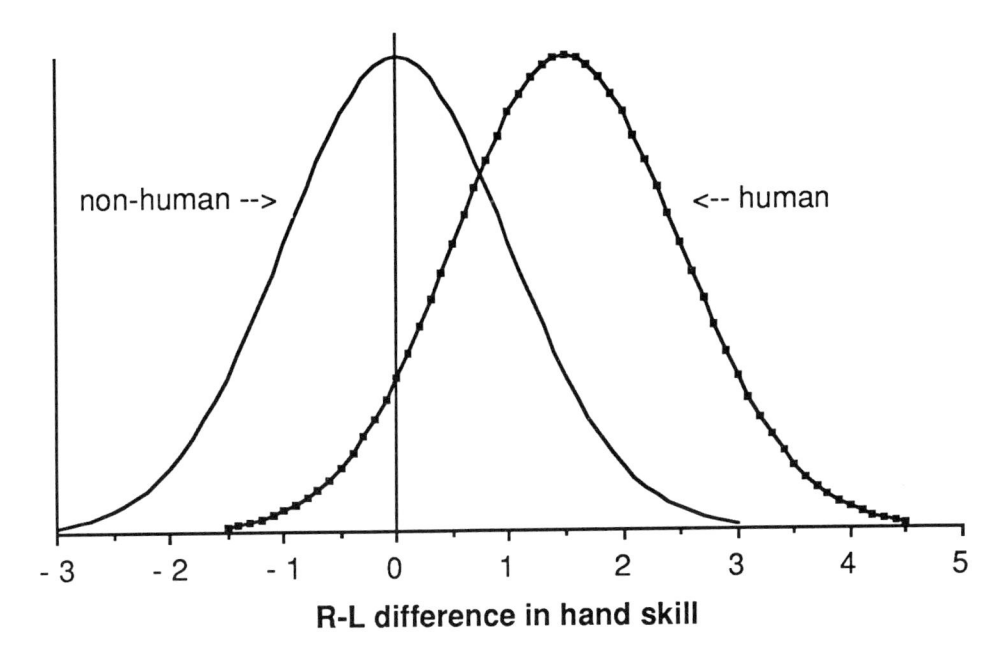

Fig. 3.4. Theoretical distributions of right–left difference in hand skill for humans and non-humans. (Redrawn from Annett 1985.)

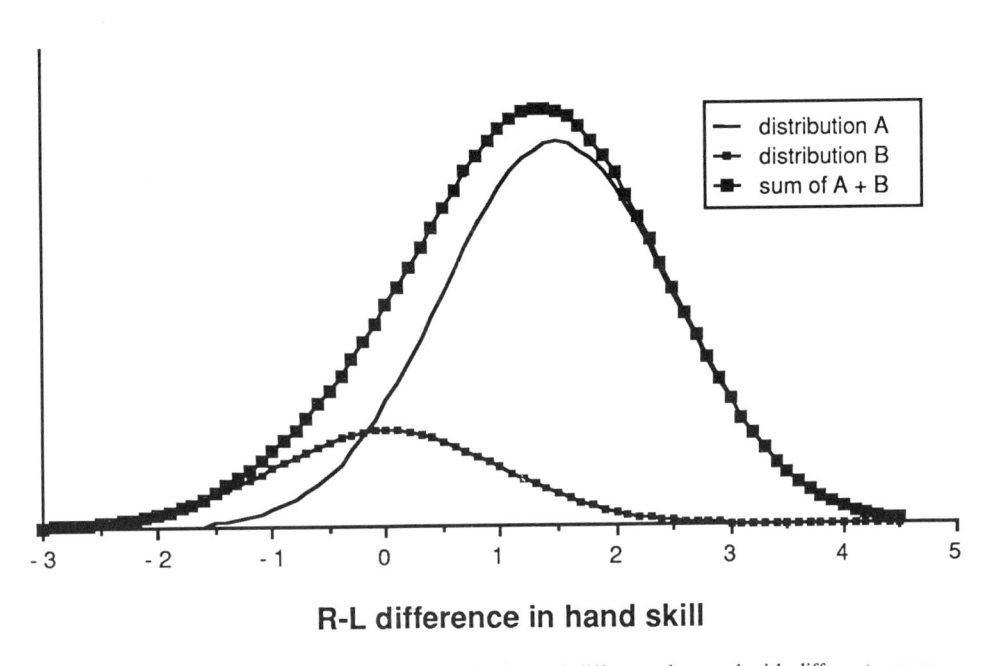

Fig. 3.5. Effect of summing two normal distributions of different sizes and with different means.

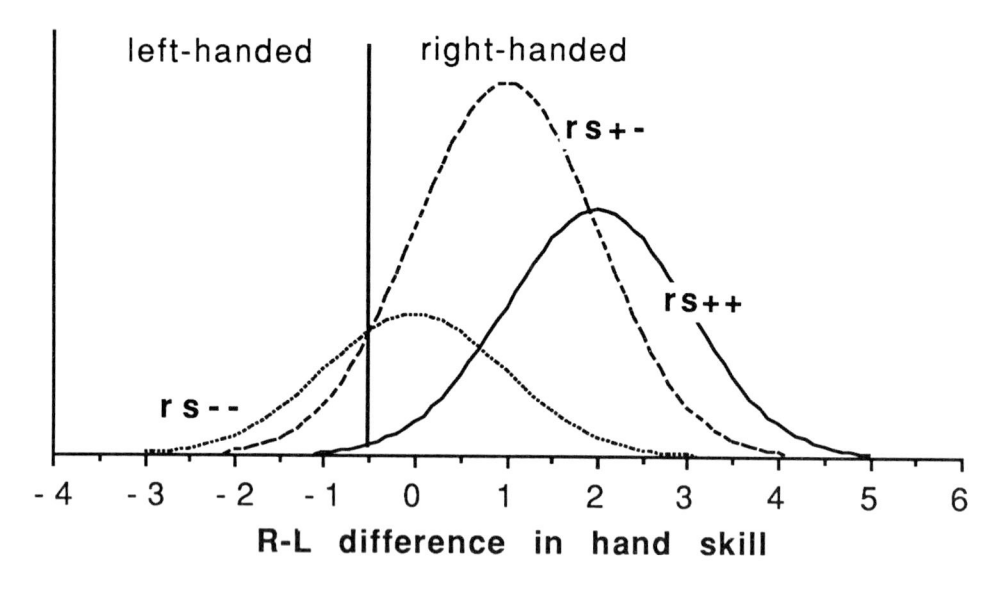

Fig. 3.6. Postulated distributions of right–left hand skill differences for three genotypes of the right shift model, assuming additivity. Relative hand skill is expressed as a z score. (Based on Annett 1985.)

left-hander may be someone who lacks the right shift factor, or may fall in the left-hand tail of the rs+− or rs++ distribution.

The right shift model has the advantage that it is not tied to one definition of left-handedness. One can use the observed frequency of left-handedness to specify where on the distribution of relative hand skills a cut-off must be placed to distinguish left- from right-handers, and this cut-off can be altered according to the handedness assessment used.

Precise predictions of the proportions of left-handed children from different matings can be made provided one assumes that hand skill differences for different genotypes are normally distributed as in Figure 3.6, and one has estimates for (i) the population frequency of the rs+ gene, and (ii) the distance of the mean of each genotype from the cut-off point which divides phenotypic left- and right-handers. Although genotypes cannot be observed and bear only an indirect relationship to handedness groupings, this model provides all the information one needs to predict relationships between parents' and children's handedness. Annett (1985) reviewed family data on handedness in relation to the right shift theory, showing that it could predict the numbers of left-handed sons and daughters born to right–right, right–left and left–left matings in two of her own samples, and in two out of three samples published by other authors. Note that the model easily accommodates the finding of discordant handedness in MZ twins: such cases are expected for individuals with the rs−− genotype, where left- and right-handedness are equally likely.

This theory has more flexibility than the model of Levy and Nagylaki, which treats handedness as a binary characteristic and consequently has problems in handling such findings as the secular increase in left-handedness during this century. However, it could be argued that, because the right shift model has so many degrees of freedom, by appropriate adjustment of parameters it could be made to fit almost any data set. One way of testing the model to rebut such criticism would be to move away from treating left- vs. right-handedness as the phenotype and to look at family relationships in the distributions of differences in hand skill, the underlying quantitative dimension that Annett regards as the determinant of hand preference. This poses obvious practical problems, because data on hand skill, especially for previous generations, are not readily available. Annett did look at relative hand skill, however, in a study of children of two left-handed parents. According to the right shift theory, the majority of left-handers are of the rs− − genotype and hence have no genetic bias towards one side. Offspring of two rs− − parents must be rs− −, and so should also show no bias to right or left. Annett obtained results consistent with this prediction in two separate samples, finding that the mean hand difference was slightly but not significantly biased in favour of the right hand. She discussed how the right shift theory can explain relationships between handedness and cerebral lateralization, and proposed that, for individuals lacking the right shift factor, handedness and cerebral lateralization are independent, both being determined by chance factors. However, those affected by the right shift factor will almost always have left hemisphere language representation except in cases of brain damage. Thus in the whole population we will observe a link between handedness and cerebral lateralization because the probability of right-handedness is increased by the same right shift factor that determines left hemisphere language representation.

Because the right shift model conceptualizes handedness as a continuous variable, the definition of left-handedness is essentially arbitrary: one could place a cut-off on the distribution of L–R hand skill well to the left of zero to include only those with very strong sinistral tendencies, or well to the right to select as left-handed anyone who departed from consistent right hand preference. Although arbitrary, the cut-off used is crucial when predicting the relationship between handedness and cerebral lateralization. Annett (1975), using an early version of the right shift model, illustrated that, where 20 per cent of the population are rs− − and the mean of the rs+−/rs++ is 1.5 standard deviations to the dextral side of zero, the relationship between cerebral lateralization and handedness varies as shown in Table 3.IV. The model assumes that 50 per cent of those who are rs− − and all of those who are rs++/rs+− will have left hemisphere language representation. From this we would predict the basic results from studies reviewed in Chapter 2, *i.e.* the majority of both left- and right-handers have left hemisphere language representation, but departure from this form of cerebral lateralization is much more common in left-handers than in right-handers. Annett went on to investigate how well the right shift theory fitted data obtained from five clinical series in which the incidence of dysphasia after unilateral brain lesions had been studied in patients unselected for laterality. This gave estimates of 18 per cent rs− −, with rs+−/rs++ individuals showing a shift of $1.937z$ to the right.

TABLE 3.IV

Language lateralization in right- and left-handers as a function of the criterion of left-handedness*

Location of threshold of left-handedness	Incidence of left-handedness in population %	Right hemisphere language In L-handers %	In R-handers %
$-1.0\ z$	3.7	43	9
$-0.5\ z$	8.0	36	7
$0.0\ z$	15.3	33	6
$+0.5\ z$	26.5	26	4
$+1.0\ z$	41.5	20	3

*Based on Annett (1985; Table 14.1).

The right shift theory can explain why the cerebral lateralization of left-handers is not a mirror-image version of that observed in right-handers, either in behavioural or morphological terms. Data from the Wada test and from procedures such as dichotic listening consistently find evidence that left-handers are less strongly biased towards left hemisphere language representation. The same picture is given by studies of morphological brain asymmetries: for those brain areas where right-handers show greater development on the left side, left-handers typically show less difference between the two sides (see Chapter 2). The right shift theory predicts such results because it maintains that there is no systematic factor biasing towards right hemisphere language representation or towards left-handedness.

Other threshold models

Although the right shift theory provides an adequate fit to family data from several sources, this does not prove that it is correct.

Falconer (1965) showed that when dealing with conditions that appear to have a hereditary basis but which do not show simple patterns of recessive or dominant inheritance, it can be useful to adopt a model that assumes an underlying normal distribution of liability to develop the condition, with a threshold beyond which it is manifest. Even where the observed phenotype is an all-or-none condition, one can apply a quantitative model that assumes its underlying basis is a graded characteristic. Computer programs have been developed that allow one not only to test the overall fit of such a model to family data, but also to partition the variance in liability into that arising from environmental and genetic sources, and to contrast models that attribute genetic variation to the effects of single genes, or to multiple effects of many genes. The right shift theory can be regarded as a variant of this general model in which genetic variation in liability is determined by a single gene whose alleles have additive effects, and where non-genetic factors also account for a substantial amount of variance. Alternative formulations of threshold models are, however, possible. In particular, inheritance of liability could be polygenic rather than determined by a single gene. Risch and Pringle (1985) showed that a polygenic threshold model fitted family segregation data just as well as the right shift theory, and Neale (1988) made a similar point with twin data. In neither case was a polygenic model superior to a single gene model: the problem was rather that the different models could not be distinguished.

Annett (1985) argued that a polygenic model would predict high correlations between family members in left-minus-right peg-moving scores, and she provided data showing weak and usually non-significant correlations between related pairs of individuals. However, this point is valid only if polygenic influences are regarded as the major determinant of liability. Provided one accepts that environmental factors also play a substantial role, then a polygenic model is no more likely than a single gene model to predict high intercorrelations between family members.

There are two ways in which the different models may be discriminated. One way forward would be to gather sufficiently large samples of family data to test between models. However, it is salutary to note that in this context a sample of 1000 individuals is grossly inadequate. Risch and Pringle (1985) pointed out that better discrimination between models might be obtained without needing astronomical sample sizes if handedness were measured as a quantitative variable rather than as a dichotomy. An alternative approach would be to seek a biological marker of a single gene. If we could identify some all-or-none characteristic whose presence is indicative of the right shift factor, this would provide firm support for a single gene effect.

McManus's single gene model
McManus (1984, 1985*a*) postulated that handedness is determined by two alleles at a single locus, D (dextral) and C (chance). Individuals who are DD are right-handed, while those who are CC have handedness determined by chance: 50 per cent left and 50 per cent right. Heterozygous individuals, DC, are intermediate, with 75 per cent right-handed. The frequency of the C allele is estimated at 0.155, giving population frequencies of 0.714, 0.262 and 0.024 for the DD, DC and CC genotypes respectively.

McManus showed that if one assumes that the probability of left-hemisphere language representation for a given genotype is the same as the probability of right-handedness, with the two being independently determined, then the predicted distribution of cerebral lateralization in left- and right-handers is close to obtained values. He went on to demonstrate that his model also predicts a relationship between cerebral lateralization and parental sinistrality, with a higher proportion of right hemisphere language representation expected in those with one or both parents left-handed. One problem for McManus was how to handle the phenomenon of bilateral language representation. He did so by postulating that more than one language function may be lateralized, with laterality of each function being independently determined. Thus some individuals have language A represented in the left hemisphere and language B in the right hemisphere. Although McManus did not speculate about the nature of these biologically dissociable functions, it is interesting to note that this formulation is compatible with at least some of the descriptions of individuals with bilateral language who have been studied using the Wada test (see pp. 21–22).

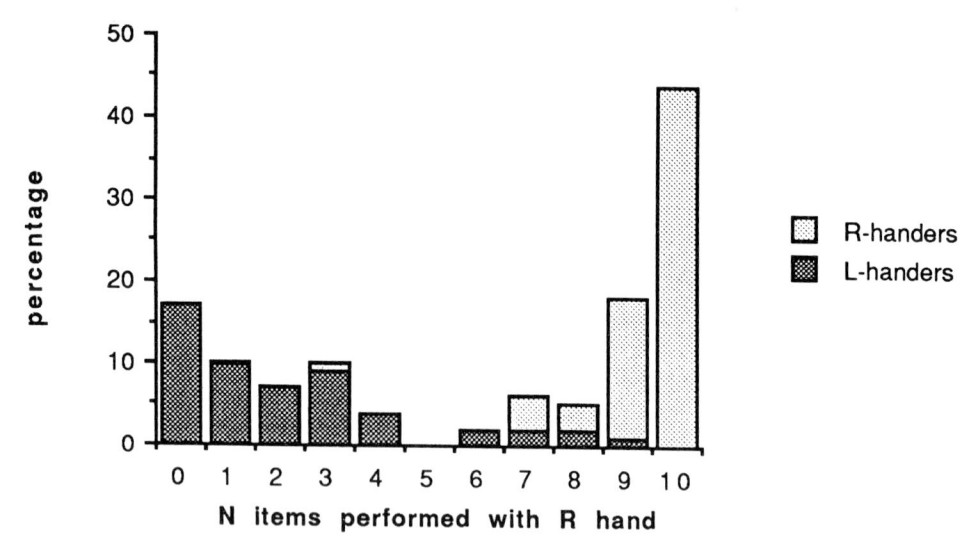

Fig. 3.7. Distribution of hand preference scores for self-classified left- and right-handers. (Based on data from Satz et al. 1967.)

According to McManus, handedness is appropriately treated as a categorical variable with two values: left-handed and right-handed. Within each category there will be some variability in degree of handedness, but he argued that this individual variation is not determined by genetic factors, and may simply reflect error of measurement or environmental experiences.

It can be seen that this model has much in common with the right shift theory in its characterization of genotypic variation underlying handedness. Like Annett, McManus proposed that genotype determines whether an individual is biased away from chance determination of handedness towards dextrality: there are no genetic factors inducing a bias towards sinistrality. McManus differed from Annett, however, in his conceptualization of the phenotype. The difference from the right shift theory is a subtle one: whereas Annett maintained that an *individual* inherits either a skill bias to the right or no bias, McManus argued that lack of bias to either side characterizes the *population* with genotype CC, but individuals constituting the population do show bias, to left and right in equal proportions.

One problem for this formulation is that we need to explain why left-handers do not behave like mirror-image right-handers. Left-handed writers on average perform more activities with their non-preferred hand than do right-handed writers (Downey 1933, Humphrey 1951, Satz et al. 1967) (Fig. 3.7). McManus answered this objection by arguing that the hand preferences of left-handers will be subject to pressures from living in a right-handed world. It is harder, however, to explain why left-handers also show less strong foot preferences than right-handers (Peters 1988), and why their brains show less morphological asymmetry than those of right-handers (see Chapter 2).

McManus suggested that the distribution of relative hand skill scores can be

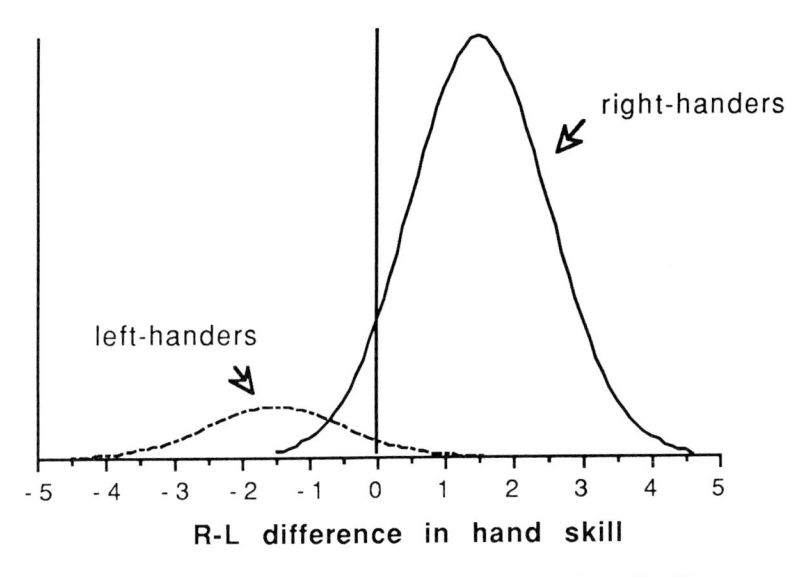

Fig. 3.8. The bilateral symmetrical model of McManus (1985b).

used to test between his model and the right shift theory. It will be remembered that the right shift theory postulates that the total population distribution will be the sum of three underlying distributions, as shown in Figure 3.6. McManus, in contrast, regards the distribution as comprising two underlying distributions: one with a mean to the right and the other with a mean to the left (Fig. 3.8). He (McManus 1985b,c) reanalysed peg-moving data from Annett and Kilshaw (1983) using a maximum likelihood procedure to compare the fit of the right shift model with that of his own model. His 'bilateral symmetrical' model gave the best fit. Other data sets analysed by McManus gave variable results, but in general his model gave a better fit than any form of the right shift theory.

However, this debate is complicated by the fact that the type of hand skill distribution obtained will depend on the task used. Peters (1987) noted that practice was a crucial variable. Prolonged practice with one hand on a task will emphasize differences between the two sides. For example, if one plots distributions of relative hand skill on a task involving holding a pen, then the skill distribution is bimodal, with one mode well to the left of zero, and the other at the corresponding point to the right (Fig. 3.9). If, however, one takes a relatively unpractised task, then bimodality is not apparent. Peters argued that in order to assess how far relative skill is a determinant of preference, it is important to minimize effects of unequal practice of the two sides. He devised a task to meet this requirement. Both hands tap a regular rhythm, with one hand tapping twice for each single tap of the other hand. Even though subjects were not paced but were asked to tap at a comfortable rhythm, significant differences were found depending on which hand tapped at the faster rate. For right-handers, tapping was faster when the preferred hand tapped at double the rate of the non-preferred hand. However,

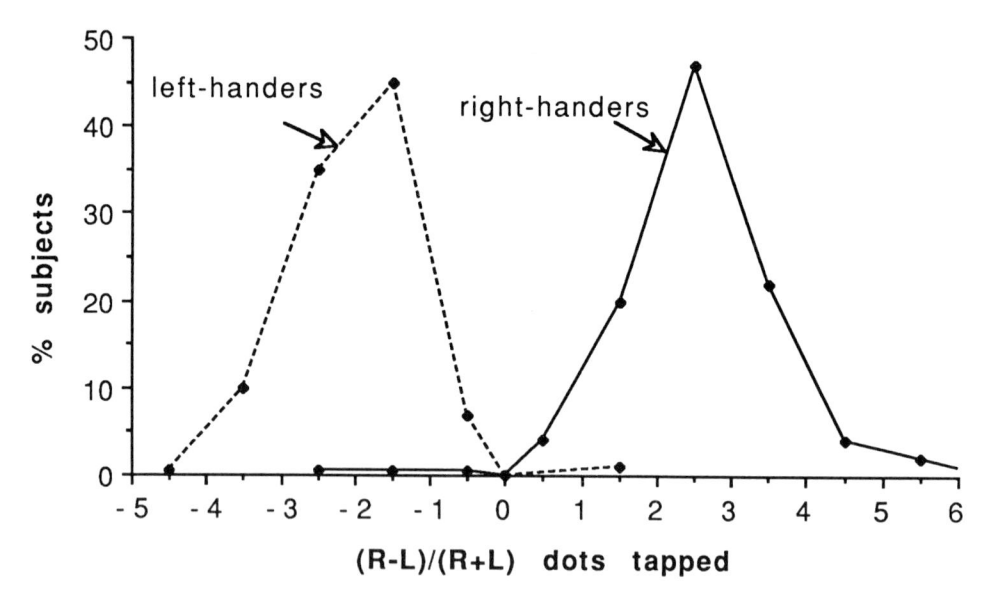

Fig. 3.9. Distinct distribution of right–left hand skill differences for left- and right-handers on a task involving pencil use. (Based on data from Tapley and Bryden 1985.)

for left-handers, no such difference was observed. Peters showed that this group effect reflected the fact that individual subjects in the left-handed group showed weaker laterality effects on this task. He interpreted his results as offering support to the right shift theory.

Non-genetic biological inheritance?
Collins (1970) argued against genetic explanations of handedness. He showed that selective breeding for pawedness in mice did not affect paw preference distributions, even if continued over many generations. This in itself does not constitute strong evidence against inheritance of the species-specific preferences shown by humans. Morgan (1977), however, took the argument a step further, maintaining that there was *no* known case in any species where direction of a morphological asymmetry was determined in an individual by its own genetic material.

Furthermore, according to Morgan and Corballis (1978) this is to be expected, because there is no way in which the direction of an asymmetry *could* be coded in a gene. We know that there is no intrinsic difference between cells on the two sides of the body, so that, for instance, by appropriate grafting, an early left limb bud from a chick can be converted wholly or partly to a right limb bud. This phenomenon is not difficult to explain: one need assume only that the pattern of development is affected by the position of a cell in relation to other cells. The problem is how does a cell recognize whether it is on the left or the right side? If there were perfect symmetry, this information would be irrelevant, but for asymmetrical development to occur, embryonic cells on the two sides of the body must have information about left–right position, so that they can differentiate along separate pathways. This problem is specific to the left–right axis and does not apply to up–down or back–front dimensions (Wolpert 1978). There is no difficulty in creating an organism in which the two sides are different from one another: the problem is in defining the left side as opposed to the right side, which is necessary if a species is to show asymmetry in a consistent direction.

Of course, this problem is not confined to human handedness, but concerns all aspects of asymmetrical development of animals, including siting of organs such as the liver and heart in humans, and more esoteric asymmetries such as the disproportionate growth of the left tooth in the narwhal and the extra digit often found on the left foot of domestic chickens. Morgan and Corballis postulated that all vertebrates have a cytoplasmic left–right gradient running orthogonal to the midsagittal plane that provides the genes with information about left and right, and so can account for all these species-specific asymmetries. They suggested that the human bias towards right-handedness is caused because the cytoplasmic gradient favours more rapid growth of the left side. Individual variation in expression of this gradient will be determined partly by the cytoplasm inherited in the oocyte from the mother, but largely by environmental influences. There was, they concluded, no need to postulate specific genes that determined left- vs. right-handedness. Although the notion of a cytoplasmic gradient has been criticized (*e.g.* Wolpert 1978), the general argument that genes do not code left–right direction is persuasive.

However, we may note that this argument is problematic only for models such as that of Levy and Nagylaki which maintain that bias to either left or right can be inherited. More recent models, such as the right shift theory, treat the genetic distinction as being between symmetry and asymmetry, rather than left and right. Expression of the gene for asymmetry would presumably be controlled by the same influences that determine other consistent bodily asymmetries, such as location of the viscera. The logical problems of coding direction in genes do not therefore apply to this type of model. The Levy–Nagylaki model, on the other hand, must answer the charge that genes do not encode asymmetry because they cannot. Levy (1977*b*) defended her position by producing a counter-example. There is a mutant gene in the fruitfly that can cause rotation of the entire abdomen. Direction of rotation (clockwise or anticlockwise) shows a Mendelian pattern of inheritance. It would seem, then, that although it is rare for direction of asymmetry to be inherited, and the mechanism is not understood, this can occur. The Levy–Nagylaki model may be criticized on other grounds, but it does not go against nature.

Overview
The puzzle posed by human handedness is that although there are clear relationships between handedness of parents and offspring, these are not easily fitted to any Mendelian pattern of inheritance, nor are they easy to explain in terms of specific environmental influences. Against a genetic explanation we have the fact that concordance for handedness is low in twins, and seems unrelated to zygosity.

However, an account of handedness as learned behaviour has difficulty explaining parent–offspring similarities in very early lateral preferences and in children separated from their parents in infancy. An influence of uterine environment on the fetus, or maternal non-genetic inheritance might seem plausible possibilities, until we consider that both Carter-Saltzman (1980) and Liederman and Kinsbourne (1980*a*) showed parent–offspring relationships for fathers as well as mothers.

Annett's right shift theory made a conceptual leap forward in suggesting that what was inherited was not direction of asymmetry, but whether or not there was symmetry. Once this assumption is accepted, it is easy to account for findings such as the less than perfect concordance in MZ twins, because the phenotypic distinction is between random determination of handedness and a bias to the right. The theory has been criticized because it is difficult to differentiate its predictions on breeding ratios and twin concordance from those of other models, including some models that assume little or no genetic component and others that argue for polygenic inheritance. However, even critics of the right shift theory tend to agree with its major postulate: the appropriate conceptualization of the phenotype is as random vs. right-biased, rather than right-biased vs. left-biased. Until there is clear evidence that another theory can better account for existing data, Annett's right shift theory is likely to remain popular because of its conceptual simplicity and its ability to account for a range of findings in different domains.

4
THE DEVELOPMENT OF HANDEDNESS

Handedness is not an obvious characteristic of young babies, but is usually evident by the time the child starts school. Does this mean that lateral preferences are not present in infancy, or can they be revealed by appropriate assessment procedures?

Hildreth, in a review written in 1949, concluded that in early infancy the physically normal child is bilateral, and that a consistent preference can first be observed at around 7 to 9 months of age. The difference between sides is initially slight, but increases gradually and becomes pronounced around 3 years of age. She summarized the results from several investigations, to show a sharp increase in the proportion of right-handers between the ages of 0 to 3 years, followed by a stabilization (Fig. 4.1). Her conclusions survive broadly intact after a further 40 years of research, but require some modification on points of detail.

Below 6 months of age
There is some evidence of differential usage of the two hands in infants under the age of 6 months. Cobb *et al.* (1966) categorized spontaneous hand positions in 360 newborn infants as tightly fisted, loosely fisted, partly open, open, or moving. They found that fisting of the right hand was significantly more common than of the left. Interpretation of this finding is complicated by the fact that the fisted hand is not traditionally regarded as a more mature posture than the open hand—in fact, quite the contrary.

Caplan and Kinsbourne (1976) measured how long infants grasped a rattle placed in either hand before dropping it. They studied 21 babies aged from 1 to 4 months, and reported that the grasp was maintained for longer in the right hand than in the left. A further five babies with a family history of left-handedness in a first-degree relative did not show any difference between the two sides. Petrie and Peters (1980) obtained similar results using a slightly different task with infants tested longitudinally from the age of 17 to 105 days, although Yu-Yan *et al.* (1983) failed to replicate the small effects reported by Caplan and Kinsbourne with a Chinese sample, despite following closely similar procedures.

Newborn infants frequently make spontaneous movements that bring the hand to the mouth. This appears to be an intentional movement, rather than a random occurrence, as the mouth opens before the hand reaches it (Butterworth and Hopkins 1988). Hopkins *et al.* (1987) found that whereas hand–face contacts in newborns were equally likely to involve left and right hands, hand–mouth contacts were much more common with the right hand, although two out of 12 infants showed a pronounced left hand preference (Fig. 4.2). The asymmetry in hand–mouth contacts was related to another motor asymmetry, that of head position, which will be discussed below.

Gesell and Ames (1947) reported that hand preference passed through distinct

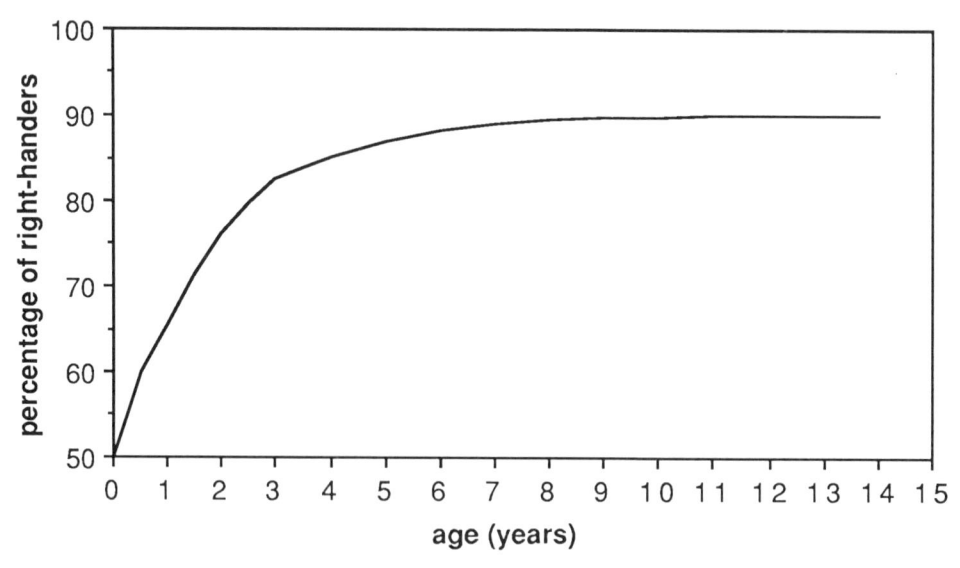

Fig. 4.1. Theoretical development of hand preference. (Redrawn from Hildreth 1949b.)

phases in early childhood, with most children showing a tendency to *left-handedness* in the first 3 or 4 months of life. However, in a comprehensive review of the literature, Young *et al.* (1983) found that the overall trend among 1- to 4-month-old infants was for the right hand to be used more than the left, although differences seldom reached statistical significance. One reason why it is difficult to show hand preferences in infants may be that reaching for objects is not yet properly established: under the age of 3 months, visual stimulation may elicit arm movements, but the infant lacks the ability to direct these to attain a goal (Michel 1983).

Although it is difficult to demonstrate reliable lateral differences in hand use in early infancy, other motor behaviours appear to be lateralized from a very early age. Peters and Petrie (1979) found that a group of infants tested at 17, 51, 82 and 105 days old had a significant tendency to lead with the right leg when the stepping reflex was elicited by lowering the infant to a flat surface so that the feet established contact. Melekian (1981) replicated this result using a larger sample, although Korczyn *et al.* (1978) found no motor asymmetry when stepping was elicited by placing a restraining bar in front of the infant's shins.

In a series of studies Turkewitz and his collaborators revived interest in a phenomenon that had been described by Gesell and Ames (1947):

> If one goes into a nursery for healthy, full-term newborn infants and is attuned to the phenomenon, two things will be noted. First, the posture of the infant is assymetrical; the infant lies with its head turned out of the midline. Second, this asymmetry is highly uniform; almost all the infants lie with their heads turned to the right. (Turkewitz 1977, p. 252)

Saling (1979) replicated initial studies by Turkewitz and his colleagues (Turkewitz

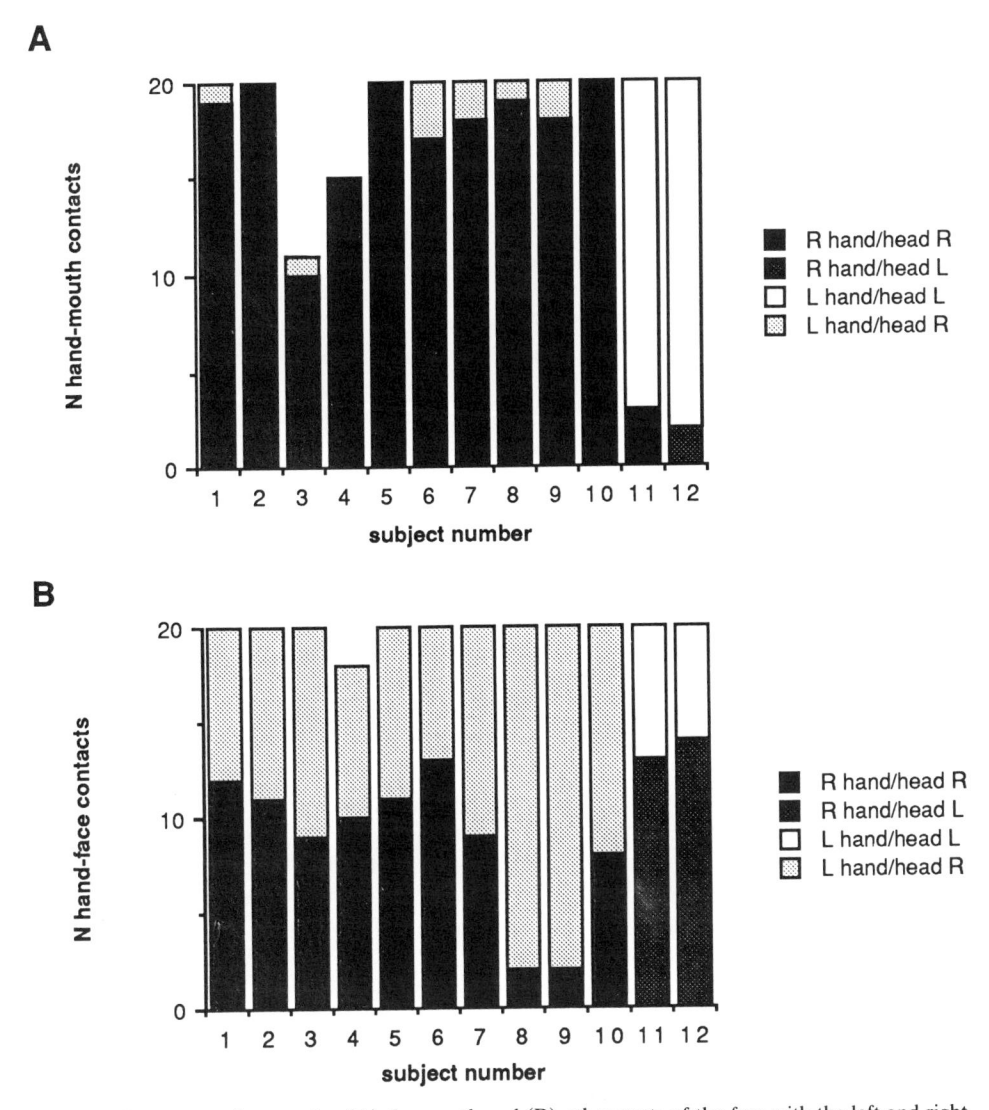

Fig. 4.2. Frequency of contacting (A) the mouth and (B) other parts of the face with the left and right hand in 12 newborn infants, classified according to direction of head turn. (Data from Hopkins *et al.* 1987.)

et al. 1965, Turkewitz and Birch 1971) demonstrating this phenomenon, and also showed that infants were usually consistent in their direction of head-turning across two occasions. It is hard to attribute this bias to the effects of handling by nurses, since Hopkins *et al.* (1987) found a right-sided head-turning bias in newborn babies within one hour of delivery. Furthermore, Gardner *et al.* (1977) found the same bias in preterm infants at a conceptual age of 35 weeks, with the proportion of right-sided turns increasing steadily up to 39 weeks. Fox and Lewis (1982) found right-biased head posture even earlier than this, in a group of infants born at 33 to 34 weeks gestation. This lateral bias does not seem to be caused by asymmetrical passage through the birth canal: unpublished observations cited by Gardner *et al.* found the same head-right posture in infants delivered by caesarian section.

Is asymmetry pathological?
Trehub *et al.* (1983) noted that these normal postural asymmetries seem to contradict conventional teaching in paediatric neurology, where motor asymmetry in neonates is regarded as indicative of neurological dysfunction (*e.g.* Prechtl 1977). They conducted a study to address this apparent paradox, studying the frequency of asymmetrical reflexes in full-term and preterm neonates, using Prechtl's protocol for elicitation of reflexes. Contrary to expectation, they found very little evidence of asymmetry in either group of infants, not even for those behaviours, such as head-turning, which had previously been demonstrated to be right-biased by other workers. Some evidence of asymmetry was found for the stepping reflex, but this was in the opposite direction to that reported by Peters and Petrie. There are several points to take into account when explaining these findings.

POPULATION VS. INDIVIDUAL BIAS
Statements about asymmetrical tendencies in normal infants are typically statements about population biases. One looks at a large number of infants and notes that significantly more than 50 per cent are asymmetrical in a particular direction. This does not necessarily mean that individual infants show consistent bias to one side. The study by Trehub *et al.* involved 12 trials of elicited head turning for each of 20 infants. When all turns were added together across all children, there was only a weak trend for a right-sided bias. However, 16 out of the 20 infants did turn more frequently to the right than to the left. Thus, while the strength of lateral bias was not impressive within individuals, there was consistency of direction of bias within the sample. It is normal for there to be a significant bias towards one side in the population of infants as whole. What is abnormal is for an individual infant to show a highly consistent bias in favour of one side.

EFFECT OF INITIAL POSTURE
There is mounting evidence that the extent to which postural and reflex asymmetries are observed depends on the infant's initial posture. If the head is held in the midline or positioned leftward, the natural tendency to turn the head to the right can be disrupted and take some time to reappear (Turkewitz and Creighton 1974, Liederman and Kinsbourne 1980*b*, Fox and Lewis 1982). Another way of drastically reducing head-turning asymmetries is by habitually positioning infants face down rather than on their backs (Konishi *et al.* 1987). Swaddling may also have an effect: this could explain why Saint-Anne Dargassies (1977) regarded postural symmetry as the norm in newborn babies.

The relatively weak lateral biases observed by Trehub *et al.* (1983) could have been affected by the procedures used to prepare infants for examination, which were designed to minimize postural biases. While the baby was sleeping, its natural

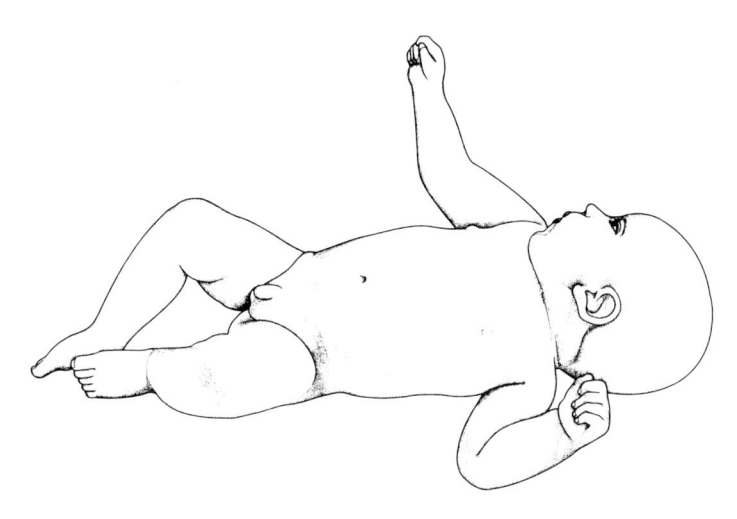

Fig. 4.3. The asymmetric tonic neck reflex: the arm and leg are extended on the side to which the face is turned, with flexion of the limbs on the opposite side. (Reprinted from Baird and Gordon 1983, p. 141.)

head position was reversed for 10 minutes, before it was picked up and gently woken by 'rotation through various planes' for 10 to 30 minutes, prior to undressing and examination. This contrasts with most other studies of normal infants where no attempt was made to reduce natural postural asymmetries prior to testing.

Initial posture, then, seems to be an important determinant of reflex asymmetry. Michel (1983) suggested that hand fisting of the kind noted by Cobb *et al.* (1966) may be a consequence of general postural asymmetry, and noted that a change in the fisting pattern can be observed when the head of the infant is turned, either spontaneously or as a result of experimental manipulation. In a clinical context, Saint-Anne Dargassies (1977) noted an interaction between prior head position and the asymmetry of the Moro reflex.

SPONTANEOUS VS. ELICTED ASYMMETRIES
Most studies of normal developmental trends have considered spontaneous postural asymmetries rather than elicited reflexes. While it is not abnormal to have a postural preference for one side, it is pathological to show marked differences in strength of response to eliciting stimuli presented to left and right.

Gesell and Ames (1947) noted that when an infant lies with its head to one side, the limbs tend to assume the posture of the asymmetrical tonic neck reflex (ATNR), whereby the turned head results in extension of the limbs on the face side and a flexion of those on the skull side of the body (Fig. 4.3). Because there is a bias towards right-sided head turn, it follows that this spontaneous posture will be observed more frequently on the right than the left.

If, however, one elicits this posture by turning the infant's head to one side and holding it there until there is no active resistance, then the ATNR can be elicited on either side in normal infants, and may, indeed, be more reliably seen on the opposite side to that for which the infant shows a spontaneous bias (Liederman and Coryell 1981, Liederman 1987). An imposed ATNR which is consistently stronger with the head to one side than to the other is abnormal and is often followed by the emergence of a motor deficit (Paine *et al.* 1964).

Saint-Anne Dargassies (1977) noted a further source of confusion about this particular reflex. The term 'tonic neck reflex' suggests similarities to reflex behaviour first described in experimental animals, in which head rotation produces an immediate, constant, rapid and inexhaustible reflex. Although this reflex can be observed in infants it is unusual and highly pathological. The normal postural changes associated with head rotation in infants are slow, inconstant, incomplete and appear only after a very long latency. Furthermore, this normal form of ATNR is not observed in newborn babies but gradually develops around 1 month of age, disappearing at 3 to 5 months.

In sum, it would seem that there is really little conflict between paediatricians and developmental psychologists in the interpretation of asymmetry. The concern of the medical specialist is with the infant who regularly responds much more strongly to stimulation on one side than the other, or who gives an asymmetrical response when the reflex that is elicited usually involves symmetrical body posture. The asymmetries that have been described in normal children are much less consistent and more easily modified than those observed in cases of neurological impairment.

Relationship of infant asymmetries to later handedness
Several investigators have considered whether habitual head position in infancy is related to later handedness. An early study relating reflexes in infancy to handedness in later childhood was by Gesell and Ames (1947), who found that of nine infants with a tonic neck reflex on the left, four were left-handed at 10 years of age, whereas all seven with a tonic neck reflex to the right were right-handers at 10 years. A small study by Coryell (1985) found that infants who tended to turn their heads to the right became right-handers, while a tendency to turn to the left or to show no bias was not predictive of later handedness. Clearly, more research is needed to extend these observations, but it is intriguing to find yet another example of the phenomemon whereby those with left-sided tendencies do not behave like the mirror-image of those with right-sided tendencies, but rather appear to be more bilateral.

More recently, modest but significant links have been demonstrated between head turning and hand preference for reaching in early childhood (Michel 1981, Konishi *et al.* 1986).

The mechanism whereby head-turning might influence handedness remains a matter of debate. One possibility is that an asymmetrical head posture leads to asymmetry in motor activity of the arms. An alternative view is that the head position leads to more sensory experience for one side than the other (Turkewitz 1977).

Certainly, there is evidence that asymmetrical head-turning is linked to asymmetrical arm movement. At around 3 to 10 weeks of age, a supine position with the head turned to one side tends to elicit the ATNR. Coryell and Michel (1978) attempted to relate the ATNR to hand preference by recording hand activity when the infant was confronted with a chequered ball within arm's reach, but this procedure was not very successful in eliciting hand movements except in the final assessment when the children were aged 12 weeks. However, on this one occasion when the ball elicited hand activity, the right hand was significantly more active than the left.

As well as causing asymmetrical motor behaviour, the ATNR results in one hand (usually the right) being placed in the visual field more often than the other, and it has been suggested that this provides more opportunity to establish eye–hand coordination on that side. Peters (1983a) noted that if asymmetrical visual experience were an important determinant of hand preference, then blind children should show less of a relationship between habitual side of ATNR and handedness. Although this prediction has not been tested, there is evidence that blindness does not affect the distribution of hand preferences (Ballard 1911–12), suggesting that any role of asymmetrical visual experience is minor.

6 to 18 months of age
Evidence for reliable hand preferences in reaching has been found in children just over 6 months of age. Harris (1983) described an early German study carried out by Voelckel in 1913. Over a period of several days, infants were tested while supine with a small toy held in the midline. Those aged 3½ to 6½ months reached equally with either side, but infants aged 7 months and over had clear hand preferences, usually for the right. Similarly, Lippman (1927) noted that when extending a hand to accept an object, children aged around 4½ months used left and right hands equally, but there was a progressive trend towards lateralization, and by 12 months use of the right hand occurred on 70 per cent or more of occasions. Goldfield and Michel (1986) tested 57 infants aged from 7 to 12 months, observing the hand used to reach and manipulate a range of toys. Each child was categorized according to whether the preference for one hand was significantly above chance level. 26 children had a right hand preference, 12 had a left hand preference, and 19 had no preference. There was no evidence of an age trend in this study. Similar results were reported by Young *et al.* (1985), who found a bias in favour of right-sided actions and gestures in 80 infants aged from 8 to 15 months.

What is responsible for the emergence of hand preference? With so many aspects of behaviour developing rapidly, the problem is not in thinking of candidate explanations, but in choosing between them.

Development of a precision grip
One aspect of motor development that alters dramatically in the first year of life is the infant's ability to adopt a precision grip. It was noted in Chapter 1 that hand preference in adults is most apparent for activities requiring precise fine motor control. Mebert (1983) found that for infants aged between 4 and 10 months, both hands generally engaged in the same amount of activity and the relative frequency with which a hand was used was largely a function of which hand first made contact

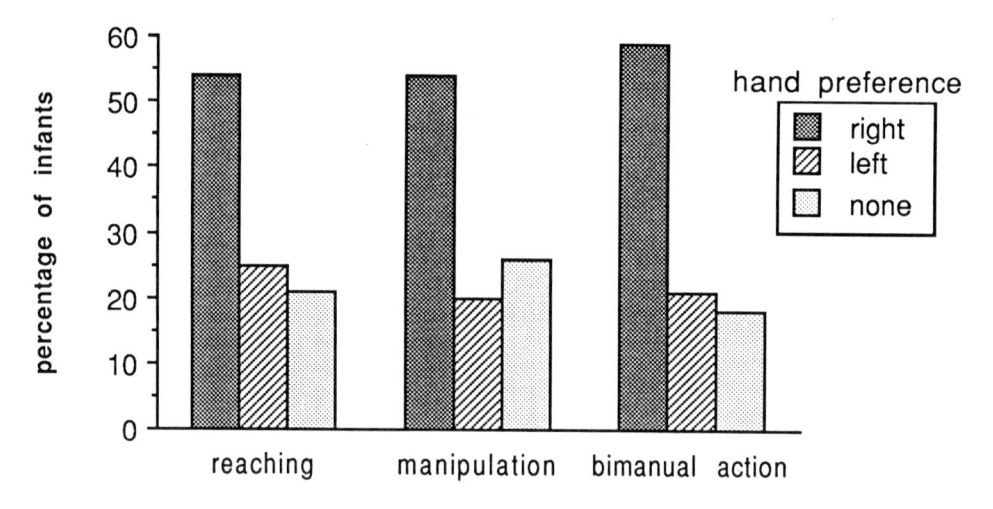

Fig. 4.4. Percentages of infants showing hand preference for three activities. (Based on data from Michel *et al.* 1986.)

with an object. However, in these same children, she observed a significant preference for the right hand in precision grasping.

Bimanual coordination
Ramsay *et al.* (1979) noted that bimanual coordination, a capacity which is not demonstrated until the end of the first year of life, may play an important role in the development of handedness, yet most assessments of infant handedness restrict consideration to unimanual activities. 24 infants were observed monthly from 10 months of age when playing with toys which were specially selected to encourage manipulation. Most children showed a clear tendency to hold the toy in one hand while using the other to manipulate it, and this preference was stable over a five-month interval. A further 100 children were given a longer assessment procedure, in which the hand used to manipulate nine toys was recorded. On first testing, at 14 to 16 months of age, 71 per cent used the right hand at significantly above chance frequency, 14 per cent used the left hand, and the remaining 15 per cent showed no clear preference.

Michel *et al.* (1986) investigated lateral preferences for three different activities: reaching for objects, manipulating objects with one hand (banging, shaking, fingering, etc.), and complementary bimanual actions. They presented 96 infants aged from 6 to 13 months with a range of toys selected to elicit these behaviours. In addition, for 64 of the children, spontaneous hand use was recorded when playing with blocks. Figure 4.4 shows the percentages of children in different handedness categories, where lateral preference was credited if the probability of the obtained hand difference occurring by chance was 0.16 or less. For all activities, the majority of children showed a preference for the right hand. There was no age trend in the proportion of infants with hand preferences for reaching and

TABLE 4.I
Contingency coefficients in infants aged 6–13 months (Michel et al. 1986)

	Pick up blocks Coeff.	(N)	Manoeuvring blocks Coeff.	(N)	Reaching Coeff.	(N)	Manipulation Coeff.	(N)
Manoeuvring blocks	0.74**	(64)	—	—	—	—	—	—
Reaching	0.62**	(64)	0.33	(64)	—	—	—	—
Manipulation	0.45*	(64)	0.36*	(64)	0.52**	(96)	—	—
Coordinated bimanual action	—	—	—	—	0.10	(32)	0.61**	(32)

*$p<0.05$; **$p<0.01$.

unimanual manipulation. Preference for bimanual action could not be assessed in the youngest children because this activity was engaged in only by those aged 9 months and over. Test–retest reliability was significant though not substantial. To assess stability of hand preference over time, 10 children were seen on three occasions: nine showed consistent preferences for reaching on all three assessments, but only six were consistent for one-handed manipulation. Table 4.I shows agreement in handedness categorization across the different tasks. While for most of the activities lateral preferences were significantly associated, handedness for reaching was not related to preference in coordinated bimanual action. This study confirmed that a population bias towards right-handedness can be observed in children as young as 6 months of age. However, the proportion of infants showing hand preferences was lower than in older samples, and those preferences that were observed were less stable across time and less consistent between activities than in adults.

Voluntary and intentional acts
Peters (1983b) argued that a major difference between the 6-month-old and the 12-month-old infant is that the older child is capable of attending to an object and intentionally reaching for it in order to manipulate it. The younger child may engage in behaviour that appears superficially similar, but its meaning is quite different, without the goal-directed volitional quality of later reaching. He proposed that the presence or absence of lateral biases will depend on the meaning of a movement as well as on its superficial characteristics.

In this regard it is interesting to note that Strauss (1982) failed to find lateral differences in grasp duration when 4- to 16-month-old infants were given a tongue depressor to hold, whereas Caplan and Kinsbourne (1976) did find such differences using a rattle. This suggests that the interest a child shows in an object might affect lateral bias even as young as 4 months. Further studies contrasting lateral bias for grasping different objects are needed.

Emergence of language
It was noted in Chapter 2 that there is a relationship between hand preference and cerebral lateralization for language. This has led some investigators to look for

relationships between emerging hand preference and language development. Ramsay (1983) found that 6-month-old children who had started to use reduplicated syllable babbling (*e.g.* baba, dada) showed signs of developing preference for one hand earlier than those who had not yet reached that stage. In this preliminary account, Ramsay was not able to find clear evidence linking age at onset of babbling to emergence of handedness, but in a more detailed later study he argued that there was a sharp increase in the proportion of right-handed toy contacts in the week that parents reported the onset of duplicated syllable babbling (Ramsay 1984). However, right hand preferences that were observed in this period were not very stable and subsequently disappeared in many infants.

Bates *et al.* (1986) raised the question of whether right-handedness might reflect the extent to which manual activity is compatible with left hemisphere language processing. They argued that symbolic actions involved in pretend play (such as using a spoon to stir an empty bowl) are more language-like than non-symbolic actions (such as moving a spoon from one position to another), and that one might therefore expect to find differences in the extent to which right-handedness is observed for these classes of activity. Their longitudinal observations on 27 infants aged from 13 to 28 months confirmed this prediction, in finding that right-handedness was more pronounced for symbolic than non-symbolic actions. Furthermore, pointing, which is not symbolic but serves a communicative function, was also more likely to be right-handed than were non-symbolic actions.

Although these findings are compatible with the view that right-handedness is primarily a secondary consequence of left hemisphere specialization for language functions, the detail of the theory proposed by Bates *et al.* may need modification. They argued for inhibition of right hand use for non-symbolic actions because these competed for limited left hemisphere resources that were used for language functioning. However, competition would only seem relevant if the child were attempting simultaneously to use language and to perform an action. Furthermore, if there were such competition, then one would expect to find left hand preference for non-symbolic actions, and this was not observed. Rather, the child tended to use the right hand more than the left for all types of actions, but this trend was more pronounced for symbolic than non-symbolic movements. It seems more parsimonious to account for these findings in terms of facilitation of right hand use for actions that engage and/or accompany left hemisphere language functions. Other actions would lack this facilitatory effect and so show less bias in favour of the right hand.

Over 18 months
One of the few longitudinal studies to follow children from early infancy to middle childhood was conducted by Gesell and Ames (1947), who documented the development of handedness in seven children who were studied at regular intervals between 8 weeks and 10 years of age. They claimed that their data revealed systematic shifts of handedness in the course of development, with left-handed, bilateral and right-handed phases emerging at particular stages. This interpretation does not seem justified by the data: rather, it seems likely that the children they observed were progressing gradually from an initially random hand choice to a

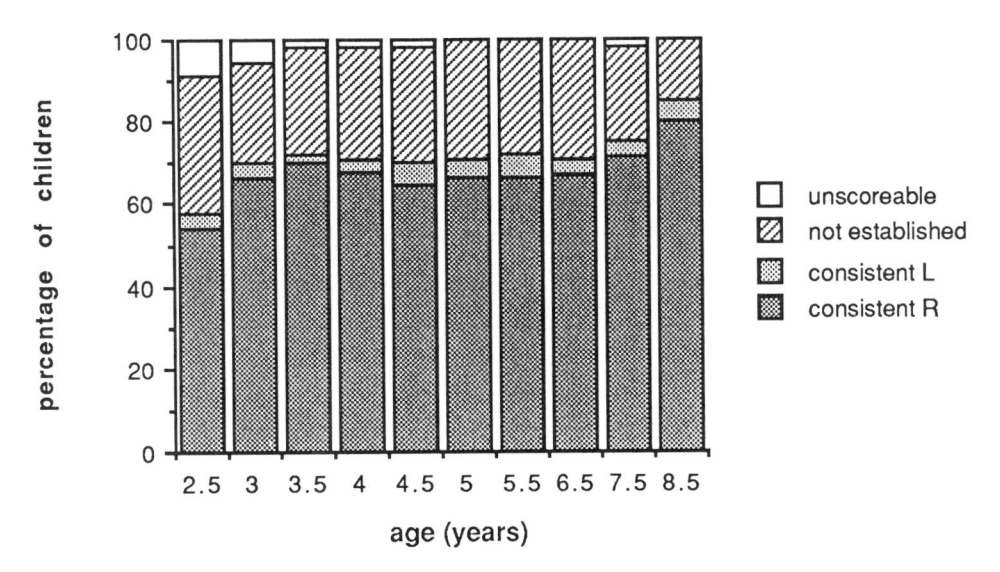

Fig. 4.5. Percentages of children with different forms of hand preference in McCarthy's (1970) standardization sample.

stable hand preference.

This is the conclusion reached in an early study by Jones (1931), who measured the time for which each hand was active in a series of motor tests given to 60 children aged from 18 to 66 months. The proportion of total time using the right hand was 68 per cent for children aged from 18 to 30 months, rising to 69 per cent for those aged 31 to 37 months, 76 per cent for ages 38 to 45 months, and 82 per cent for those aged 46 to 66 months. The published data are not adequate for statistical analysis, but the overall picture is consistent with a gradually increasing trend towards dextrality over this age range. This interpretation was supported by a longitudinal study of 272 children by Rice *et al.* (1984), who assessed hand preference at the ages of 12 and 24 months. Less than 10 per cent of infants exhibited a clear preference at 12 months, whereas 30 per cent did so at 24 months.

There are several recent cross-sectional studies which confirm that the frequency of mixed handedness decreases gradually with age (Belmont and Birch 1963, McCarthy 1970, Coren *et al.* 1981; but cf. Annett 1970*b*, Longoni and Orsini 1988), and, more recently, similar trends have been documented in prospective longitudinal studies (Fennell *et al.* 1983, Gaillard and Satz 1989). Fennell *et al.* found that 154 out of 159 right-handers identified in kindergarten (around age 6 years) had the same handedness classification at grade 5 (around 11 years), compared with 17 out of 23 left-handers and only one of 26 ambidexters.

While the majority of studies agree in finding that handedness gradually stabilizes with age, there is disagreement about the age at which this occurs. Data from the standardization of the McCarthy Scales of Children's Abilities (McCarthy 1970) are shown in Figure 4.5.

Degree vs. stability of handedness
As in most studies in this field, degree and stability of hand preference are not distinguished in McCarthy's study. A child is coded as having 'dominance not established' if there is any inconsistency in hand preference across four activities (ball bouncing, bean-bag catch, bean-bag throw and drawing). Thus a child who always draws using the left hand but performs the other three activities with the right will be coded as 'dominance not established' together with a child who is random in hand preference and likely to shift laterality from one occasion to another. Furthermore some children who are coded as 'dominance established' may in fact be children whose hand preference is labile and affected by temporary situational factors. Indeed, McCarthy provided evidence that this was the case: for a subset of children retested one month after initial testing, only 71 per cent of those originally categorized as having 'dominance established' were placed in the same category at second testing.

McCarthy also found that the proportion of children who were classified in the same handedness category on retest showed a developmental trend, from 61 per cent in 3-year-olds, 70 per cent in 5-year-olds and 76 per cent in 7- to 8-year-olds. Similarly, Bruml (1972), in an experimental study in which hand preference for a range of activities was assessed on four occasions, found that between the ages of 5 and 10 years there was a modest increase in stability of hand preference for a given activity (see Table 1.I). There is evidence that in the young child, choice of hand to perform a skilled action on a given occasion may be more subject to temporary situational influences than in an older child (Hildreth 1948, Connolly and Elliott 1972). Adults, in contrast, usually have stable preferences for particular activities, even if they are inconsistent across activities (Steehuis and Bryden 1989, Peters and Servos 1990). It seems probable that the major aspect of laterality that changes with age is stability of hand preference for a given activity across different occasions and that clearer developmental trends would be apparent if investigators distinguished this aspect of laterality from between-task consistency.

Rather than assuming that development involves a progressive trend towards either consistent right-handedness or consistent left-handedness, it seems more accurate to view development as involving gradual stabilization of lateral preference for any given activity. Thus we can use Annett's (1975) right shift theory (see pp. 40–46) to propose that there are two types of individual: a large set who are biased to prefer the right hand for most activities and who will progress from initial random behaviour to reliable preference for the right side for the majority of activities, and a smaller set who lack bias favouring one side and who progress from initial random behaviour to systematic preference for one side or the other for any given activity, but with little relationship between side of preference across activities. This model is shown in Figure 4.6.

On the assumption that the population consists predominantly of individuals with a right shift, we would not predict much change with age in the frequency of individuals who use the right hand more than the left, but the number of actions performed with the right hand would increase as children grew older. This was exactly what was found by McManus *et al.* (1988) in both cross-sectional and

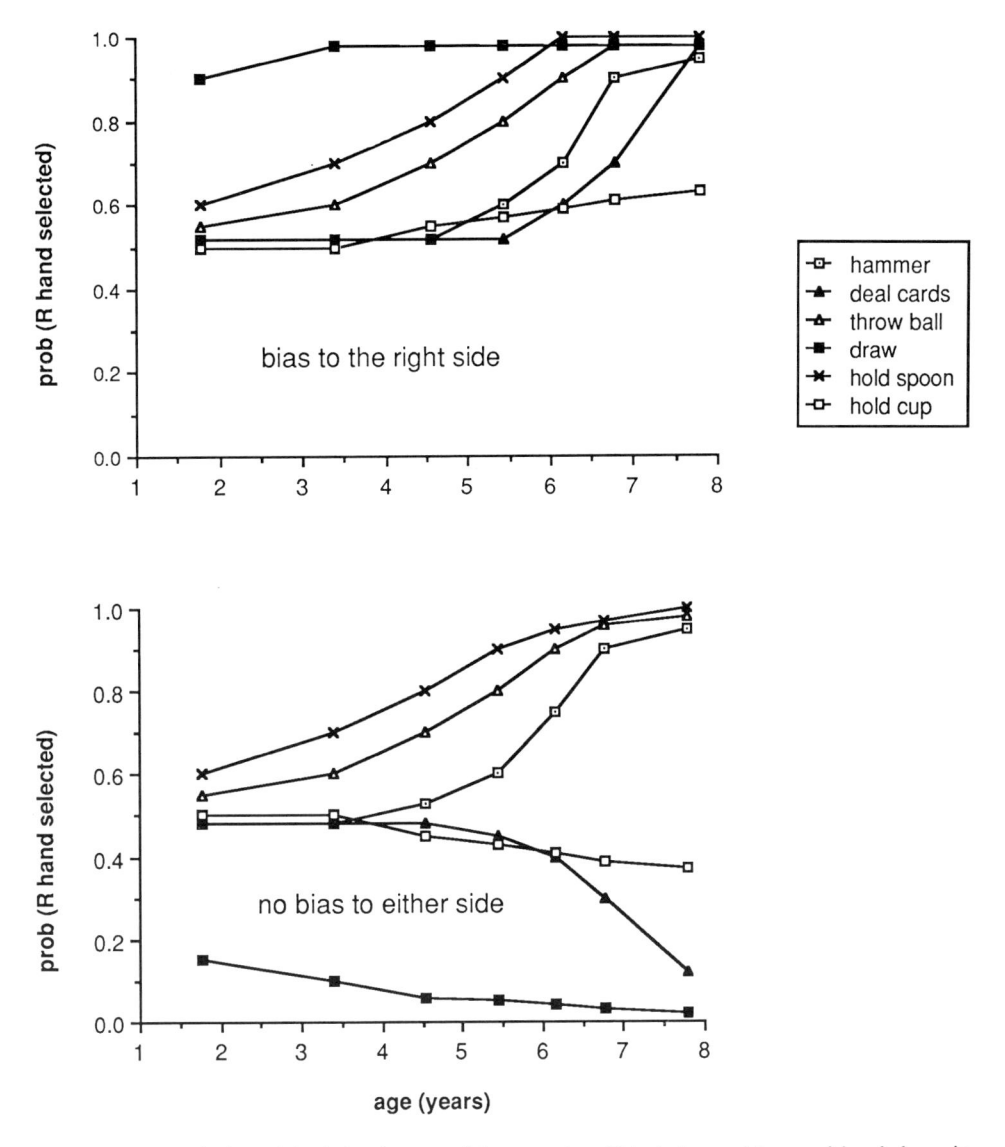

Fig. 4.6. Theoretical model of developmental increase in within-task consistency of handedness in individuals with and without a bias to prefer the right side.

longitudinal samples. Similarly, Auzias (1984) reported that between 3 and 5 years of age there was a trend for right-handers to become more consistent across activities in their right-handed preference, whereas left-handers showed no such trend for increasing left-handedness. However, measuring degree of hand preference (*i.e.* how many actions are performed by the preferred side) is an indirect way of testing this model: ideally one would like to see a longitudinal study in which consistency of hand preference was directly assessed by giving children repeated trials of the same activity. The prediction is that what changes with age is the extent to which the individual is consistent in choice of hand for a given activity.

Practice and maturation as determinants of developmental change in handedness
Provins (1967) noted that acquisition of a motor skill involves a process of 'paring down': initially one can only produce gross actions involving many related muscles, but with practice one reaches a state where precise control of single motor units is achieved. He argued that handedness was most marked in practised tasks which require appreciable fine coordination of muscle activity. Implicit in this formulation are two possible explanations for developmental trends in handedness. According to the first, hand preference develops as the child becomes increasingly practised in particular activities. Whether or not a spoon is consistently held in one hand will be a function of the child's experience of spoon use. A second, but not mutually exclusive view is that consistent handedness is largely a result of neuromotor maturation. The more capable the child is of fine motor manipulations, the more likely it is that consistent handedness will be observed. If the predominant determinant of handedness were practice on a task, then we might expect that familiar everyday activities such as using a comb or toothbrush should show hand preferences earlier than actions such as dealing cards, in which few small children are experienced. In general, the evidence reviewed in Chapter 1 goes against this view. In adults, level of practice alone is not able to account for consistency of hand preferences: some very frequent activities show weak hand preferences whereas other actions, especially those involving a precision grip, are invariably executed with one side, even though they may be performed only rarely. It seems likely that neuromotor status and consequent ability to perform precise movements is a more important factor than practice in determining whether hand preference is shown for an activity.

Neurological bases of developing motor skills
Liederman (1983) proposed that manifest hand preference might depend on the relative maturity of medial and lateral motor systems. The lateral system controls contralateral distal extremity musculature, whereas the medial system effects ipsilateral control of the trunk and proximal extremity musculature. Superiority of left hemisphere motor control would be reflected in a left side preference for whole arm movements, such as those involved in reaching, but as fine motor coordination, mediated by the lateral system, developed, right-handedness would become increasingly apparent. Liederman further proposed that maturity of the corpus callosum may be a crucial factor affecting hand preference. Until interhemispheric callosal connections are functional, hand movements that cross the body midline are seldom observed. Young infants, like split brain patients, typically use the left hand to reach for locations on the left side and the right hand to reach to the right. Once the corpus callosum is functional, the child is able to use the preferred hand regardless of the location of an action relative to the body. A mature corpus callosum is also probably important for the inhibition of symmetrical bilateral

movements ('mirror movements'). Such inhibition seems necessary to enable asymmetrical bimanual actions to occur (Fog and Fog 1963).

There have been few studies relevant to the issue of neuromotor maturity and handedness, although Cohen (1966) showed that consistent hand preference at 8 months of age was significantly related to advanced developmental status, and lack of preference to below average development. Kaufman *et al.* (1978) and Tan (1985) confirmed that preschool children with 'unestablished' hand preference (assessed on the McCarthy scales) had lower levels of motor skill than those with consistent handedness, and Tierney *et al.* (1984) found a link with lower overall scores on the General Cognitive Index. Gottfried and Bathurst (1983) gave 6-monthly handedness assessments between 12 and 42 months of age. They found that girls whose hand preference for drawing was consistent across assessments were more advanced in development than those who were inconsistent, although this was not confirmed for boys. Much more research remains to be done. The hypothesis that relates handedness to callosal maturity generates a number of testable predictions. It would, for instance, be of interest to see whether at a given age, children with unestablished hand preference were less competent at crossing the midline, showed more mirror movements, and were less able to perform bimanual asymmetrical actions than those with established hand preference. The prediction is not that non-right-handedness *per se* is associated with deficits in these areas, but rather that lack of consistent hand preference within a given task is a sign of callosal immaturity.

Sex differences
As well as looking at interrelationships between motor competence and handedness, it may be instructive to consider sex differences. Males are slightly more likely than females to be non-right-handed, and they also mature rather more slowly, as evidenced by lags in language milestones. There is little evidence from cross-sectional studies of lateralization differences between boys and girls early in life (*e.g.* Gardner *et al.* 1977), although Humphrey and Humphrey (1987) found that females aged from 5 to 8 months had a right-sided reaching bias whereas males of this age did not. It would be interesting to monitor development of hand preference longitudinally in boys and girls, because, according to the theory outlined here, if one restricted consideration to children who ultimately became right-handed, the age at which stable hand preference is observed should be later for the males than the females.

Does cerebral lateralization develop?
In adults we know that there is a link between hand preference and cerebral lateralization. As discussed in Chapter 2, non-right-handers are less likely to have strongly lateralized language functions than right-handers. This argument has been extended to the developmental context. The notion that cerebral lateralization develops gradually was proposed by Lenneberg (1967) in his influential book *Biological Foundations of Language*. He maintained that early in development both cerebral hemispheres participate in language functions, but that as the child matures, cerebral lateralization gradually develops, with this process being

completed around puberty. Following Orton's (1925) early speculations, it became popular to regard delay of this postulated maturational progression (or its total failure to occur) as a cause of developmental reading and language disorders (see Chapter 11). Furthermore, again largely due to Orton's influence, mixed handedness in children came to be regarded as an indirect indicator of undeveloped cerebral lateralization.

There is, however, mounting criticism of the view that cerebral lateralization develops with age (Kinsbourne and Hiscock 1977, Witelson 1987). Lenneberg's main source of evidence for this position came from studies of the frequency of aphasia in children after unilateral brain lesions, where he argued that in early childhood, language disturbances were as likely to result from right as from left hemisphere lesions. However, because of the rarity of aphasia in young children, Lenneberg was forced to gather evidence from a range of published sources, and it has been argued that at least some of these were misleading, (a) because the lesion was not strictly unilateral, and (b) because the criteria for aphasia were neither objective nor clearly specified. More recent analyses using stricter criteria for inclusion of cases tell a different story. Although it seems to be broadly true that the right hemisphere can mediate language functions if the left hemisphere is damaged early in life, there is little support for the idea that in normal development the right and left hemispheres participate equally in early language functioning (see Bishop 1988 for a review).

Behavioural studies of functional asymmetry support this view. There is no doubt that it is much harder to demonstrate cerebral lateralization by behavioural means in young children than in adults. When the child's language capacities, concentration and cooperation are limited, techniques such as dichotic listening are difficult to apply (Bryson *et al.* 1980). Where these problems have been overcome, the evidence is that cerebral lateralization is not something that gradually develops, but is present from the earliest stages of language acquisition (see review by Best 1988). New techniques, such as measurement of lateralization of evoked responses to linguistic stimuli, have also shown predominantly left hemisphere processing of language, even in infancy (Molfese and Betz 1988). Although this area is fraught with methodological problems, and results must be looked at with a critical eye (see, for instance, the comments made by Michel 1983), the balance of current evidence supports the view that in most infants the left hemisphere is already specialized for language processing in the first few months of life. As Witelson (1987) has argued, it is not cerebral lateralization that increases with age, but 'the amount of cognition available to be asymmetrically mediated by the hemispheres' (p. 679).

If cerebral lateralization does *not* develop in childhood, then one cannot interpret mixed handedness in a child as a sign of a maturational delay in establishing brain asymmetry. There is no doubt that mixed handedness *is* more common in children than in adults, but this phenomenon can be explained in terms of neuromotor maturation and/or motor experience, without assuming a link with development of asymmetrical language representation.

5
THE DEFINITION AND MEASUREMENT OF HANDEDNESS

It may seem illogical to defer consideration of the definition of handedness to this point. The more general rule is that definitions precede explanations. The reasons for this counterintuitive sequence should become clear in the course of this chapter: quite simply, one cannot consider how handedness should be measured without first understanding something about the causes and correlates of the phenomenon.

The reader might think that in any case measurement of handedness should be a simple procedure: it seems sensible and straightforward to categorize people as left-handed or right-handed on the basis of the hand used to hold a pen when writing. Indeed this is exactly the approach favoured by McManus (1984), who argued that people are easily dichotomized according to writing hand, and so few individuals are truly ambidextrous for writing that it makes sense to treat handedness as a binary categorical variable.

Others, however, have argued that there are several ways in which this definition is unsatisfactory when considering the neuropsychology of handedness. One problem is that handedness for writing may be strongly influenced by teaching, with explicit discouragement of left-handedness. While this is less pronounced in Britain and the USA than it was in the past, it is still an important influence in many cultures, especially those that associate the left hand with unclean activities. For those of us whose interest is in handedness as a manifestation of underlying biological constitution, it is desirable to find a way of assessing handedness which is relatively unaffected by cultural pressures, and which could be administered to young children or illiterate adults. Another objection is that a simple dichotomy may be too insensitive: some people carry out virtually all one-handed actions with the same hand, whereas others may prefer different hands for different activities. For example, I am left-handed for writing, eating with a spoon, combing my hair and sewing, but hold a toothbrush, a tennis-racquet and scissors in my right hand. It has frequently been suggested in the neuropsychological literature that *degree* of hand preference as well as *direction* may be important, and that it might be more fruitful to treat handedness as a continuous variable, ranging from extreme right-hand preference, through equal preference for both sides (ambidexterity or 'mixed handedness'*) to extreme left-hand preference. On such a scale I would be distinguished from a left-hander who used the same hand for all activities.

The objections to reliance on writing hand were stated 50 years ago by Burt (1937): '. . mere casual observation of some particular stereotyped action, like

---

*These terms are often used interchangeably to refer to intermediate degrees of handedness, although some authors prefer to reserve 'ambidexterity' for cases where the person is equally skilful with either hand for a given activity such as writing.

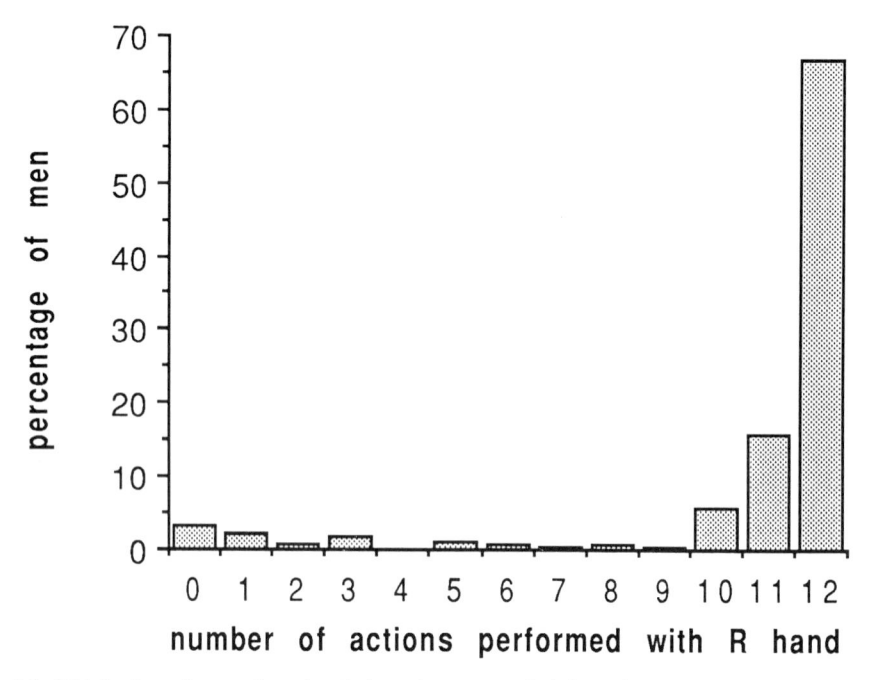

Fig. 5.1. Distribution of scores from handedness inventory administered to 241 servicemen. (Redrawn from Annett 1985.)

writing or drawing, will be of little value by itself . . [Handedness] must be judged . . . not so much by long-standing habits as by an unfamiliar task, and not by a single action, but by several' (p. 271).

Handedness inventories

Inventories were designed in an attempt to refine handedness assessment. Rather than simply classifying people as 'right-handed' or 'left-handed', lateral preferences for a wide range of different activities are combined, in most cases to give a 'laterality quotient'. As well as yielding a quantitative index of handedness, an inventory can avoid undue reliance on activities that are subject to cultural pressures by including items for which hand preference is unlikely to be specifically taught (*e.g.* cutting with a knife, brushing the teeth). Details of three published inventories (Crovitz and Zener 1962, Annett 1970*a*, Oldfield 1971) are given in the Appendix.

A variety of formulae have been proposed for computing a laterality quotient, with most yielding a score ranging from −100 for extreme left-handedness, through zero, corresponding to equal preference for either side, up to +100, corresponding to extreme right-handedness. The distribution of laterality quotients is typically J-shaped, with most scores clustering at the extremes, and relatively few individuals without a strong preference for left or right (Fig. 5.1).

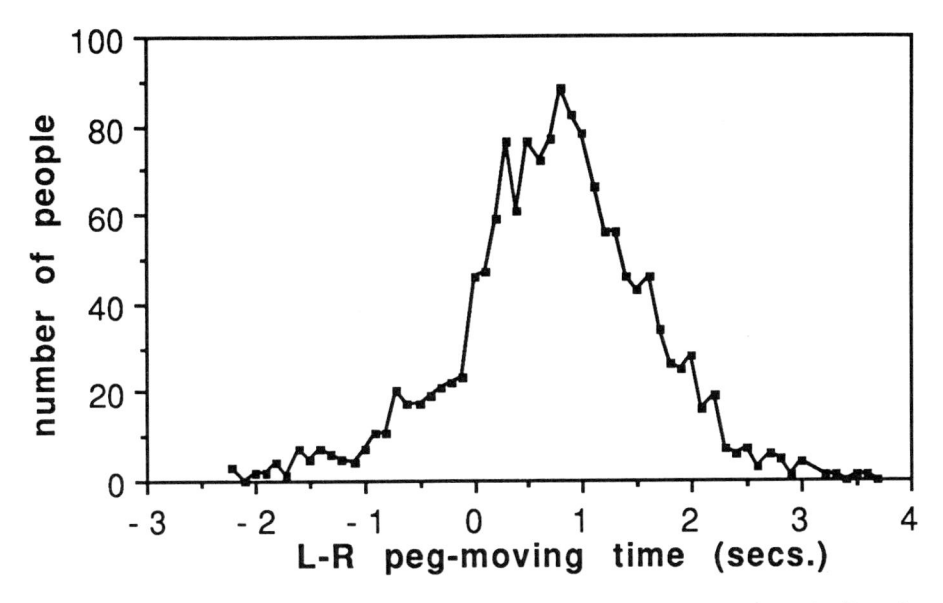

Fig. 5.2. Distribution of left–right difference in hand skill on Annett's peg-moving task. (Data from Annett and Kilshaw 1983, both sexes combined.)

Preference inventories have the advantage that they require little or no apparatus and are quick and easy to score. Data can be gathered at a distance by questionnaire, and large groups can be easily assessed.

Studies of various inventories have found that in most cases test–retest reliability is reasonable (Raczkowski *et al.* 1974, McMeekan and Lishman 1975, Coren and Porac 1978) and, provided one avoids unpractised and infrequent activities (*e.g.* sweeping with a broom—Hull 1936), self-reported preference for left and right are reasonably consistent with preferences observed on behavioural testing, at least in adults (Raczkowski and Kalat 1974, Coren and Porac 1978).

Relative proficiency measures
An alternative approach to handedness assessment is to measure relative proficiency of the two hands in carrying out skilled activities. There are various ways of converting raw scores into a laterality index, a popular one being to compute $100(R-L)/(R+L)$, where R is the score for the right hand and L the score for the left. Unlike the handedness inventory, relative proficiency measures typically yield normal or near-normal distributions of scores (Fig. 5.2). Furthermore, test–retest reliability has been shown to be acceptable for a range of measures (Annett *et al.* 1974, Todor and Doane 1977).

One drawback of hand proficiency measures is that they are considerably less practical than inventories: equipment is typically required to assess relative hand skill, and individual testing is usually necessary, although Tapley and Bryden (1985) have devised a reliable procedure that can be administered to groups.

Which is the best measure? The question of validity
We have, then, three different approaches to handedness assessment: binary categorization by writing hand, preference inventories, and direct measurement of relative proficiency. The question for researchers in this field is which is the best measure to use. Here the most important consideration must be test validity.

According to Guilford and Fruchter (1973), we say a test is valid when it measures what it is presumed to measure. It is possible for a procedure to have high reliability and sensitivity but no validity whatsoever: for example, I may claim that the relative length of a person's arms is indicative of degree of handedness: the measure is practical, reliable and sensitive—but totally invalid. Although validity is clearly the most important property we should look for in a handedness assessment, it is the most difficult to establish. As Guilford and Fruchter pointed out, validity is a highly relative concept: rather than asking of a procedure 'is it valid?' we need to ask 'is it valid for this particular purpose?' Thus we cannot decide which handedness measure is best until we consider what we want to use it for. If, like Porac and Coren (1981), we are interested in lateral preferences in their own right, then the most valid procedure would be one that involves direct measurement of preference behaviour. However, most neuroscientists are not particularly interested in hand preference for its own sake. Rather, we want to assess handedness because it can tell us something interesting about individual differences in underlying neurological organization. However, our criteria for identifying this 'something interesting' remain poorly defined. To date the quest for better measurement procedures has proceeded largely in an opportunistic hit-and-miss fashion. We have used those procedures that are convenient, hoping that they may shed some light on neurological processes, and when the results have been unsatisfactory, we have tried something else. Because we have no clear criterion against which to validate our measures, selection of assessment procedures has been guided largely by personal predilection. Consequently there is variability from one study to the next in the precise way in which handedness is assessed, and this makes it difficult to determine whether differences between studies are meaningful or just a consequence of procedural variations.

Quantitative or categorical?
A crucial question is whether handedness should be regarded as a quantitative or a qualitative variable. Many studies treat handedness as a binary categorical variable, but usually as a matter of convenience rather than for any logical reason. McManus (1984), however, explicitly advocated a categorical view of handedness. He opposed the notion of quantitative measurement for the reason that when we look at the most strongly lateralized activity, handwriting, we do not observe a continuum ranging from strong preference for the right hand, through equal preference for both hands, to strong preference for the left hand. He took the position that direction of hand preference, left or right, is influenced by genetic factors and is related to cerebral lateralization, but that strength of hand preference is a relatively uninteresting variable, not under genetic control, and at least partly reflecting error of measurement. He advocated the use of writing hand as the index

of handedness, on the grounds that this is extremely stable, and virtually no individuals show equal proficiency with both sides. He recognized that there will be problems with this measure in societies where right-handed writing is enforced, or indeed where written language is not used, but he maintained that difficulties in applying the measure in such situations should not lead us to abandon it in Western societies where there is widespread tolerance of left-handedness. According to McManus, one is only muddying the waters by measuring handedness quantitatively in terms of different degrees of hand preference or relative hand skill: 'That a few individuals are not as clearly lateralized as the rest should not mean that we dispose of the conceptual advantages of a simple dichotomy' (p. 127).

How, then, did McManus account for the fact that on handedness inventories we find different degrees of handedness? He argued that the extent to which hand preferences depart from chance in other tasks will depend on how far they utilize the mechanisms involved in handwriting. Behaviours which do not overlap at all with handwriting may be strongly lateralized, but the direction of lateralization will be independent of writing hand. Try clasping your hands with fingers interlaced, or crossing your arms, and then perform each action in the opposite direction. For most people, the positions feel natural with one thumb or arm uppermost, and quite unnatural with the thumbs or arms reversed. Hand-clasping and arm-folding are instances of behaviours which are strongly lateralized but independent of handwriting (Beckman and Elston 1962, Bruml 1972, Porac *et al.* 1980). Similarly, Coren *et al.* (1981) have shown that perceptual preferences for eye and ear are stable and reliable, but not highly correlated with preferences for hand or foot. It cannot be the case, however, that overlap with writing hand is the sole factor determining preference for other manual activities. If this were so, we would expect left- and right-handed writers to be symmetrical in their preferences for other activities. This is not the case. As McManus himself has demonstrated, in general, left-handed writers perform more activities with the non-writing hand than do right-handed writers (McManus *et al.* 1988; see also p. 48). To explain this finding in terms of his theory, McManus has to argue that environmental pressures and tool design produce a bias towards right-handed usage.

Annett has taken the opposite stance, arguing that handedness is best understood if treated as a continuous variable. In her view, 'to talk about asymmetry in terms of left and right might be like talking about height in terms of "tall" and "short"' (Annett 1970*a*).

This debate cannot be resolved by argument alone. Conceptualization of handedness as a continuous variable will be validated if it can be shown that degree of hand preference relates to cerebral function in an interesting way, *e.g.* if there are reliable neuropsychological differences between left-handed writers who are left-handed for all activities and those who have less strong hand preference. Some evidence for such differences was presented in Chapter 2 (*e.g.* Satz *et al.* 1967). Although some studies give contradictory results, it seems unjustified to abandon quantitative assessment of handedness. If degree of handedness really is an important variable, then we incur heavy costs if we persist in treating handedness as categorical because we lose critical information by collapsing together different types of handedness. If, on the other hand, degree of handedness ultimately proves to be unimportant, then we will have introduced unnecessary complexity, and possibly some error, by using a quantitative measure, but we will not have not lost vital information. McManus makes the salutary point that just because we *can* measure something quantitatively, it does not follow that we *should* do so: we need to adopt a healthy scepticism about the value of distinguishing degrees of handedness, and make every effort to validate this approach to assessment. However, as yet the arguments against a quantitification of handedness do not seem forceful enough to merit abandoning this potentially useful approach.

Preference or proficiency?
Accepting that handedness should be measured quantitatively still leaves un-answered the question of what type of measure is most suitable. Annett *et al.* (1974) have argued in favour of proficiency measures on theoretical grounds: 'It seems probable that preferences depend on underlying differences in skill and if the appropriate skills could be identified, studies of their distribution would be highly relevant to studies of laterality.' Using her peg-moving task, Annett (1970*b*) showed that hand difference scores formed a continuous distribution and relative proficiency of the two sides was significantly correlated with strength of hand preference as assessed by an inventory. Peters and Durding (1978) reported similar findings using a finger-tapping task. Annett's view is that degree of hand preference is determined by the underlying continuous distribution of relative hand skill, and to quantify handedness she recommended direct performance measures of relative proficiency rather than preference inventories.

Porac and Coren (1981) have argued against this view, stating:

There has been a tendency to view skill, strength, and preference as relatively interchangeable indicators of the dominant hand; however, evidence suggests that they are separable aspects of behavior perhaps mediated by different mechanisms . . [The evidence] suggests that *skill*, *strength* (or general *proficiency*), and *preference* might be orthogonal dimensions. (p. 12)

These authors used two facts to support their case. First they noted that correlations between relative proficiency measures and degree of hand preference are far from perfect. Todor and Doane (1977), for instance, obtained correlations around 0.6 to 0.7 between proficiency and preference measures. Second, as noted above, the shapes of distributions obtained with the two types of measure are quite different: normal or near-normal for proficiency measures, and J-shaped for preference. If these criticisms are justified, then in so far as one type of measure is valid, the other must be invalid. Bishop (1989*a*), however, questioned whether their arguments are correct. For a start, the correlations between hand preference and proficiency, while not perfect, are far too strong to justify the claim that these correspond to orthogonal dimensions of handedness, and indeed correlations of the size cited by Porac and Coren as evidence for independence have been interpreted by others as *supporting* the view that preference and proficiency have a common basis (Annett 1970*b*, 1976). Porac and Coren's case is based on the implicit assumption that, if preference and proficiency are indices of a common factor,

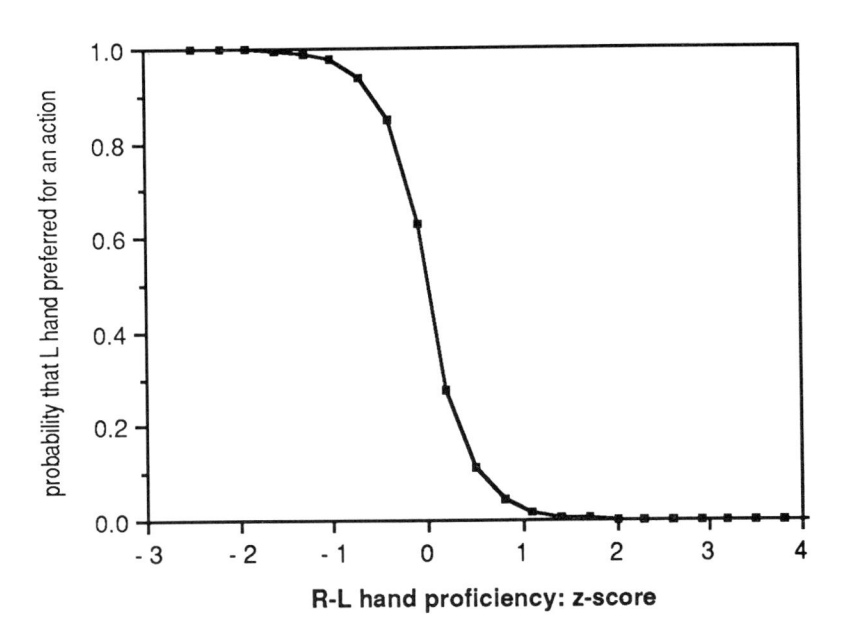

Fig. 5.3. Postulated relationship between relative hand proficiency and hand preference. When there is equal skill of the two hands, either hand is equally likely to be selected, but the probability of preferring one side increases rapidly as imbalance in skill of the two sides increases.

there must be a linear and very strong relationship between the number of activities a person carries out with one hand, and the degree of superiority of that hand on a proficiency measure. However, an alternative and perhaps more plausible view is that, for any task, there is a direct relationship between the *probability* that the more proficient side will be preferred, and the size of the difference between hands in proficiency.

Figure 5.3 illustrates a hypothetical situation where for individuals equally proficient with both hands, the probability of preferring one hand on a given task is 0.5, but as one moves away from this point of equal proficiency, the probability that the more proficient hand will be preferred increases exponentially. Thus when the two hands are equal in skill, either hand is equally likely to be selected to perform a task, but it needs only a slight skill advantage of one hand to strongly bias the individual to prefer that side for unimanual tasks. We can use such a hypothetical relationship to simulate the situation where a person is presented with several different tasks, and compute the distribution of hand preference scores that we would expect for individuals with a given proficiency score. If we know the probability of preferring the left hand for any one activity, then we can use the binomial theorem to compute the probability that the person will be left-handed for n out of m activities. Figure 5.4 shows the hypothetical distribution of hand preference scores in relation to relative skill of the two hands, assuming that the latter variable is normally distributed, with the mean shifted to the right of zero.

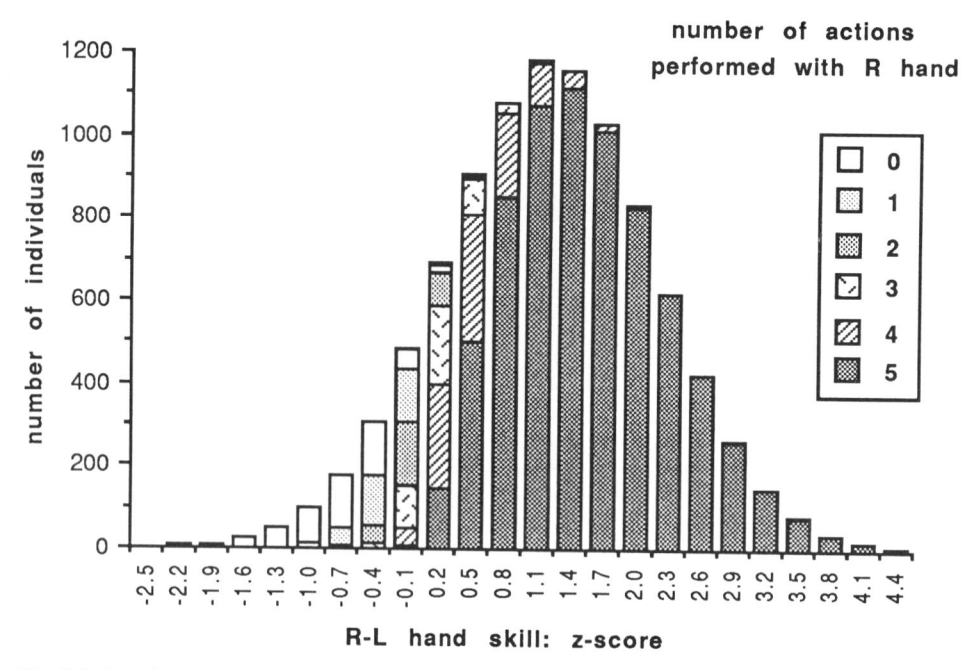

Fig. 5.4. Postulated normal distribution of right–left hand skill, with mean shifted 1.2 z units to the right, showing the proportions of handedness types expected at each skill level. (Redrawn from Bishop 1989*a*.)

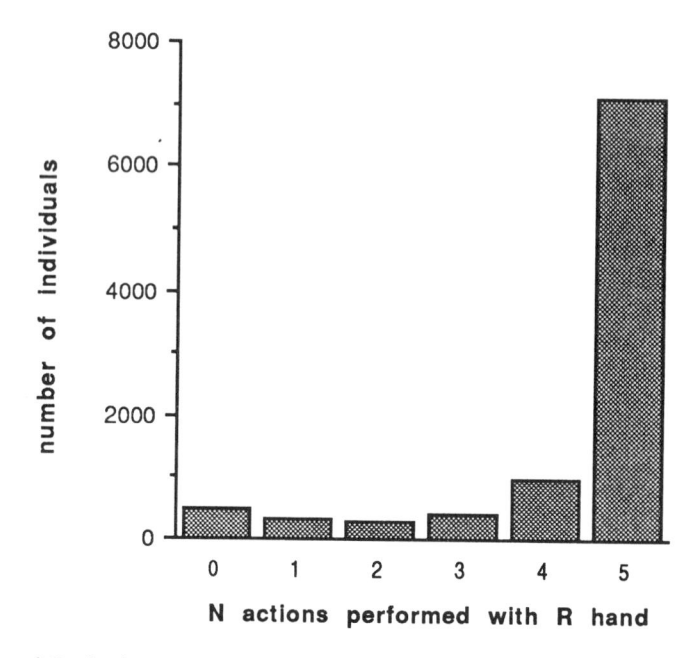

Fig. 5.5. J-shaped distribution of preference scores derived by summing across all columns of Figure 5.4.

Bishop (1989a) used this simulation to illustrate that one can derive a J-shaped distribution of preference scores directly from a normal distribution of proficiency scores (Fig. 5.5), provided one assumes that the relationship between proficiency and probability of preferring one hand on a task is of the form shown in Figure 5.4. Under these assumptions, one also finds that the correlation between preference scores and relative proficiency scores is significant but not perfect. With a five-item preference scale, the correlation is 0.70, and with a nine-item scale it is 0.72. These figures, derived from a computer simulation, are closely comparable to those obtained with real data on proficiency and preference, and indicate that lack of perfect correlation between these two measureable aspects of handedness does not necessarily mean that they have different origins. Of course, such a simulation cannot *prove* that hand preference is determined by relative proficiency, but it does demonstrate that moderate correlations between measures are compatible with a common cause.

This analysis highlights one peculiarity of hand preference as measured quantitatively by inventories. Although handedness inventories are often described as measuring *strength* of hand preference, what they in fact assess is *consistency* of hand preference across different activities, which is logically quite separate. As Boklage (1980) put it:

Attempts to generate quantitative measures . . . have all been based on lists of dichotomies, quantitative only in summing over the list and fitting the sum to a quasicontinuous distribution. (p. 117)

This distinction between strength and consistency of hand preference may be illustrated with a fictional example. Child A invariably uses the left hand for hammering and eating, but the right for cutting and throwing, whereas Child B has no preference for either side, and is equally likely to use left or right for all four activities. The laterality quotients for these two individuals would be the same, despite the fact that A has a very strong preference which is inconsistent between activities, whereas B has no preferences.

Some inventories do allow one to categorize preference into more than two categories (*e.g.* 'always', 'usually', 'seldom' and 'never' responses). However, this does not solve the problem, because the scoring procedure invariably collapses responses across items, once again confounding strength and inter-item consistency. For instance, a person who replied that they always used the right hand for eating (score +2) and always used the left hand for writing (score −2) would obtain the same laterality quotient as one who had a weak right preference (+1) for one activity and a weak left preference for the other (−1) or one who had no preference for either (score 0 on both). In any case, validity of self-reported strength of hand preference is questionable. There is some latitude in how such terms as 'always' or 'usually' are interpreted. Suppose a man invariably writes with his right hand, but did learn to use the left for a period while his right arm was in plaster. Will he answer that he 'always' uses his right hand to write, or that he 'usually' does so? Bryden (1977) reported that males were much more likely than females to answer 'usually' rather than 'always', and he suggested that sex differences in degree of handedness could arise from different reactions to the wording of the handedness inventory.

One motivation for the development of handedness inventories was dissatisfaction with a simple binary categorization of handedness, and the feeling that quantification would yield a more sensitive index. However, to quantify by measuring consistency of preference across items is an unsatisfactory solution. The J-shaped, non-normal distribution of laterality quotients limits the types of statistical analysis that can be applied. Indeed, it is common to find that, having used an inventory to quantify handedness, when analysing data researchers revert to a categorical classification, dividing people in terms of broad ranges of laterality quotients defined by arbitrary cut-off points which vary from study to study. Results are then analysed using contingency table analysis, a procedure which ignores any quantitative relationships between categories.

Selection of activities

Boklage (1980) raised a further criticism of the handedness inventory as measuring instrument thus:

> . . its real worst fault seems to lie in the arbitrarily equal weights assigned to the various dichotomies. Writing . . . takes its place alongside hammer and spoon as equally considered indicators. Although it is conceivable that this might not be wrong, I can not be comfortable with its arbitrariness. (p. 117)

Choice of items in an inventory can substantially affect the recorded rate of left-handedness (Annett 1970a). In my own case, I obtain a laterality quotient of −13, 0 and +20 on the Oldfield, Annett, and Crovitz and Zener inventories respectively, which means that with a cut-off placed at zero, I would be classified as left-handed by one questionnaire, right-handed by another, and mixed-handed by a third. The inclusion of items often seems decided by a mixture of tradition and idiosyncratic preference, rather than because of any theoretical considerations. Items recommended for handedness batteries include such diverse activities as swatting a fly (Simon 1948), spreading glue on the edge of a piece of glass with a toothpick (Hardyck 1977), playing the ukelele (van Dusen 1939), and using a nailbrush, the last of these being recommended by Critchley and Critchley (1978) as 'perhaps the most reliable simple test of hand preference'. Some inventories go beyond manual activities and include items covering lateral preferences for foot, eye and ear to give an overall laterality index.

One criterion that can be used to judge whether a given item should be included in an inventory is reliability. Exclusion of items that people answer in an inconsistent manner rules out many unskilled and uncommon activities. Most inventories include an item concerned with writing or drawing, but Tan (1983) argued that changing cultural pressures made this unsuitable when considering handedness in different generations: among Australians born before 1945 the proportion of left-handed writers was much lower than for those born after that date.

Should an inventory include items testing lateral preferences for eye, ear or foot? Inclusion of eye preference items (*e.g.* eye preferred for sighting down a tube) was for a long time regarded as a useful way of detecting 'left-sided tendencies' in an activity that was unlikely to be influenced by training. However, more recent research has shown that even when left-handedness is widely tolerated, lateral preferences for eye and hand are not closely associated. Porac *et al.* (1980) concluded that laterality for sensory processes (eyedness and earedness) and motor functions (handedness and footedness) should be regarded as separate dimensions of human behaviour rather than as common indices of a general lateral bias.

Whether or not footedness should be included together with handedness items is more debatable. Following the logic developed in Chapter 1, one can argue that the functions of the foot have few of the characteristics associated with lateral differentiation: the foot is not used for skilled manipulations of objects, nor is it usual for feet to assume complementary roles in acts of bipedal coordination. However, despite these limitations, foot preferences show high stability and are related to handedness. A case can therefore be made for using footedness as an index of motor laterality that is relatively uncontaminated by effects of practice or training (Peters 1988).

Relative proficiency measures avoid many of the logical and statistical problems of handedness inventories, but the issue of task selection remains a serious one. Relative proficiency cannot be treated as a single dimension. There is a wide range of different hand functions that may be measured, including speed, steadiness, dexterity, sensory sensitivity and strength, and these are by no means interchangeable. Buxton (1937) found that while pursuit rotor, motility rotor and tapping tasks had acceptable levels of test–retest reliability, intercorrelations between hand difference ratios for these three tests were close to zero. Further, whereas measures of speed and dexterity correlate reasonably well with hand preference, measures of strength and sensory sensitivity do not (Finlayson and Reitan 1976).

Recognition of this problem led to a search for a common property of those tasks which give reliable differences between the two hands. Flowers (1975) suggested that handedness might be more apparent in movements that were ballistically preprogrammed than in those under feedback control, whereas Provins (1956) proposed that lateral differences would be clearest for activities where serial organization of muscle movements was crucial. However, neither hypothesis has received convincing support, and both have difficulty in explaining why the same task may show greater or smaller differences between hands depending on the level of difficulty (Steingrueber 1975). Peters (1980) noted that the extent to which a task like tapping shows hand differences may vary depending on the precision of force modulation required.

Another way in which hand differences can be altered within a single task is by changing the length of the test. It is a well-known statistical principle that the larger a sample one collects, the more reliable the estimate of the population mean. Thus, unless fatigue starts to affect behaviour, we can in general predict that the more trials and/or longer time period that is used, the easier differences between hands will be to detect.

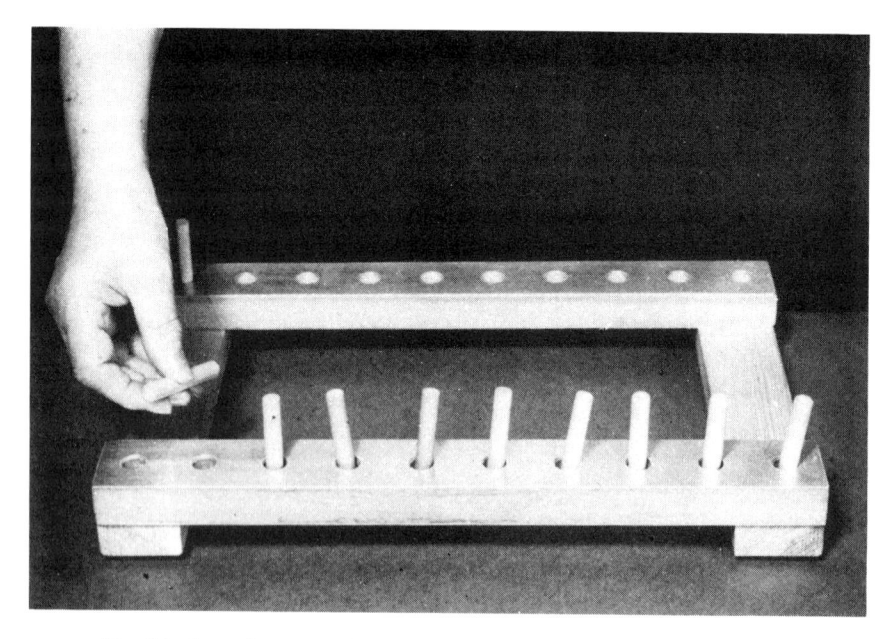

Fig. 5.6. Annett's peg-moving task. (Reprinted from Annett 1985, p. 208.)

Nor can the effect of practice upon performance be ignored. For most investigators, practice is a nuisance factor because measures that are affected by differential practice of the two sides will confound biological variation and experiential differences between individuals. Accordingly, researchers have looked for a task which yields reliable hand differences but which will be unfamiliar to subjects. Annett *et al.* (1974) used a peg-moving task in which the subject is required to transfer a row of dowelling pegs from the back to the front of a pegboard (Fig. 5.6). Even though subjects will not have performed this particular activity in everyday life, it could still be argued that components of the movements involved in peg-moving overlap with those involved in more familiar activites, so there will be some transfer of training. For instance, experience of handwriting may determine the ease with which a person picks up and places a dowelling peg using a pincer grip. Annett (1970*b*) argued that if practice in handwriting affected relative hand proficiency, then the differences between hands should be accentuated with age: such a change was not found for her peg-moving task between the ages of 3 and 15 years, although absolute speed improved for both hands.

Concluding comment
The traditional approach to handedness assessment involving a single administration of a preference inventory does not come out of this analysis very well. Preference inventories are reliable and practical, but their validity is questionable, and, although designed with the aim of quantifying handedness, they are far less

sensitive than proficiency measures in this regard, and yield data that cannot readily be analysed using parametric statistics. Laterality quotients from such instruments fail to tell us anything about the stability of hand preference, or about the absolute or relative skill of the two hands. These criticisms of inventories are not new: Barnsley and Rabinovitch described handedness questionnaires as 'psychometrically inadequate' back in 1970. However, inventories persist as the predominant procedure for assessing handedness. One reason may be that, although proficiency measures have much in their favour, an enormous amount of work needs to be done to develop valid and reliable instruments. At present, we do not even know how far differences beteen motor proficiency measures are a function of task content, how far they result from differential practice, and to what extent they reflect scaling factors and test length. We need both theoretically motivated experimental work (*e.g.* Peters 1987), and more normative data on motor proficiency at different ages that would allow us to apply research findings with confidence in clinical settings.

6
COGNITIVE CORRELATES OF HANDEDNESS

Handedness would not have attracted much attention from psychologists were it not for the claim that hand preference is related to intellectual function. In this chapter, studies comparing cognitive abilities of left- and right-handers from normal populations will be reviewed. Chapters 7 to 14 will consider the related question of whether there is a raised prevalence of non-right-handedness in groups with various developmental disorders.

Overall intellectual level and attainment
The first question to consider is whether left-handers differ from right-handers in terms of overall intelligence or attainment.

One of the earliest systematic studies on this topic was conducted by Haefner (1929), who found no differences in IQ or attainment between 68 left-handers and a matched group of right-handers drawn from a Brooklyn high school. This lack of relationship was subsequently confirmed in much larger-scale studies. Douglas *et al.* (1967) analysed the relationship between handedness and attainment in the National Survey Sample, a stratified sample of over 5000 British children drawn from the total population born in a particular week in 1946. Handedness was rated on the basis of preference for writing, drawing and picking up a ball. Left-handers did not differ from right-handers on group tests of mental ability and school attainment. Hardyck *et al.* (1976) looked at hand preference (for writing), figure copying, listening attention, speed and persistence, intelligence, reading, spelling and arithmetic in the total population of 7688 schoolchildren in a medium-sized Californian community. They found 'a resounding lack of any relationships at all' between handedness and mental tests. Similar conclusions were drawn by Clymer and Silva (1985) in a study in which intellectual (Wechster Intelligence Scale for Children—Revised), language (Illinois Test of Psycholinguistic Abilities) and articulation skills were tested in a sample of 890 7-year-olds. Handedness did not account for a significant proportion of the variance on any of these measures. Satz and Fletcher (1987) compared 431 extreme right-handers with 48 extreme left-handers on a range of reading tests as well as the Peabody Picture Vocabulary Test and Beery Test of Visual–Motor Integration. They found no difference between these groups on any test.

Other studies have considered degree and consistency of lateral preference, rather than direction. In a study of 302 first-graders, Balow (1963) found no association between reading attainment, handedness, degree of hand preference or crossed eye–hand dominance. Ullman (1977) reported data on IQ, reading, arithmetic and spelling achievement in 648 elementary school children and found no evidence that inconsistent or mixed hand preference was associated with low overall performance.

Familial and non-familial left-handers
Left-handedness is, of course, a very indirect index of cerebral lateralization, and it has been suggested that more orderly relationships with cognitive abilities would become evident if we could distinguish handedness subgroups which corresponded to different patterns of cerebral lateralization. One suggestion is that familial sinistrality is important, and it has become popular to divide non-right-handers according to whether or not they have left-handed relatives.

Bishop (1980*a*) drew attention to a methodological problem in this area, noting that familial sinistrality was typically confounded with family size. If left-handers are regarded as familial sinistrals if they have *any* blood relative who is left-handed, then the likelihood of being so categorized will increase with family size. We know that large family size is associated with low socioeconomic status and relatively poor educational attainments, and so this could be an important confounding variable. To avoid this bias, researchers who make distinctions between familial and non-familial sinistrals should either ensure that groups are matched on family size, or should judge familial sinistrality only on the basis of relatives common to all individuals, *i.e.* parents and grandparents.

Even if this possible artefact is taken into account, one cannot equate familial and non-familial sinistrality with particular types of cerebral lateralization. Bishop (1990*c*) used the right shift theory to show that the expected proportion of familial sinistrals is not very different for left-handers who are rs− − , rs+− or rs++.

Although familial sinistrality has frequently been used to subdivide left-handers, the logic of this approach does not appear to have been thought through, and it is perhaps not surprising that results based on this distinction have been inconsistent from one study to another (Soper *et al.* 1988).

Intellectual profile
The notion that left-handers have a distinctive intellectual profile was popularized by two studies of university students conducted by Levy (1969) and Miller (1971), which concurred in finding that non-right-handers scored lower than right-handers on tests of non-verbal visuospatial abilities, but not on verbal intelligence. Levy (1976) accounted for these findings in terms of cerebral lateralization, arguing that 'when verbal and perceptual processing are each confined to a single and separate side of the brain the two patterns of neural connections underlying these abilities can evolve optimally for the functions they serve.' Essentially, this is an explanation in terms of competition for resources: Levy proposed that in a proportion of left-handers 'both sides of the brain [have] developed, to a certain degree, according to the verbal blueprint' and that this impedes the mediation of visuospatial abilities by the right hemisphere. This explanation rests on the questionable assumption that in individuals with bilateral language representation, visuospatial skills remain confined to the right hemisphere (cf. Bryden *et al.* 1983, see p. 21).

The sample sizes in these investigations were small (15 right-handers and 10 left-handers in Levy's study, and 29 right-handers and 23 'mixed-handers' in Miller's). Subsequent larger-scale studies have found little support for Levy's hypothesis. Gibson (1973), like Levy, used the Wechsler Adult Intelligence Scale

(WAIS) with a university sample and found no evidence for a specific deficit in performance IQ in left-handers. Newcombe *et al.* (1975) studied 928 adults enrolled in a demographic study, classified according to direction of hand preference, within-task consistency and between-task consistency of preference on the basis of a seven-item questionnaire. Non-right-handers and right-handers obtained similar scores on both WAIS verbal IQ and performance IQ. The only significant finding in relation to handedness was a slight superiority in verbal IQ for those who reported that they could use either hand for at least one activity.

Heim and Watts (1976) analysed data collected in the course of standardizing an intelligence test. To look at the relationship between intellectual profile and handedness, each left-hander was matched with a right-hander on overall test score, and pairs then compared on each subtest to see whether the left-hander or right-hander obtained the higher score. The only significant finding was that left-handers tended to score higher on the numerical scale than did right-handers of similar overall ability. However, when a more powerful analysis using the whole sample of nearly 2000 subjects was conducted to consider the contribution made by each subtest to the total score, there were no consistent differences between handedness groups.

Mascie-Taylor (1980) studied 687 people living in a Cambridge suburb. In contrast to Levy, he found that left-handers scored significantly higher on verbal IQ than did right-handers, but did not differ on performance IQ.

One problem with relying on Wechsler's IQ test is that it was not designed to assess lateralized cognitive functions. Although, in general, we would expect verbal and performance scores to reflect strength of left- and right-hemisphere processing, the relationship is far from perfect, given that some of the performance tests (*e.g.* Picture Arrangement) implicate left hemisphere skills, and at least one verbal test (Arithmetic) probably involves some right-hemisphere processing. It has been argued that clearer evidence of intellectual differences between left- and right-handers might emerge if different cognitive tests were used, specifically selected to contrast the functions of the two hemispheres (Sanders *et al.* 1982).

Initial reports from studies adopting this approach were promising: Nebes (1971) claimed that left-handers were selectively impaired in a spatial reasoning task, designed to tap right hemisphere functions. However, this result was not replicated in two independent studies (Kutas *et al.* 1975, Hardyck 1977). Other studies involving mental rotation tasks (Fig. 6.1) gave similarly inconsistent results, with some reporting deficits in left-handers (Freedman and Rovegno 1981), others finding superior performance (Herrmann and van Dyke 1978), and yet others finding no relationship (McKeever and VanDeventer 1977, Fennell *et al.* 1978). One drawback of all these studies was that subjects were recruited from student populations. Although verbal ability is likely to be much more important than visuospatial skills in determining university entrance, the possibility remains that level of right hemisphere proficiency may influence whether a person goes into higher education. If so, we would expect to find clearer results in unselected populations.

A large-scale study of this kind by Yen (1975) did find some evidence of

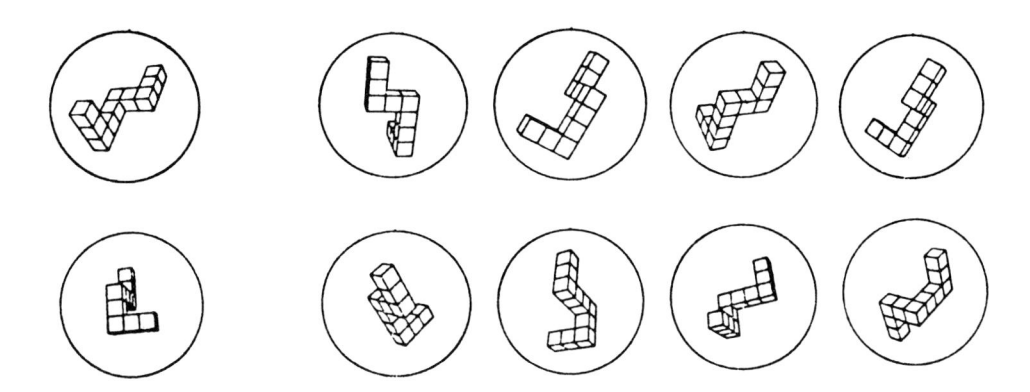

Fig. 6.1. Sample items from the Mental Rotations Test, used to assess competence in visuospatial skills mediated by the right hemisphere. The subject must judge which of the alternatives corresponds to a rotated form of the index figure. In the first item, the first and fourth alternatives are correct. In the second item, the second and third alternatives are correct. (Reprinted from Vandenberg and Kuse 1978, p. 600.)

deficient spatial ability in left-handed males, but not in females. However, this was not replicated by Sanders *et al.* (1982), who analysed spatial factor scores derived from a battery of cognitive tests given as part of the Hawaii study of cognition. The main effect of sex was highly significant, but the main effect of handedness and the interaction between handedness and sex were not reported (and so were presumably non-significant). The authors noted a significant interaction between sex, ethnicity and handedness. They did not report specific comparisons, but the graphical representation of the data indicated that left-handed males of Chinese and Japanese ancestry scored higher than other males, whereas left-handed females from these ethnic groups scored lower than other females. However, when we see that, despite an impressive overall sample size, there were in the Japanese group only four left-handed males and three left-handed females, and in the Chinese group, two left-handed males and three left-handed females, confidence in this interaction evaporates. Complex analysis of variance can give misleading results when cell sizes are grossly unequal, as in this case.

Harshman *et al.* (1983) noted the ambiguous and often contradictory evidence for spatial and verbal differences between left- and right-handers, and asked:

We are forced to wonder whether the inconsistent results are real, or simply an accumulated series of type I errors. Could there be unexplored factors which will explain the inconsistencies? (p. 151)

Recognizing that if one does enough statistical tests, some significant associations are bound to turn up sooner or later, they took the sensible step of attempting to cross-validate findings across three independent samples, all of whom had been given various spatial and verbal tests in the course of different research studies.

On the spatial tests there was no suggestion of a main effect of handedness in any sample. In only one out of seven analyses did the interaction between sex and handedness reach conventional levels of significance, and here the result went in the opposite direction to that reported by Sanders *et al.*, with left-handedness associated with inferior performance in males, but superior performance in females. Similarly unimpressive results were obtained for the verbal tests and for a group of 'other' tests which could not be clearly categorized as verbal or spatial. Only one out of 26 comparisons was significant at the 0.05 level: exactly what would be expected by chance.

Undismayed, Harshman *et al.* proceeded to look for moderator variables that might make more sense of the results. They noted that one factor which varied from study to study was intelligence level: some samples were drawn from a pool preselected for high ability, *i.e.* university students, whereas others were more representative of the general population. Pursuing this idea, Harshman *et al.* reanalysed their own data, dividing the samples according to scores on a reasoning test. Their conclusion was that reasoning ability acted as a moderator variable which could explain some of the inconsistent results reported previously, and that once this variable was taken into account, the data made a strong case for handedness-related differences in cognitive abilities. However, this conclusion does not seem justified. The main problem is that, even after subdividing for reasoning ability, very few of the main effects or interactions analysed were statistically significant. Harshman *et al.* were impressed by the fact that when trends for three-way interactions between sex, handedness and reasoning ability were observed, they tended to go in the same direction in all three samples. While one does not want to be so blinkered as to totally disregard any trend that does not achieve some conventional criterion of significance, it seems unwise to put much faith in findings that could easily have arisen by chance, and which, in any case, could account for only a minute proportion of the variance. Such caution is particularly relevant in this case where, as with the Sanders *et al.* study, three-way analysis of variance was conducted in a situation where there were massive inequalities in cell sizes, with some cells containing only five or six subjects. Confidence in the replicability of a particular pattern of results is further shaken when we read that quite different patterns of three-way interaction between handedness, sex and ability were obtained when different tests were used to divide subjects into high and low ability groups. Finally, there is every reason to believe that the ability groups that were formed were not comparable in the three data sets that were examined. Each group was subdivided at its median score on a reasoning test, but two groups were already preselected for ability (university samples), whereas the other was not. Indeed, where data from different samples were presented for the same test, it is apparent that the high ability group of one sample scored in the same range as the low ability group of another. The conclusions that I would draw from this study are quite the opposite from those given by the authors. Main effects of handedness on spatial ability simply do not stand up. Some complex interactions with sex and other variables were reported, but they were neither large nor robust and they tended to be found in situations where the use of conventional analysis of variance is questionable. There seems every reason to believe that what we are seeing is indeed 'an accumulated series of type I errors'.

Marshall (1981), in reviewing the literature on handedness and ability, concluded: 'All in all, there seems to be little cause at the moment to give up the hypothesis that left-handers differ from right-handers solely by virtue of preferring their left hands' (p. 78). There is little in the more recent research literature to alter that conclusion.

Population versus clinical studies

Hardyck and Petrinovich (1977), on the basis of a literature review and their own data, concluded that the belief in an association between left-handedness and ability arose because of the influence of small-scale and poorly conducted clinical studies which were open to sampling bias. Suppose a researcher decides to do a study of handedness and dyslexia, and so compares a sample of dyslexic children with an equal number of controls. There are several drawbacks to this type of study. First, a number of biases may conspire to yield a spurious result. The most obvious one is that if the object of the study is known and one is seeking suitable subjects to include, people may be biased to refer 'interesting', *i.e.* non-right-handed cases. This sort of bias can be overcome if one samples from a clearly defined population, such as all children attending a particular school or clinic. However, there are other more subtle ways in which bias can be introduced. Because people believe that left-handedness is an indicator of an unusual and possibly disadvantageous neurological organization, a left-handed poor reader may be more likely than a right-handed poor reader to be referred to a neurologist. Further, given that there is a belief that left-handedness is part of the symptom complex of developmental dyslexia, this diagnosis may be more readily made if a poor reader is left-handed. Thus a link between dyslexia and left-handedness may be forged by people's preconceptions about the significance of left-handedness.

Are there then any benefits from conducting small-scale clinical studies? Hardyck and Petrinovich (1977) imply that there are not, and that epidemiological surveys are the only reliable source of data. Bishop (1983), however, pointed out that one should be cautious in extrapolating from average results on unselected populations to rare clinical conditions. Suppose we have a condition X, which impairs development of some cognitive function Y, so that those who suffer from X perform on average three standard deviations below the normative mean on some objective test of Y. For example, X could be developmental dyslexia, and Y, reading ability. Further suppose that X affects 1 per cent of the population, and that 30 per cent of people with condition X but only 10 per cent of unaffected individuals are left-handed. This three-fold increase in left-handedness would be fairly easy to demonstrate in a clinical study in which equal numbers of affected and unaffected individuals were compared on handedness. A statistically significant difference would be found using a sample size of 50 per group. Suppose, however, we adopted the alternative research approach of taking an unselected population and comparing scores on Y for left- and right-handers. Because the base rate of disorder X in the population is low (1 per cent), the mean scores are not much influenced by affected individuals, and differences between left- and right-handers

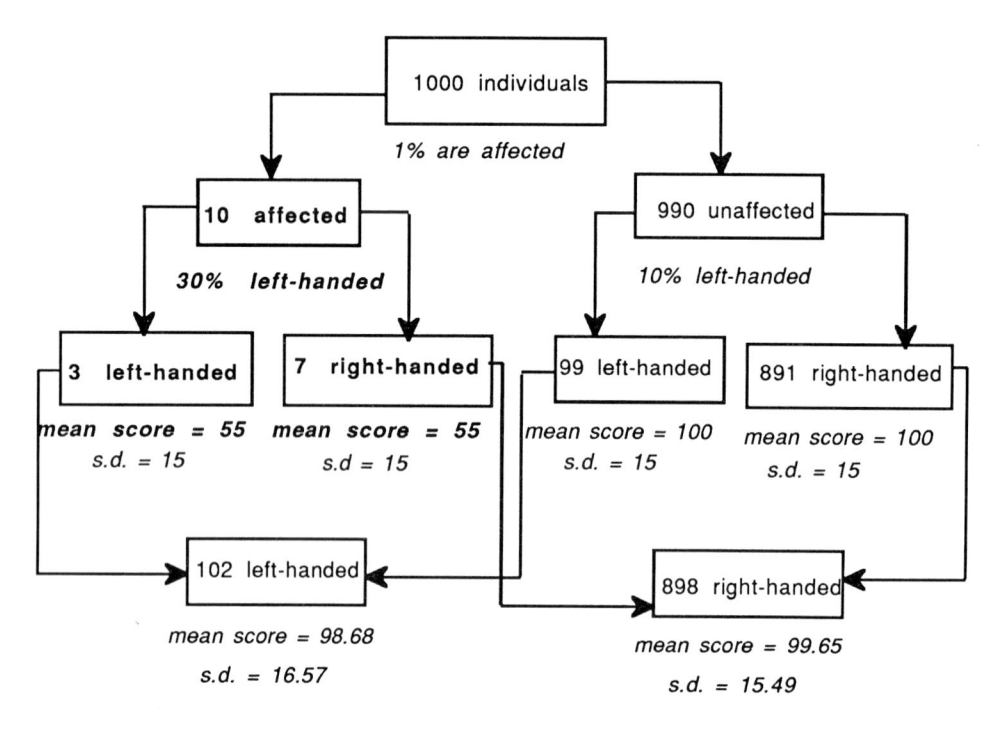

```
                        ┌──────────────────┐
                        │ 1000 individuals │
            ┌───────────┴──────────────────┴───────────┐
            │            1% are affected               │
            ▼                                          ▼
    ┌──────────────┐                          ┌──────────────┐
    │ 10  affected │                          │ 990 unaffected│
    └──────────────┘                          └──────────────┘
        30%  left-handed                        10%  left-handed
    ┌──────┴──────┐                          ┌──────┴──────┐
    ▼             ▼                          ▼             ▼
┌────────────┐ ┌──────────────┐         ┌──────────────┐ ┌────────────────┐
│3 left-handed│ │7 right-handed│         │99 left-handed│ │891 right-handed│
└────────────┘ └──────────────┘         └──────────────┘ └────────────────┘
 mean score = 55  mean score = 55        mean score = 100  mean score = 100
   s.d. = 15       s.d = 15                s.d. = 15         s.d. = 15
```

Fig. 6.2. Negligible impact on average scores of left- and right-handers in a population when a rare condition affecting 1 per cent of individuals is associated with a three-fold increase in left-handedness. Affected individuals obtain test scores three standard deviations below the mean.

(Combined: 102 left-handed, mean score = 98.68, s.d. = 16.57; 898 right-handed, mean score = 99.65, s.d. = 15.49)

will be small. For the situation shown in Figure 6.2, a population sample of several thousand would not reveal a significant difference between left- and right-handers.

We can see then that the possibility that rare conditions may be associated with left-handedness is not incompatible with a finding of no mean difference between left- and right-handers in population studies. The data obtained in two large British surveys are consistent with this view. As noted above, in the National Survey sample (Douglas *et al.* 1967), there were no differences in mean attainment scores for different handedness types. However, there was a significant excess of children with inconsistent hand preferences among those scoring more than one standard deviation below the mean. In the National Child Development Study, where the sample size was over 16,000, mean differences between left- and right-handers, although numerically tiny, did reach statistical significance (Calnan and Richardson 1976). In this same sample, Bishop (1984) was able to show an association between mental impairment and left-handedness. Even where the average performance of left-handers is very close to that of right-handers, there may be a significant increase in the proportion of left-handers among those with marked impairment.

Annett and Turner (1974) carried out a study which further illustrates this point. When left- and right-handed children were compared on a vocabulary test, there was no difference in mean scores. However, among those with very low vocabulary scores there was a significant excess of left-handers. Hardyck (1977) failed to confirm this pattern, finding only marginal trends in the predicted direction when examining the tails of distributions from the large-scale study of Hardyck *et al.* (1976). However, there was a striking lack of low achievers in this sample: *e.g.* in several grades no children scored more than one standard deviation below the mean on a reading test.

To summarize, in evaluating evidence for a link between handedness and disorder it is important to recognize (i) the limitations of the conclusions that one can draw from population studies, and (ii) that a bigger study is not necessarily a better one: this will depend on the question one is asking. What we can say from population studies is that left-handers do not on average have a significantly different intellectual profile from right-handers. This does *not* rule out the possibility that certain cognitive disorders with low base rates may be associated with a raised rate of left-handedness. The evidence for such links will be examined in the following chapters.

7
EARLY BRAIN DAMAGE AND PATHOLOGICAL LEFT-HANDEDNESS

Perinatal hazards and handedness
Genetic influences on individual variation in hand preference were considered in Chapter 3. A very different type of aetiological theory was advanced by Bakan, who maintained that left-handedness is a manifestation of underlying brain damage sustained around the time of birth. His evidence, however, was indirect. In an initial study (Bakan 1971), he noted that left-handers were more likely than right-handers to be either first-born, or fourth or later-born. He argued that the birth ranks with a high rate of left-handedness were those associated with increased risk of perinatal problems. In a second study (Bakan *et al.* 1973), students were asked to specify which of the following perinatal problems had applied to their birth: multiple birth, preterm birth, prolonged labour, caesarian birth, breech birth, blue baby, breathing difficulty at birth, other. It was found that left-handers reported a higher rate of perinatal hazards than right-handers. Bakan concluded that left-handedness is caused by highly localized brain damage affecting the giant Betz cells of the motor cortex, which are particularly sensitive to anoxia.

Bakan's views have been criticized on two counts. First, in regarding all cases of left-handedness as the consequence of brain damage, his theory is too extreme. It cannot explain family associations in handedness (see Chapter 3), nor can it account for the fact that, on average, left-handers show neither cognitive deficit (see Chapter 6) nor impaired motor proficiency (Kilshaw and Annett 1983, Rudel *et al.* 1984).

A second problem is that it has proved difficult to replicate Bakan's original observations. The association between birth rank and left-handedness has not been confirmed (Hicks *et al.* 1978*a*, Dusek and Hicks 1980, Smart *et al.* 1980, Tan and Nettleton 1980), although effects in the predicted direction are occasionally found if one considers extreme cases, such as first-born children to mothers aged over 39 (Smart *et al.* 1980) or sixth or later-born children (Leviton and Kilty 1976). In any case, birth order is a very indirect index of perinatal hazard, and it is preferable to use more direct measures, and to gather data from hospital records rather than relying on maternal recall. In a meta-analysis of published data, Searleman *et al.* (1989) found that certain indices of birth stress (*e.g.* low birthweight, rhesus incompatibility, caesarian delivery) were associated with decreased right-sidedness, but effects were tiny and only reached significance with the huge samples generated by combining data from many sources.

The clearest evidence for a link between left-handedness and perinatal condition comes from studies of infants of extremely low birthweight. O'Callaghan *et al.* (1987) reported that 21 out of 39 children with birthweight below 1000g were left-handed at 4 years of age, compared with 8 per cent of other infants admitted to intensive care. None of the very low birthweight group had cerebral palsy. Ross *et al.* (1987) found that while 80 per cent of a full-term control group were right-handed, only 63 per cent of preterm children with very low birthweight were, this being a statistically significant difference. Furthermore, the two groups did not differ in the distributions of parental handedness. Only six children in this sample had asymmetry of body tone, but four of these were left-handed. In addition, within the preterm group, the non-right-handed children had significantly lower IQs, impaired expressive language and a higher frequency of articulation defect relative to right-handed children. Although this study appears to provide strong support for the notion that very preterm children are vulnerable to brain damage affecting handedness, it should be noted that not only was left-handedness more frequent in this sample, but so too was mixed handedness.

Few studies have obtained direct measurements of the infant's condition at birth and related this to handedness in childhood. Schwartz (1988) confirmed a relationship between low Apgar score and non-right-handedness at 2 years of age in a sample of 290 children for whom information was available from medical records. Nine out of 33 children (27 per cent) with Apgar scores below 7, compared with 45 out of 207 (18 per cent) with Apgar scores of 7 or over, were non-right-handed. However, Smart *et al.* (1980) found no relationship between fetal distress or delay in onset of regular respiration and subsequent handedness (asssessed by parental questionnaire) in a sample of 6-year-olds, and Ehrlichman *et al.* (1982) found no association between Apgar score and handedness at 7 years of age in the Collaborative Perinatal Project.

Perinatal hazards and infant motor asymmetries
The research considered so far has concentrated on links between perinatal hazards and subsequent handedness. A related body of research has looked for relationships between birth status and motor asymmetries in infancy. The literature on lateral biases in normal early motor development was summarized in Chapter 4. Is there any evidence that asymmetries favouring the left side are more marked in those with high perinatal risk? Such studies as exist do not confirm this prediction. Typically, they find that infants with poor condition at birth fail to show the usual patterns of lateral differentiation seen in healthy infants, but rather than showing a bias in the opposite direction, they tend to show no bias to either side. In one of the earliest studies to address this question, Turkewitz *et al.* (1968) studied lateral differentiation in a group of 130 infants, 32 of whom had Apgar scores of 6 or less, indicating suboptimal condition at birth. When the corner of an infant's mouth is touched with a camel-hair brush, the usual response is to turn the head in the direction of the stimulus. Whereas infants with good condition at birth (Apgar score of 9 or 10) showed lateral differentiation of this response and were more responsive to stimulation of the right side, those with low Apgar scores showed no lateral differentiation. Liederman and Coryell (1982) obtained similar findings with 4- to 10-week-old infants. Whereas those with unexceptional birth histories showed a clear preference to turn the head to the right, infants with a history of complicated

birth did not. In other studies, low birthweight and preterm birth have been shown to lead to reduced lateral differentiation of head turning, whether spontaneous (Kurtzberg *et al.* 1979) or in response to tactile stimulation (Lewkowicz *et al.* 1979).

If, as argued by Bakan, all left-handedness were attributable to brain damage around the time of birth, then one would have to assume that around 10 per cent of the population suffered such damage. Yet, as we have seen, there is little evidence that the more common perinatal problems influence handedness. When we turn to cases of extreme perinatal stress, a link with handedness is somewhat stronger, although it is noteworthy that many studies find weak lateralization rather than left-handedness in high risk infants. The significance of this point will be considered further in Chapter 9.

Pathological left-handedness as an explanation for a minority of left-handers
Although few would accept Bakan's hypothesis that attributes all left-handedness to pathological factors, it seems plausible to suppose that brain damage plays a role in determining handedness in some individuals.

Satz (1972, 1973) made an important logical point in demonstrating that, in so far as neurological damage determines handedness, more left- than right-handers will be affected. Although there is some evidence that the left hemisphere is more vulnerable to hypoxic insult than the right (see reviews by Liederman 1983, Harris and Carlson 1988), one does not need to postulate an excess of left hemisphere lesions to account for a higher frequency of pathology in left-handers than in right-handers. The simplest way of explaining his argument is to take an extreme example. Suppose we had a group of 100 individuals, half of whom had suffered brain damage around the time of birth resulting in paralysis of one side (hemiplegia), and half of whom were neurologically normal. In the normal group, we would expect around 10 per cent of individuals to be left-handed, but in the hemiplegic group this would rise to 50 per cent, as hemiplegia will lead to the individual preferring the unimpaired side. The combined sample would consist of five normal left-handers, 45 normal right-handers, 25 hemiplegic left-handers and 25 hemiplegic right-handers. Thus the overall rate of left-handedness is increased from the 10 per cent found in normal populations to 30 per cent, and 25 out of 30 left-handers (83 per cent) would be brain-damaged, as opposed to 25 out of 70 right-handers (36 per cent). Furthermore, while the majority of hemiplegic left-handers would be natural right-handers who had shifted hand preference, only a minority of hemiplegic right-handers would be natural left-handers now forced to use the right hand.

There is no doubt that pathological left-handedness does occur in individuals with cerebral palsy (although interesting examples of persistence in preferring a hemiplegic limb are sometimes reported). Galliford *et al.* (1964) found 18 left-handers and 14 right-handers in a group of children with athetoid cerebral palsy, and Rutter *et al.* (1970*a*) found a significant increase in left-handedness in a sample identified as abnormal on neurological examination in an epidemiological survey. Even where there is no overt hemiplegia, early damage to the left hemisphere can result in left-handedness. Vargha-Khadem *et al.* (1985) studied 53 paediatric patients with unilateral cerebral lesions. All had had a measureable degree of hemiparesis that had been shown to be a consequence of a unilateral brain lesion but in several cases this had substantially or completely resolved. Patients with prenatal and early postnatal left hemisphere lesions were invariably strongly left-handed, even though in several cases there was minimal hemiparesis affecting only the lower limb, with no motor or sensory impairment of the hand. In contrast, three out of four patients who had acquired a left hemisphere lesion after the age of 5 years remained predominantly right-handed.

Orsini and Satz (1986) reported a frequency of 43 per cent left-handedness in individuals with early left-hemisphere brain lesions. Left-handers with early left-hemisphere damage were far more likely than other left-handers to have atypical ear asymmetry on dichotic listening. This is consistent with findings from studies using the Wada test which show that a lesion which shifts hand preference usually also affects language lateralization (Rasmussen and Milner 1977, Woods *et al.* 1988). Like Vargha-Khadem *et al.*, Orsini and Satz noted that signs of pathological left-handedness were seen in patients with subtle motor impairments who were able to use the right hand adaptively.

Such cases of pathological left-handedness without frank hemiplegia raise the question of whether the phenomenon of pathological left-handedness occurs only when there is clear evidence of brain damage, or whether less evident neurological abnormality might be responsible for increases in the frequency of left-handedness in certain clinical conditions where there is no obvious brain damage.

Population studies comparing average scores of left- and right-handers are not very useful for addressing this question. Even if we postulate that a proportion of apparently non-brain-damaged left-handers are pathological and have low test scores, we would still expect these to be in the minority, and so to have a relatively small effect on the average performance of the group of left-handers (see Fig. 6.2).

An alternative approach is to subdivide the population into disordered and normal subgroups (perhaps on the basis of some test of cognitive function), to see whether there is an excess of left-handers in the disordered group. One can see that if unilateral neurological impairment is implicated in a particular disorder, then a comparison of a disordered group with a control group should show an increase in the proportion of left-handers in the former sample. However, this will not be substantial unless the proportion with underlying motor impairment is very high. Figure 7.1 shows the incidence of manifest left-handedess in two populations. In population A, 5 per cent of individuals are affected by unilateral brain damage, whereas in population B, 20 per cent are so affected. Despite this four-fold increase in underlying brain damage, the rate of manifest left-handedness is only slightly higher in population B than in population A, and one would need a large sample from each population to show a statistically significant difference in handedness. Thus, looking for an increase in manifest left-handedness as evidence for pathological left-handedness is a relatively insensitive approach. Furthermore, if we do find an increased frequency of left-handedness associated with disorder, pathological left-handedness is not the only possible explanation (see Chapters 9 and 15).

Population A

```
                    1000 individuals
                  8% naturally left-handed
         ┌──────────────────┴──────────────────┐
  80 natural left-handers            920 natural right-handers
              5% with brain damage
              that impairs contralateral hand
   ┌────┬────┬────┐              ┌────┬────┬────┐
  76    2    2                  23    23   874
unaffected L brain R brain    R brain L brain unaffected
        affected affected    affected affected
 L-handed L-handed R-handed   R-handed L-handed R-handed
```

| 101 manifest left-handers | 899 manifest right-handers |
| 25 with poor right hand | 25 with poor left hand |

Population B

```
                    1000 individuals
                  8% naturally left-handed
         ┌──────────────────┴──────────────────┐
  80 natural left-handers            920 natural right-handers
              20% with brain damage
              that impairs contralateral hand
   ┌────┬────┬────┐              ┌────┬────┬────┐
  64    8    8                  92    92   736
unaffected L brain R brain    R brain L brain unaffected
        affected affected    affected affected
 L-handed L-handed R-handed   R-handed L-handed R-handed
```

| 164 manifest left-handers | 836 manifest right-handers |
| 100 with poor right hand | 100 with poor left hand |

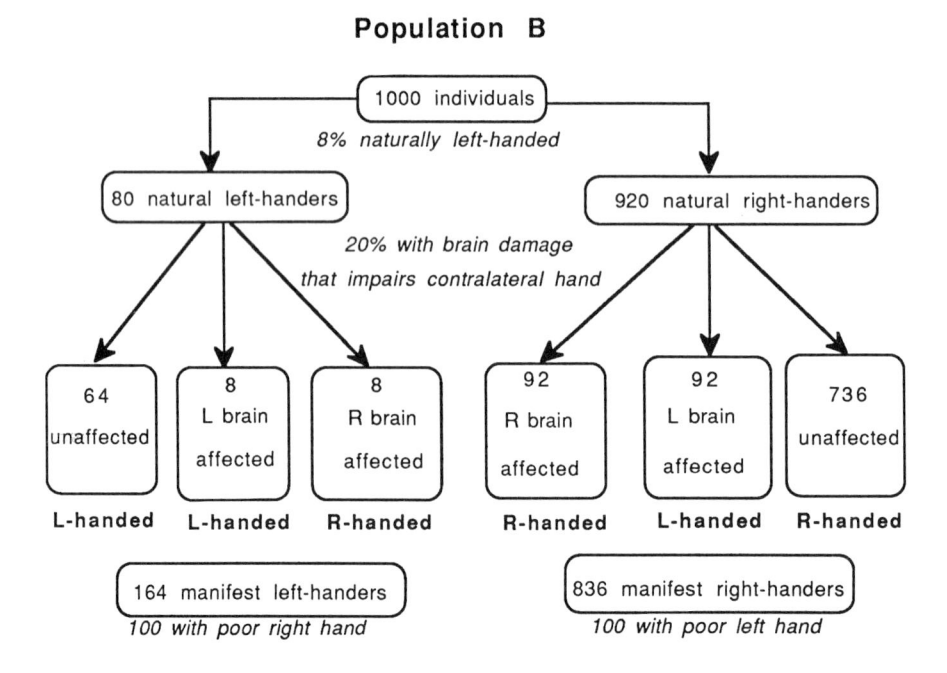

Fig. 7.1. Model of pathological left-handedness, illustrating how manifest left-handers include a higher percentage of pathological cases than manifest right-handers, even when there is no laterality bias in brain lesions.

Possible indicators of pathological left-handedness
What is needed is some way of distinguishing pathological and non-pathological left-handers.

Familial sinistrality
One suggestion is that familial sinistrality can be used as an index, on the assumption that if a left-hander is born into a family with no other left-handers, then the left-handedness is unlikely to be genetic, whereas a person with left-handed relatives has evidence of a genetic predisposition to left-handedness (Briggs *et al.* 1976). However, if one works out the predictions from any current genetic model in detail, one can see that familial sinistrality would act as a very inaccurate index of genetic tendencies to left-handedness. For instance, we can use Annett's (1985) calculations based on the right shift model to show that for a left-handed child, the probability of having at least one left-handed parent is around 0.24 (slightly less for sons, and slightly more for daughters). In contrast, if there were no genetic relationship between handedness of parents and children, then with a population frequency of 12 per cent left-handed, the probability of having at least one left-handed parent would be 0.159. Classification of individuals into 'genetic' or 'pathological' left-handers on the basis of whether they had a left-handed parent would be highly inaccurate. Increasing the number of relatives considered raises the probability that at least one relative will be left-handed, but, as argued by Bishop (1990c), it does not improve the power of familial sinistrality to discriminate genetic and non-genetic left-handers.

This does not mean that data on handedness of family members is worthless: only that it is totally inadequate as a basis for dividing left-handers into 'genetic' and 'pathological' subgroups. If we had some reliable independent means of identifying pathological left-handers, we would predict that they should have fewer left-handed ancestors than other left-handers; however, many in the pathological group would have at least one left-handed relative, and many in the non-pathological group would not.

The problems of using familial sinistrality as an indicator of 'genetic' left-handedness were recognized as long ago as 1958 by Bingley-Wennström, but his cautions have been largely ignored. In treating familial left-handedness as an index of whether the handedness is genetically determined, investigators have applied a logic that works well when the condition under consideration is very rare. For instance, if a deaf person has a deaf parent, then the odds are very low that this is a spurious association, and a genetic explanation is by far the most plausible. However, the argument does not hold up if the base rate of the condition under consideration is so high that its presence in two members of the same family could easily arise by chance.

Strength of hand preference
One might wonder whether strength of preference could be used to distinguish pathological and non-pathological left-handers. The problem for this approach is that the predictions are unclear. One could argue that very strong hand preferences

for either right or left are indicative of underlying pathology (Subirana 1969), on the assumption that a person whose handedness is determined by neuromotor impairment will be sufficiently poor with the non-preferred side to make it unlikely that this hand is used for any skilled task. However, another line of reasoning could be used to make the opposite prediction: a child with a natural tendency to prefer the right side who suffered from damage impairing skill of that side might prefer the left hand for performing intricate manipulations, but persist in right hand use in other activities. Similar contradictory arguments could be applied when considering development of hand preference. One could predict that a child whose preference was determined by pathological factors might show a highly consistent hand preference from an unusually early age, but if the degree of motor impairment was mild, then just the opposite might be observed, with a natural tendency to right hand use competing with a pathologically induced superiority of the left hand. It seems likely that when hand preferences are observed unusually early, or when they are exceptionally pronounced, this is indeed an indication of underlying pathology. However, the converse cannot be assumed, and there may well be some pathological left-handers who have only weak hand preferences which stabilize late in childhood.

Restricted growth of one limb
Lateralized brain injury early in life is frequently associated with restricted growth on the affected side (Aram *et al.* 1986). This observation has led to the suggestion that unilateral restriction of growth of the hand or foot may be a marker for pathological influences on handedness (Satz *et al.* 1984), even in individuals with no known history or sign of neurological injury (Yanowitz *et al.* 1981).

Clumsiness of the non-preferred side
Bishop (1980*b*) looked at functional rather than anatomical restriction of the non-preferred side. It can be seen from the model in Figure 7.1 that left-handers with neurological impairment are expected to have poor right hand function, and, conversely, right-handers with such impairment should have poor left hand function. It therefore follows that, if pathological factors are affecting handedness in a population to a significant extent, there should be an association between poor performance with the non-preferred hand and left-handedness. Note that it is not predicted that the average non-preferred hand skill of left-handers will be lower than that of right-handers: rather there should be a excess of left-handers among those with very poor non-preferred hand skill. The test of this view is to subdivide a population in terms of non-preferred hand skill, to see if there is an association with side of hand preference.

Bishop (1980*b*) carried out such a study with 170 unselected 8-year-olds. The sample comprised all children of this age who were registered at a rural general medical practice in England over a two-year period. Skill of both preferred and non-preferred hands was assessed by asking the children to use a ball-point pen to draw a square between guidelines without hitting the edges (Figure 7.2). This task was performed with both preferred and non-preferred hands (two trials per hand),

Fig. 7.2. Square tracing task used by Bishop (1980a). The squares are secured on a blotter as the child draws between the guidelines, continuously in one direction. Separate tests are conducted for the right and left hands, and using both simultaneously. (The length of the side of the outer square is 102mm, and the distance between the inner and outer squares is 5mm.)

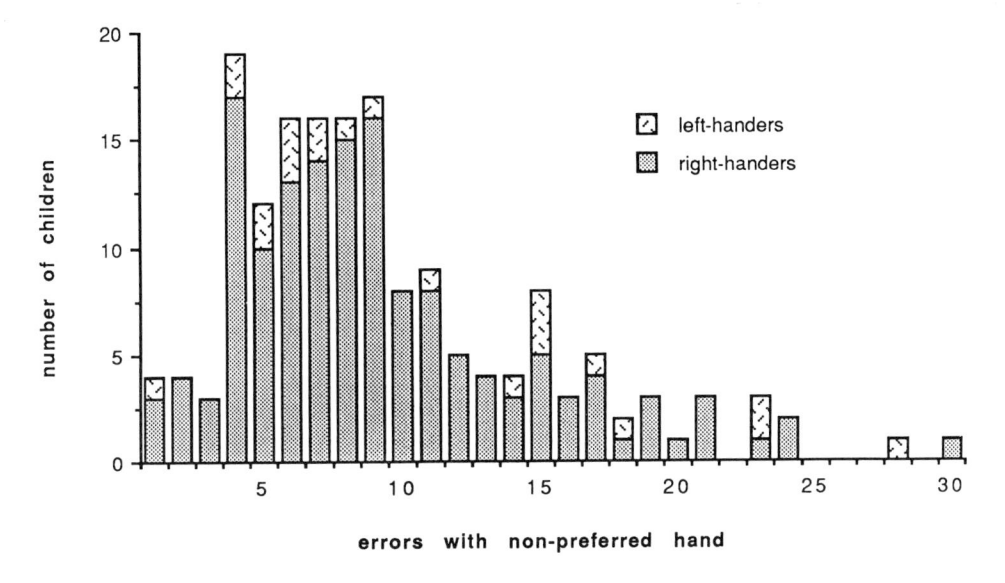

Fig. 7.3. Distribution of square-tracing errors committed by the non-preferred hand in Bishop's (1980a) sample of 8-year-olds.

and bimanually. The score was the total number of times the pen departed from the track. Results are shown in Figure 7.3. It was found that children who were impaired with the non-preferred hand (defined as a score falling at or below the 20th centile) were significantly more likely to be left-handed than those whose scores were above this level. In contrast, there was no link between poor performance of the *preferred* hand and left-handedness. This study suggested that pathological factors played some part in determining handedness even in a non-clinical population. Furthermore, those left-handers with poor non-preferred hand scores had fewer left-handed relatives than other left-handers. In general, children with poor scores of the non-preferred hand were more likely to have had a history of neurological impairment, and obtained lower scores on tests of intellectual function, than did other children. The picture was thus consistent with the view that underlying neurological impairment can alter the balance of skill between the hands sufficiently to shift hand preference if the naturally preferred hand is affected, even in children without obvious motor impairment.

The link between poor non-preferred hand performance and left-handedness has since been replicated by Gillberg *et al.* (1984), using the same square-tracing task with Swedish 10-year-olds. Left-handers were over-represented among those who made many errors or who performed the task very slowly with the non-preferred hand. Children with poor non-preferred hand scores had significantly more evidence of neurological dysfunction than other children. Gillberg *et al.* also replicated Bishop's findings on familial sinistrality, showing that presumed 'pathological' left-handers had significantly lower familial sinistrality scores than did those with normal non-preferred hand scores.

Estimating the frequency of pathological left-handedness

Bishop (1984) went on to analyse data from 12,000 children in the National Child Development Study in the same way. Data were available on two tasks of motor skill administered at the age of 11 years. A link between poor performance of the non-preferred hand and left-handedness was not found for a square-marking task but was found for time taken to transfer 20 matches from one box to another.

Figure 7.4 shows a more precisely defined model of the relationship between handedness and non-preferred hand skill. The abscissa is a standard scale of non-preferred hand skill. Individuals whose hand proficiency is unaffected by pathological influences have scores normally distributed around a mean of zero with a standard deviation of one. Those whose hand proficiency is affected by pathology have a much lower mean proficiency score for the affected hand. Using this simple model, one can use the logic shown in Figure 7.5 to make precise estimates of the expected numbers of children whose motor proficiency of the non-preferred hand falls below some cut-off level (*e.g.* fifth centile or less), provided one estimates three parameters: (i) the probability that an individual will be left-handed, provided no pathological influences operate; (ii) the difference in mean hand proficiency score between affected and unaffected children; and (iii) the probability that an individual is affected by lateralized motor impairment sufficient to shift hand preference if the previously preferred side is affected. By fitting the model shown in Figure 7.5 to data obtained with this large sample, it was estimated that in a normal population, 1.4 per cent of individuals are affected by some underlying abnormality that impairs performance of the contralateral hand. From this it follows that around one in 20 of all left-handers are pathological left-handers, and just over one-third of left-handers with very poor non-preferred hand skill are

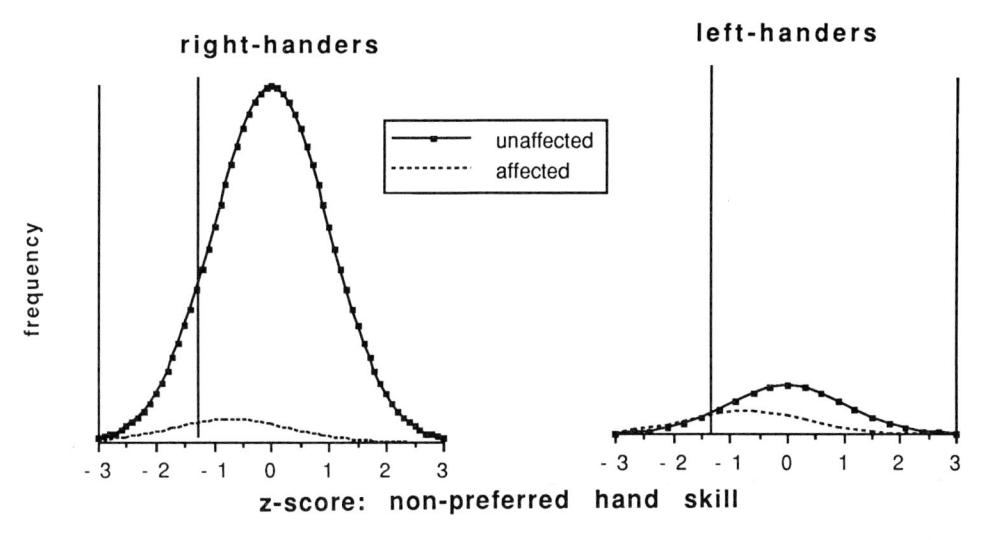

Fig. 7.4. Theoretical distribution of non-preferred hand skill for individuals affected and unaffected by brain damage. The cut-off at $z = -1.33$ is an arbitrary threshold below which the non-preferred hand is designated as clumsy.

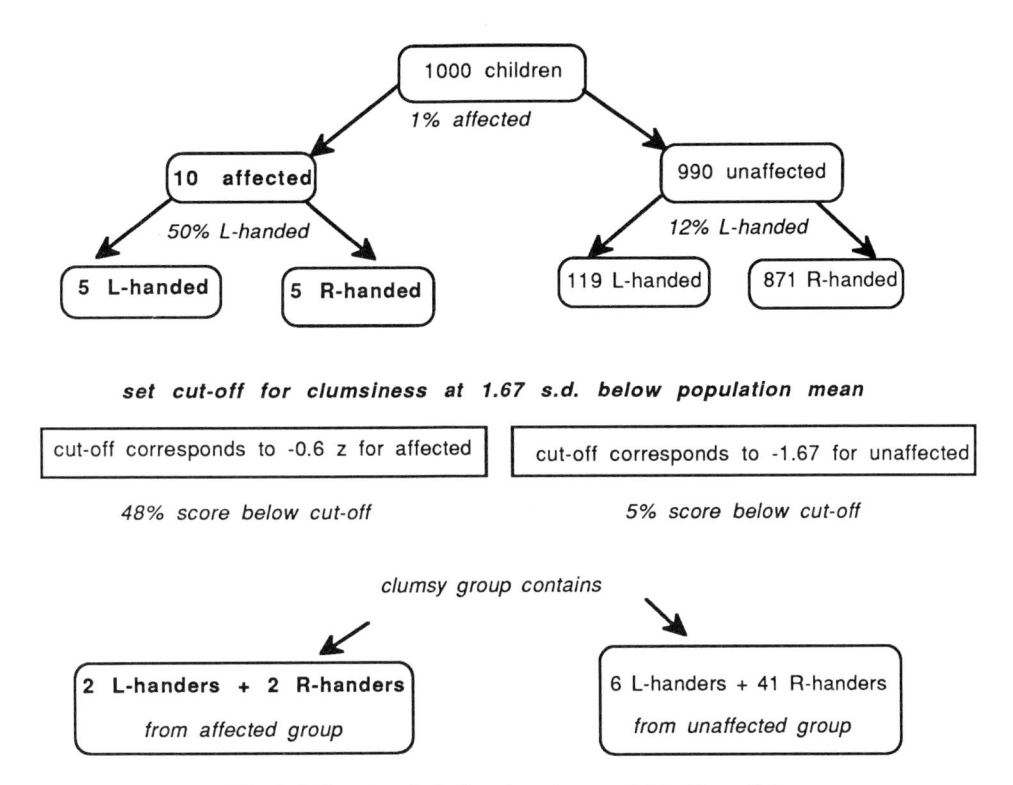

Fig. 7.5. Sample calculations based on model in Figure 7.4.

pathological left-handers. This study indicated that it is not implausible to postulate that an increase in left-handedness due to pathological influences may be found even in populations where frank neuromotor abnormality is not evident.

Concluding comment
It is not reasonable to regard all left-handedness as pathological. However, hand preference can be affected by underlying neurological impairment, and when this occurs it raises the proportion of left-handers in a population. Pathological left-handedness is not confined to groups with obvious signs of brain damage but can occur in more subtle forms in cases where there is no hemiplegia or hard neurological sign. Bishop's (1984) study estimated that in the general population about one in every 20 left-handers is a pathological left-hander. We need to develop better ways of distinguishing pathological from non-pathological left-handers. Familial sinistrality, the most widely used index, yields such a high rate of misclassification as to make it worthless. Hypotrophy of one limb, strength of hand preference and poor motor skill of one side are all promising indices.

8
EPILEPSY

The claim that there is a raised frequency of left-handedness in epileptic populations was one factor that led Satz (1972, 1973) to formulate a model of pathological left-handedness (see Chapter 7). Yet this claim is controversial, and several epidemiological studies have failed to find any link (Douglas *et al.* 1967, Rutter *et al.* 1970*a*, McManus 1980*b*). The discrepancies in findings may have to do with the severity and aetiology of epilepsy and whether focal seizures are common in a sample. Douglas *et al.* excluded children with known brain damage, CNS abnormalities and petit mal. The study by Rutter *et al.* restricted consideration to epileptic children who were normal on neurological examination. McManus did find a trend for a link with handedness in children who had been absent from school for more than one week due to 'convulsions, fits and turns' (among these children, 27.2 per cent of boys and 23.5 per cent of girls were left-handed); however, numbers were small and the effect did not reach statistical significance.

Handedness relative to laterality of lesion
According to the pathological left-handedness model of Satz, any increase in the frequency of left-handedness among epileptics should be accounted for by individuals with left hemisphere lesions acquired early in life. Data consistent with this view were reported by Ounsted (1955), who found that 10 out of 13 epileptic children with left focal discharge were left-handed, compared with four out of 13 with right focal discharge. All the children in that study were also diagnosed as hyperkinetic. Bingley-Wennström (1958) did not find any excess of left-handedness in a sample of 90 patients with temporal lobe epilepsy, but these data are difficult to evaluate in the absence of information about age at onset. Martin *et al.* (1968) did not find any handedness difference between epileptic and control samples, but the interpretation of this negative result is obscured because the control group was younger than the epileptic group and included many individuals with a mental impairment. What is of interest are the data relating laterality of brain damage and handedness. Seven out of 10 with left-sided radiographic abnormalities were non-right-handed, compared with none of the seven with right-sided abnormalities. Although the effect is diminished when hemiplegic subjects are excluded, despite the small sample there is still a statistically significant difference: five out of seven with left-sided abnormalities were non-right-handed, compared with none of the five with right-sided lesions. The majority of subjects had bilateral radiographic abnormalities, and in this group 29 per cent were non-right-handed. Data on laterality of EEG focus were less clear-cut, but showed a similar trend for non-right-handedness to be higher in those with left-sided abnormalities, even after excluding hemiplegic individuals.

Satz (1972) used data from Penfield and Roberts' (1959) Montreal series of

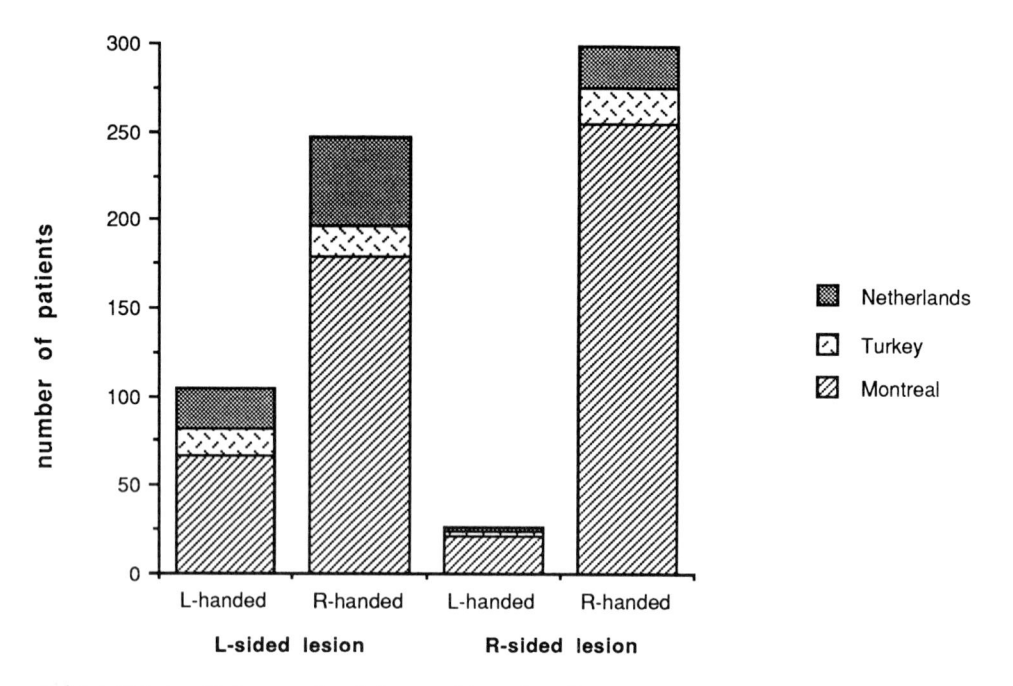

Fig. 8.1. Relationship between handedness and laterality of lesion in three samples of epileptic patients. (Based on data from Satz *et al.* 1979.)

epileptic patients undergoing unilateral lobectomy to test some of the predictions from his model. He showed that the increase in left-handedness in this group was accounted for primarily by those who sustained left-sided brain injury before the age of 2 years. Satz *et al.* (1979) went on to present data on handedness and laterality of lesion or EEG abnormality for three large populations of epileptic patients, from Montreal, Turkey and the Netherlands. Data are shown in Figure 8.1. The association between handedness and laterality of lesion was highly significant in each sample, in agreement with prediction from the model that attributes the excess of left-handers in epileptic populations to the inclusion of pathological left-handers. What was not stated in this report was how many of the subjects were hemiplegic. Clearly, if the link between lesion laterality and handedness were totally explained by the inclusion of hemiplegic individuals, this would be relatively uninteresting. We do know that some of the patients from the Penfield and Roberts series were hemiplegic, and exclusion of this subset from the analysis does weaken the association between lesion laterality and handedness.

Epilepsy associated with areas of alien tissue
Many epileptic individuals do not have signs of injury to the brain, but post-mortem studies reveal areas of abnormal development. Geschwind and Galaburda (1987) argued that the types of malformed and misplaced areas of cortex associated with epilepsy arise when the normal developmental patterns of neuronal migration in

the fetus are disrupted, and they suggested that abnormal levels of circulating sex hormones may be responsible for selectively affecting development of the left hemisphere (see Chapter 14). According to this explanation, we would expect a link between handedness and epilepsy, even in individuals who had no sign of brain injury, because the same factors that lead to neuronal migration disorders and retard left hemisphere development will also lead to left-handedness.

To evaluate this hypothesis we need much more detailed studies of handedness in relation to neuropathological findings in epileptic patients. Such data as we have are not encouraging for Geschwind and Galaburda's hypothesis. The studies reviewed above suggest that an increase in non-right-handedness in epilepsy is found only in populations in whom there are neurological signs of early damage to the left hemisphere.

Relationship of handedness to symptomatology

Geschwind and Galaburda also suggested that learning disabilities arise from abnormalities of neuronal migration. Indeed, the first patient in whom Galaburda and Kemper (1979) described cytoarchitectonic anomalies in the left hemisphere was dyslexic, epileptic and left-handed! They noted that: 'In our own clinical observations of adults with temporal lobe epilepsy we have been struck by the frequency of childhood learning disorders and evidence of anomalous dominance. Studies should be carried out to test the validity of these observations' (p. 206). Ounsted's (1955) early study of hyperkinetic epileptic children lent some support to this view. In a sample of 70 children, 10 had speech defects disproportionate to intelligence, and seven of these were left-handed. However, other studies have obtained contrary findings: Jennekens-Schinkel *et al.* (1987) found no link between spelling proficiency and handedness in a large sample of epileptic children.

Intriguing associations have been reported between left-handedness and psychiatric symptomatology. In a review of this field, Flor-Henry (1983) concluded that psychosis in patients with temporal lobe epilepsy was more common with left-sided foci, and was associated with left-handedness. The mechanism for this association remains mysterious. A methodological consequence is that if an epileptic sample is recruited from a psychiatric institution, then an excess of left-handers is likely to be found.

Concluding comment

It has become part of conventional neuropsychological wisdom that left-handedness is unusually common among people with epilepsy. Such data as we have suggest that this is true only in cases where the epilepsy is a symptom of a focal brain lesion acquired early in life. However, studies to date have failed to look at handedness in relationship to the aetiology of the epilepsy. It would be interesting to discover whether there is any evidence of excess left-handedness in individuals whose epilepsy is due to focal cortical dysplasias of the kind described by Taylor *et al.* (1971).

9
MENTAL IMPAIRMENT

A link between non-right-handedness and mental impairment has been recognized for some time (Gordon 1920, Wilson and Dolan 1931, Burt 1937, Dart 1938), with the frequency of right-handedness decreasing with the severity of intellectual retardation (Hicks and Barton 1975, Bradshaw-McAnulty *et al.* 1984, Broman *et al.* 1987). Hildreth (1949*b*), in a review paper, noted that: 'Left-handers are not duller in general than the right-handed, but left-handedness is found more frequently among the dull when that section of the population is studied' (p. 245), a conclusion that was supported by analysis of data from the National Survey Sample (Douglas *et al.* 1967), showing that while right-handers and non-right-handers did not differ on average ability and attainment, the rate of non-right-handedness increased from 14 per cent in those of average or above-average attainment to 20 per cent in those scoring more than one standard deviation below the mean, and to 30 per cent in those categorized as 'mentally handicapped'.

Explanations for the excess of non-right-handers
The finding of relatively high rates of non-right-handedness among mentally handicapped people appears to be well established, but explanations for this result remain in question. Hildreth proposed a learning hypothesis: 'the dull and mentally handicapped . . . are less responsive to social training, they receive less of it, and they do not learn so easily from incidental clues' (p. 247). However, this assumes that in normal individuals, handedness is a learned behaviour, whereas according to the evidence reviewed in Chapter 3, learning plays but a minor role in determining handedness.

Bishop (1983) distinguished two other possible explanations for the association of handedness and intellectual retardation. The first is the *pathological* hypothesis which attributes the excess of left-handers to the fact that many cases of mental impairment are the consequence of brain injury, and so are likely to have handedness influenced by lateralized pathology, as discussed in Chapter 7. The second may be termed the *increased randomness* hypothesis. Palmer (1964) regarded stable hand preference as the outcome of a process of neurological differentiation. The normal infant progresses gradually from a state of undifferentiated bilaterality, with innervation of the trunk developing first, followed by the arms and finally the hands. If this developmental process is slowed or arrested, there would be lack of differentiation and poor motor skill. On a handedness inventory, a completely undifferentiated child would respond at random. In this situation, on a binary handedness classification, left- and right-handers would be equally common, not because of any factor biasing towards the left side, but simply because the normal bias favouring the right is absent.

TABLE 9.I
Handedness in mentally handicapped subjects in relation to EEG abnormality

EEG finding	Total	Left-handed N	(%)	Right-handed N	(%)
Normal	96	9	(9)	87	(91)
Unilateral left-sided abnormality	21	7	(33)	14	(67)
Bilateral asymmetrical, predominantly left-sided	35	8	(22)	27	(78)
Unilateral right-sided abnormality	16	1	(6)	15	(94)
Bilateral asymmetrical, predominantly right-sided	27	4	(14)	23	(86)
Bilateral, no asymmetry	377	62	(16)	315	(84)

Evidence for pathological left-handedness

Lucas *et al.* (1989) presented evidence that the excess of non-right-handedness among mentally handicapped people was confined to those identified as having language problems. They argued that this could be explained in terms of pathological left-handedness, on the grounds that language difficulties were indicative of left hemisphere pathology. There are two problems with this study, one methodological and one theoretical. The methodological problem concerns the way in which degree of mental handicap and presence of language impairment were assessed. Classification was based on data from records, which included informal impressions as well as psychometric assesments. No criteria were given for defining language impairment, and it is unclear whether this was evaluated relative to test norms, or whether impairment was scored only when language problems were disproportionate to mental age. The latter seems probable, since 61 per cent of this institutionalized sample were rated as having no language impairment. The second problem is that early lesions of the left hemisphere do *not* typically result in language impairment, unless there is also damage to the corresponding areas of the right hemisphere (see pp. 136–137). It is therefore not logical to use verbal impairment as evidence of early left hemisphere damage.

More direct evidence for the biological basis of excess left-handedness in mentally handicapped people comes from a study by Silva and Satz (1979), who related electroencephalographic (EEG) results to handedness in a sample of 675 mentally handicapped people. Handedness was assessed by asking caregivers to judge whether each person was left-, mixed or right-handed, with mixed handers (N=179) being excluded from further analysis. Results are shown in Table 9.I.

Silva and Satz drew attention to the fact that for those with normal EEGs the frequency of left-handedness was similar to the rate typically reported for normal populations, whereas for those with EEG abnormalities it was considerably higher, especially where there was an asymmetrical EEG abnormality predominantly affecting the left hemisphere. They noted, however, that the rate of left-handedness was also high in those with symmetrical bilateral EEG disturbances, which was not predicted by their model of pathological left-handedness. To account for this they suggested that 'the probability of an individual being right-handed decreases with poorer levels of cortical functioning' (p. 15), a line of explanation similar to the increased randomness hypothesis.

Bishop (1984), analysing data from the National Child Development Study, tested the fit of a model of pathological left-handedness to data from two mentally handicapped groups, one with evidence of neurological impairment and one without such evidence. The data fitted the model in so far as an increased rate of left-handedness was found in the mentally handicapped group, and the rate of left-handedness was particularly high among those with poor performance of the non-preferred hand. Although these results agreed well with the hypothesis that pathological influences upset the balance of skill between the two sides, this explanation could not account for the fact that the fit of the model was as good for those *without* evidence of neurological damage as it was for those with such evidence. Although it is possible that in some cases there was a failure to detect neurological impairment, it seems improbable that such error could totally account for this result. Diagnostic categories were not recorded for this sample, but it is likely that a high proportion of cases were caused by genetic conditions, such as Down syndrome and fragile-X syndrome, which result in diffuse abnormalities of brain development rather than focal lesions (Fryns *et al.* 1986). This finding raised concern that the pattern of results may be caused by a different process, that of increased randomness.

Evidence for increased randomness
Further evidence against an explanation solely in terms of pathological left-handedness comes from a simple comparison of rates of non-right-handedness in different aetiological groups. Several studies have shown that the rate of non-right-handedness in Down syndrome is well above the level found in control populations (Pickersgill and Pank 1970, Batheja and McManus 1985, Elliott 1985, Pipe 1987). Furthermore, where a distinction has been made between mixed- and left-handedness, it is clear that in general it is *lack of hand preference* rather than left-handedness that is particularly common in mentally handicapped people (Dart 1938, Porac *et al.* 1980). These findings are consistent with the view that non-right-handedness in mentally handicapped people may indicate an increased tendency towards random behaviour.

Soper *et al.* (1987) conducted one of the few studies to investigate directly stability of hand preference. They assessed 73 severely mentally handicapped individuals with IQs in the range 11–31. Aetiology was unknown in many cases, though five individuals had Down syndrome and two had phenylketonuria. Hand preference was assessed using an eight-item inventory administered in two sessions one week apart. On each occasion, eight tasks were administered three times to establish whether the preference was stable or random. Subjects were categorized as left- or right-handed if they used that hand on 90 per cent or more of trials. It was found that 33 out of 73 (45.2 per cent) showed mixed handedness, and of these, 30 were inconsistent in their preferences both between and within items. This latter group was referred to as having ambiguous handedness.

Explanations for ambiguous handedness

Soper and his colleagues (Soper and Satz 1984, Soper *et al.* 1987) proposed that ambiguous handedness represents a pathological subtype which exists only in clinical populations with severe early bilateral brain damage which prevents development of manual dominance. This contrasts with Bishop's (1983) suggestion that ambiguous handedness is an indicator of motor immaturity. Soper *et al.* argued against this type of interpretation on the grounds that ambiguous handedness was rare in a sample of normal 5-year-olds given the same handedness assessment. However, it seems possible that, although younger than the handicapped group, these control children were superior to them on motor skills. Inconsistent handedness on repeated administration of the same items has been described in normal children aged from 18 to 42 months (Gottfried and Bathurst 1983).

It would be interesting to compare the frequency of ambiguous handedness in mentally handicapped and younger normal children at a similar level of motor competence. As shown in Chapter 1, handedness in humans is most apparent for skilled, stereotyped actions involving a pincer grip and/or bimanual coordination, and young children, who cannot perform such actions, are more random in their preferences than older individuals. If ambiguous handedness corresponds to developmental delay rather than deviance, then the extent to which ambiguous handedness is shown should be predictable from level of motor skill. Consistent with this explanation is Elliott's (1985) demonstration that right-handed individuals with Down syndrome initially showed no difference between the two hands in a tapping task, but a right hand superiority became apparent after a period of training. It is as if the skill bias favouring the right hand was present, just as in those of normal intelligence, but it only became obvious when the individual performed practised tasks.

However, another source of evidence suggests that ambiguous handedness may be indicative of particular type of brain pathology. Lonton (1976) assessed handedness for drawing and writing in 203 children with spina bifida and hydrocephalus. Despite the fact that both tasks involved pencil use, a substantial minority of the spina bifida children used both hands, a behaviour that was observed only rarely in the youngest normal control children. Although these 'mixed handers' were of significantly lower IQ than other children in the sample, the majority of them (68 per cent) had IQs above 70. Anderson and Spain (1977) suggested that while failure to develop hand preference in children with spina bifida might simply be a consequence of general motor delay, a specific neuroanatomical basis could be the stretching and thinning of the corpus callosum that often occurs in this condition. This interpretation fits well with contemporary views on the role of the corpus callosum in normal development of handedness (see Chapter 4). If the callosal thinning hypothesis is correct we would predict that children with spina bifida who did not develop hand preference should show mirror movements beyond the usual age and should also have difficulty in executing movements that crossed the midline or involved asymmetrical bimanual actions. We need to test these predictions in studies that compare children with spina bifida with younger children matched for level of motor ability.

The significance of familial sinistrality
Both the increased randomness hypothesis and the pathological hypothesis assume that the excess of non-right-handedness is caused by non-genetic influences. Therefore, one would expect that mentally handicapped left-handers would be less likely than other left-handers to have left-handed relatives. Bradshaw-McAnulty *et al.* (1984) concluded that the excess of non-right-handedness in mentally handicapped groups can be explained in terms of pathological left-handedness, having found that parent–proband handedness correlations were non-significant in a sample of mentally handicapped individuals. However, they did not compare the size of obtained correlations with those that would be expected in a normal sample. Also, one quarter of their sample had Down syndrome, where pathological left-handedness due to a focal lesion is unlikely. Results from this subgroup were not presented separately, so one cannot tell if their pattern of performance resembled that of other individuals of similar intellectual ability.

Two recent studies have reported results that appear to pose a problem for explanations in terms of pathological factors. Searleman *et al.* (1988) found higher rates of familial sinistrality among left-handed mentally handicapped people than among other left-handers. They came to the counterintuitive conclusion that familial sinistrality is an indicator of probable pathological left-handedness: 'The reasoning behind this position is that a family history of left-handedness may be mediated by a familial tendency to have birth stress or may be associated with an anomalous intrauterine environment for the developing fetus' (p. 133). Unfortunately, they assessed familial sinistrality in terms of whether the person had a left-handed parent or sibling, and so the likelihood of finding familial sinistrality increased with family size (see Chapter 6, p. 83). Their claim would be much stronger if it could be shown that mentally handicapped left-handers were more likely than other left-handers to have left-handed parents or grandparents.

A similar claim was made by Pipe (1987), who found that the prevalence of left-handers with familial sinistrality was higher in mentally handicapped individuals than in a control group. However, the analysis conducted by Pipe was misleading. Having demonstrated that the overall incidence of left-handedness was raised in two mentally handicapped groups, she then compared the frequency of left-handers with sinistral relatives in mentally handicapped and control groups. Even if there were no genetic influence on handedness, the number of left-handers with left-handed relatives would increase as the overall frequency of left-handedness went up. A more appropriate test would involve comparing groups in terms of the *percentage* of left-handers who had a sinistral relative, or, if numbers were too small to justify this, comparing the overall rates of left-handed relatives for all subjects in a sample. When this was done by Pipe, she found no difference between the mentally handicapped groups and a control group. For instance, five out of 25 controls (20 per cent), seven out of 21 subjects with Down syndrome (33 per cent) and 11 out of 46 individuals with some other developmental disability (23 per cent) had a left-handed parent: a non-significant difference.

Concluding comment

It is well established that there is an excess of non-right-handedness in mentally handicapped populations, but we have a long way to go before we fully understand the nature of this increase. A major step forward has been the recognition that in many mentally handicapped people lack of right-handedness does not indicate left-handedness or ambidexterity so much as randomness on hand preference inventories. Further research is needed to clarify how far this is a function of level of motor skill and how far it is a pathological phenomenon, perhaps arising as a specific consequence of callosal dysfunction. It is important that future studies distinguish between aetiological groups rather than selecting subjects purely on the basis of intellectual level.

10
AUTISM AND RETT SYNDROME

Autism
Interest in a relationship between infantile autism and handedness was sparked by Colby and Parkison (1977), who reported a high frequency of non-right-handedness among a group of preschool autistic children. They interpreted this as indicating a failure of the development of cerebral lateralization due to bilateral brain damage.

Barry and James (1978) criticized the Colby and Parkison study on a number of points. (1) The control group was not matched on intellectual level, so it was not possible to tell whether the increased rate of non-right-handedness was specific to autism or whether it was a correlate of mental impairment. (2) The criterion for right-handedness was unusually generous in that a child was regarded as right-handed if the right hand was used on 60 per cent or more of occasions. (3) Children in the sample were young enough for their non-right-handedness to have been a temporary condition associated with motor immaturity, rather than a persisting feature. Autistic and control children were not precisely matched on age. (4) The handedness assessment procedure was biased towards finding less right-handedness among those with poor language, because different test items were weighted not only in terms of the motor dexterity they required, but also depending on whether they involved language (*i.e.* writing and drawing). Also, there was variability from child to child in the activities tested, depending on age and ability.

Since Colby and Parkison's report, several further studies which overcome some of these drawbacks have appeared. Studies by Boucher (1977), Barry and James (1978) and Gillberg (1983) all compared handedness of autistic children with that of a control group closely matched on age and ability. In Gillberg's case, the study was conducted on a total population sample identified in an epidemiological survey. Gillberg and Barry and James defined handedness as consistently left, consistently right or mixed on the basis of hand preference for five actions, whereas Boucher used seven test activities. Results from these studies are summarized in Table 10.I. One can see there are inconsistencies in the findings. Neither Boucher nor Barry and James found significant differences in handedness distributions between autistic and control children. Boucher compared her sample with a group matched on verbal ability as well as with one matched on non-verbal ability, but results were similar in both cases. Gillberg, however, did find a significant excess of left-handers among the autistic children.

Closer scrutiny of Table 10.I reveals that there are fluctuations in the proportion of left-handers from one study to another not just in the autistic group, but also among the controls. While differences in assessment procedures might account for some of this variation, it seems unlikely that this is the whole explanation. One would expect, for instance, that Boucher would have more

TABLE 10.I
Handedness in autistic children relative to controls matched for mental age

Study		Total	R-handed N	(%)	Mixed-handed N	(%)	L-handed N	(%)
Boucher (1977)	Autistic	46	21	(48)	21	(48)	3	(7)
	Controls*	46	23	(50)	16	(35)	7	(15)
Barry and James	Autistic	33	15	(47)	13	(38)	5	(15)
(1978)	Controls**	34	16	(47)	17	(50)	1	(3)
Gillberg (1983)	Autistic	26	10	(38)	10	(38)	6	(23)
	Controls**	52	33	(63)	16	(31)	3	(6)

*Matched on non-verbal IQ; **matched on full-scale IQ.

children in the mixed-handedness category, simply because she used a longer battery of items, yet in her mentally handicapped control group there are more consistently left-handed children than in the other studies. This could be a consequence of the fact that children were never scored as lacking hand preference for an item: if both hands were used equally for a given task, the test was repeated until a preference for one or the other hand emerged. Control subject selection may also play a part in explaining variation between studies: if one is matching autistic children with mentally handicapped controls, then the aetiology of the mental impairment assumes importance (see Chapter 9). However, the major reason for variability from study to study is probably just the small sample sizes that investigators are forced to use when studying such a rare condition as infantile autism. If the results from these three studies are combined, the overall proportion of left-handers is 13.3 per cent for autistic children and 8.3 per cent for matched controls, not a significant difference. However, if left- and mixed-handers are summed, then the frequency of non-right-handedness among autistic children is considerably higher than that found in age-matched normally developing children, although it is similar to that found in other children of the same intellectual ability.

A popular explanation for the excess non-right-handedness is that it is an indication of a constitutionally determined form of neurological organization in which cerebral lateralization does not develop. Several investigators have proposed this hypothesis, and it forms part of Geschwind and Galaburda's hormonal theory of the origins of cerebral lateralization (see Chapter 14). An alternative view is that excess non-right-handedness in autism can be explained in the same way as the excess in mental handicap: either in terms of randomness reflecting underlying motor immaturity, or in terms of an increased rate of pathological left-handedness (see Chapters 7 and 9).

Evidence against a genetic predisposition to left-handedness in autism came from studies by Boucher (1977), Tsai (1982) and Fein *et al.* (1985), all of which found that the overall rate of left-handed relatives in autistic individuals was similar to expected population values, and non-right-handers and right-handers had similar numbers of left-handed relatives.

Evidence for pathological left-handedness
The mounting evidence of neurological impairment in autistic children (Coleman and Gillberg 1985) makes an explanation in terms of pathological left-handedness attractive. As Satz (1972) pointed out, excess left-handedness reflecting the contribution of pathological left-handers is expected in any population where there is focal brain damage which affects either hemisphere with equal probability. Clearly, if autism is specifically associated with *left* hemisphere damage, pathological left-handedness should be particularly pronounced. Evidence for left hemisphere abnormalities in autism came from a pneumoencephalographic study by Hauser *et al.* (1975), who reported dilatation of the left temporal horn and general widening of the left lateral ventricle in 15 out of 18 children. However, Fein *et al.* (1984) noted that only seven of the 18 children in this study were clearly autistic, and six of these had evidence of bilateral involvement. They argued that most children observed by Hauser to have gross dilatation of the left temporal horn were probably not autistic. This would explain why later studies have failed to find an association between left hemisphere abnormalities and autism (Caparulo *et al.* 1981). Furthermore, in so far as Hauser *et al.* provided information on this point, left-handedness did not appear to be associated with left hemisphere damage. A similar conclusion was reached by Gillberg (1983), who found that, although several left-handed autistic children had unequivocal evidence of brain damage or dysfunction on CT scan or EEG, it was frequently the right hemisphere that was affected. The only autistic child in this study with clear evidence of damage lateralized to the left hemisphere was right-handed. Tsai and Stewart (1982) found a similar lack of relationship between handedness and lateralized abnormality in an electroencephalographic study. In all cases where EEG abnormalities were found, these were bilateral.

Ambiguous handedness
In a review of the literature, Fein *et al.* (1984) noted that the high frequency of non-right-handedness in autism arose more because of the contribution of those without established hand preference than because of excess left-handers, and they noted that this could be a transitional developmental stage rather than an indication of weak cerebral lateralization. Likewise, Prior and Bradshaw (1979), who found six mixed-handers in a group of 23 autistic children, noted: 'Those children with a mixture of preference were classed as such, generally because they were apparently developmentally immature and their preference reflected poor coordination and ability to do the task, rather than being a real indicator of preference' (p. 77). Such interpretations correspond to the increased randomness hypothesis (see p. 104), and are supported by studies finding that mixed preference is associated with generally poor mental functioning. Fein *et al.* (1985) examined handedness and hand function in 62 children diagnosed as suffering from pervasive developmental disorder. Although this category is somewhat broader than Kanner syndrome, children with this diagnosis had clear autistic symptomatology. One aim of this research was to replicate a study by Tsai (1983) in which it was reported that mixed handedness in autistic children was associated with poor mental abilities. Like Tsai,

they found that those with mixed handedness (N=18) obtained particularly poor scores on several cognitive tests. However, the stable left-handers (N=8) did rather better than the right-handers (N=36).

Data from Soper *et al.* (1986) also encourage one to think in terms of randomness of hand preference rather than pathologically enforced left-handedness in autistic children. These investigators distinguished two types of mixed handedness: that where the child's hand preference was inconsistent within an activity, and that where preference for a given activity was reliable, but direction of preference differed from one activity to another. They showed that it was the former type of mixed handedness, which they termed ambiguous handedness, that was particularly frequent in autism, especially in those with lower levels of intellectual functioning. In their original publication on this topic they suggested that ambiguous handedness was not commonly found except in autism, but, as we saw in Chapter 9, they subsequently reported that this was also characteristic of non-autistic mentally handicapped children.

The data reviewed so far point toward an explanation of increased non-right-handedness in autism arising as a consequence of generally poor motor functioning which results in a failure to learn the types of motor skills for which hand preference is normally shown. Lack of hand preference rather than stable left-handedness is what differentiates autistic from normal children. Neither pathological left-handedness nor a genetic predisposition towards decreased cerebral lateralization seem able to account for available data.

Morphological brain asymmetry
There is, however, one source of evidence that does not neatly fit in with this explanation and suggests, rather, a constitutional basis for lack of cerebral lateralization. Hier *et al.* (1979) used CT scan measurements of left–right morphological asymmetries of the parieto-occipital region in 16 autistic individuals. In nine patients (56 per cent), the right parieto-occipital region was wider than the left, whereas this pattern was observed in only 10 out of 44 (23 per cent) of non-autistic mentally handicapped patients and 25 out of 100 other neurological patients. However, later studies failed to confirm this result (Tsai *et al.* 1982, Gillberg and Svendsen 1983, Prior *et al.* 1984, Rosenbloom *et al.* 1984), although there was some indication that lack of asymmetry rather than reversed asymmetry might characterize autism (Damasio *et al.* 1980). Tsai *et al.* concluded that the previous findings of reversed asymmetry could have arisen because evaluation of CT scans was not blind, or because of bias in patient selection and failure to control for age and sex. We may also note that accurate assessment of CT scan asymmetries requires that the child's head be placed in a symmetrical position and maintained there.

As with handedness studies, even where abnormal results are obtained with autistic samples it can be difficult to establish whether the abnormality is specific to autism or is a more general concomitant of mental impairment. Prior *et al.* (1984) studied a small group of autistic individuals whose intelligence was in the normal or borderline range and found no evidence of any abnormality on CT scan. Similarly,

Harcherik *et al.* (1985), using objective assessment of ventricular volume, ventricular asymmetry and brain density in a study of 16 subjects, concluded that autistic children without other neurological abnormalities are very unlikely to have detectable CT scan abnormalities.

Functional measures of cerebral lateralization
Assessment of functional lateralization of language is difficult in autism because of the low language attainments of most individuals. Prior and Bradshaw (1979) tested 19 autistic children aged from 8 to 13 years on a dichotic listening task in which they were required to repeat words. The control group showed a clear right ear advantage on this task, whereas the autistic group did not. However, the two groups were not directly compared within the same analysis, and despite the authors' reassurances of comparability in overall performance between controls and autistic subjects, there do appear to have been some differences. The number of words repeated wrongly was closely similar for the two groups, but the total words correctly reported was not stated (*i.e.* no information was provided on omissions). Whereas no autistic child ever repeated more than one word from a dichotic pair, five of the 19 control children did so. A child was regarded as having an ear advantage if the difference between ears was three words or more, but no rationale was given for this cut-off: the difference between ears would need to be considerably larger than this to be confident that the child was not responding randomly to the two sides. The authors' interpretation that a proportion of autistic children have right cerebral dominance for language processing does not seem justified in view of their failure to demonstrate that ear difference scores depart from chance values. Those autistic children with better language skills were more likely to show an ear advantage (for either right or left), but it is unclear whether this result would hold up if ear difference scores were corrected for overall number of responses. Thus although this study found a lack of normal functional asymmetry in autistic children, it remains unclear whether this reflects the cause or the consequence of limited language skills and motivation.

Similar problems of interpretation apply to a study of lateralized EEG activation by Dawson *et al.* (1982). Whereas control subjects showed left hemisphere activation when performing verbal tasks, autistic subjects did not. The question arises as to whether low verbal competence of autistic children is a consequence of their failure to develop language in the left hemisphere, or whether the lack of left hemisphere activation is an indication that these children are not attending to or processing verbal materials normally.

Dawson *et al.* (1986) carried out a study aimed at resolving this question. They chose a technique for measuring lateralization in young children that had been used to demonstrate hemispheric asymmetries in normal infants: interhemispheric difference in average evoked response to the stimulus 'da'. Autistic children did not show the evoked response asymmetry that was observed in the control group. However, the variance in the autistic group was substantial, with some showing large differences favouring the right hemisphere, and others showing more normal responses. Furthermore, those with the normal pattern of asymmetry had better

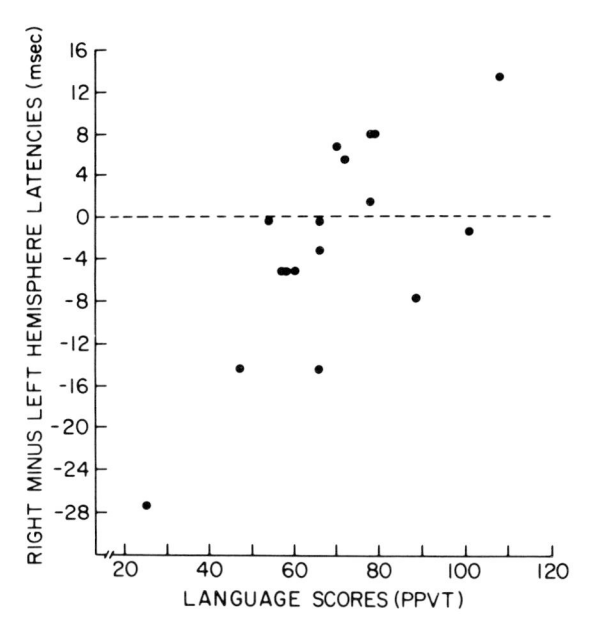

Fig. 10.1. Scatter plot displaying individual autistic subjects' scores on the Peabody Picture Vocabulary Test and patterns of hemispheric asymmetry, as measured by right- minus left-hemisphere evoked potentials to speech stimuli. (Reprinted from Dawson *et al.* 1986, p. 1451.)

language skills than those with reversed asymmetry (Fig. 10.1). Dawson *et al.* discussed two explanations for these findings. One possibility is that there is a subgroup of autistic individuals with severe left hemisphere impairment who rely on the inadequate capacity of the right hemisphere for language processing. Another possibility is that there may be developmental changes in language processing in autism: in this study, evidence of left hemisphere language functions was strongest in the older subjects.

Rett syndrome
Rett syndrome is a rare, progessive brain disorder that affects girls. After apparently normal psychomotor progress in the first nine months of life, development slows down so that by the age of 18 months there is obvious mental impairment. There is dystonia, hypotonia, loss of purposeful hand skill, and appearance of stereotypic hand-wringing. After rapid deterioration in the second year of life, there is slow progression of the disease. The syndrome is often confused with infantile autism, because the stereotypic motor behaviours are associated with social and communicative abnormalities (Olsson and Rett 1987).

Interest in handedness in Rett syndrome was fuelled by a report by Nomura *et al.* (1984) who noted that out of 11 girls with the syndrome five were left-handed, one was right-handed and five had never been observed to show a preference. Handedness ceased to be apparent as children grew older and hand function declined so that the child could no longer grasp objects. Olsson and Rett (1986) studied handedness in 33 children with Rett syndrome. A range of toys and foods was presented, with hand preference being coded if one hand was used for grasping at least three times more often than the other. Olsson and Rett reported a striking difference between children aged above and below 7 years. For the younger group, there was confirmation of the findings of Nomura *et al.*, with nine out of 14 girls using the left hand more than the right, one using the right more than the left, and the remainder showing no preference. However, for those aged above 7 years, only one out of 12 preferred the left hand, whereas nine out of 12 preferred the right. These older children had evidence of asymmetrical pathology affecting the upper limb, with the left side more abnormal than the right.

Rett syndrome would appear to be a straightforward case in which handedness is affected by pathology. What remains unclear is (i) whether hand preference is dependent on asymmetry of pathology affecting hand function, or whether the raised prevalence of left-handedness occurs because there is an increase of ambiguous handedness, as in other forms of mental impairment, and (ii) how far individual children show systematic changes in hand preference with age, *i.e.* whether the age-related trend reported by Olsson and Rett was just a chance effect in a group with predominantly unestablished hand preference, or whether it could be replicated in a longitudinal study. If the latter, then we need to explain why the underlying pathology follows this asymmetrical temporal course.

Concluding comment
Abnormal handedness distributions are reliably found in children with pervasive developmental disorders, but consistent differences have not been found between autistic individuals and controls matched for degree of mental impairment. Non-right-handedness in autism takes the form of ambiguous handedness rather than left-handedness, especially in lower-functioning individuals, and seems to reflect randomness of motor behaviour, rather than the influence of focal brain pathology leading to hypofunction of one side. However, pathological influences do seem to be a factor in a minority of autistic children, and may be the explanation for abnormal handedness distributions observed in Rett syndrome. For both Rett syndrome and autism the possibility has been raised that handedness may alter as a function of age, but we lack the longitudinal studies necessary to confirm this.

11
SPECIFIC READING RETARDATION (DEVELOPMENTAL DYSLEXIA)

> .. the following question appears to be apropos at this time—are investigations regarding the relationship of laterality to reading an area that has been substantially researched? If so, perhaps the research time that is being devoted to this area could be used more advantageously in studying other relationships in respect to reading.

This was the somewhat peevish conclusion reached by Zeman (1967, p. 123) in his review of 14 studies involving over 9000 subjects, few of which found any hint of an association between reading ability and handedness. He would be depressed to see how little notice has been taken of his recommendation. Despite the largely negative evidence from population studies, the notion persists that non-right-handedness is associated with developmental disabilities, especially disorders of spoken and written language (*e.g.* Critchley 1970). Is there any evidence to support this belief? As argued in Chapter 6, we should beware of dismissing theories linking rare disorders and left-handedness solely on the basis of negative results from studies that compare the average attainments of left- and right-handers, because these do not provide a sensitive test of such theories. We need also to consider clinical studies, while keeping in mind the methodological problems associated with these. In this chapter, attention will be focused on those theories that account for an association between handedness and reading disorder in terms of cerebral lateralization.

The concept of developmental dyslexia
It has been recognized for over a century that illiteracy is not invariably the consequence of lack of education or low intelligence. Some children have great difficulty in learning to read and spell despite normal intelligence and adequate opportunity to learn. Early accounts of such difficulties adopted a variety of terminologies: congenital word-blindness (Hinshelwood 1917), strephosymbolia (Orton 1925) and specific dyslexia (Hallgren 1950). The latter has remained popular, and 'specific dyslexia' and 'developmental dyslexia' are widely used in contemporary accounts. In reviewing this field one needs to be aware of the problems surrounding the definition of this condition. The term 'developmental dyslexia' implies a distinct syndrome with a known neurological aetiology. Rutter (1969) examined the validity of the syndrome in an epidemiological study that assessed whether the symptoms which were thought to characterize developmental dyslexia did indeed co-occur. He found little support for a coherent syndrome of dyslexia, with wide variation in signs of neurological abnormality in poor readers. Because of the lack of good evidence for a cluster of neurodevelopmental abnormalities in such children, Rutter proposed that the term 'specific reading

retardation' be used in preference to 'developmental dyslexia'. However, he has had only partial success in persuading others to adopt this theoretically neutral but less concise terminology.

Not all experts in this field would agree with Rutter that developmental dyslexia is not a syndrome. A popular view is that although there is no one condition that can be clearly identified, this is simply because there is more than one variety of developmental dyslexia (*e.g.* Boder 1973, Mattis 1978). This viewpoint has received some support from genetic studies showing that certain types of dyslexia run in families and are linked to particular gene loci (Finucci and Childs 1983). However, while the notion of heterogeneity has proved popular, there is little agreement about how dyslexia should be subclassified (Satz *et al.* 1985*a*), and there is continuing debate as to how far the reading errors of poor readers can be used to characterize neuropsychologically distinct syndromes (Bryant and Impey 1986, Baddeley *et al.* 1988).

A further question concerns how best to identify children whose reading skills are disproportionately poor relative to IQ. It is generally agreed that it is not appropriate to call children dyslexic if their inability to read is just one aspect of low intelligence. Traditionally, dyslexics have been identified as those children whose reading is poor for their age but whose IQ is in the normal range. In effect this means selecting children whose reading is below some specified level but whose IQ is above a cut-off (Fig. 11.1). However, this procedure will fail to detect those children of high IQ whose modest reading attainments, while not below cut-off, are significantly below what one would expect. Yule (1973) recommended an alternative regression approach to select those children whose reading is significantly below the level predicted from IQ. As can be seen from Figure 11.1, this procedure selects a somewhat different subset of children than the conventional cut-off procedure.

Yet another variable to consider is the measurement of IQ. All agree that a dyslexic individual is one whose reading is disproportionately poor relative to IQ, but, because reading ability is much more strongly correlated with verbal than non-verbal ability, it makes a considerable difference whether or not one uses an IQ test with a verbal component. Many children whose reading is very poor relative to non-verbal IQ have low verbal IQs compatible with their reading level (Bishop and Butterworth 1980). A sample selected on the basis of reading relative to performance IQ will be very different from one selected on the basis of verbal IQ or full-scale IQ. Finally, the type of reading measure used can also have a substantial effect on who is termed dyslexic. In a follow-up study of children with language delay, Bishop and Adams (1990) found that reading accuracy (*i.e.* ability to pronounce written words correctly) was much less impaired than reading comprehension (ability to answer questions about what had been read). When dyslexia was defined in terms of poor reading comprehension relative to IQ, many more children were identified as dyslexic than when a measure of reading accuracy was used.

Thus, those investigating the relationship between handedness and reading disability have not only to contend with a lack of consensus over the definition and

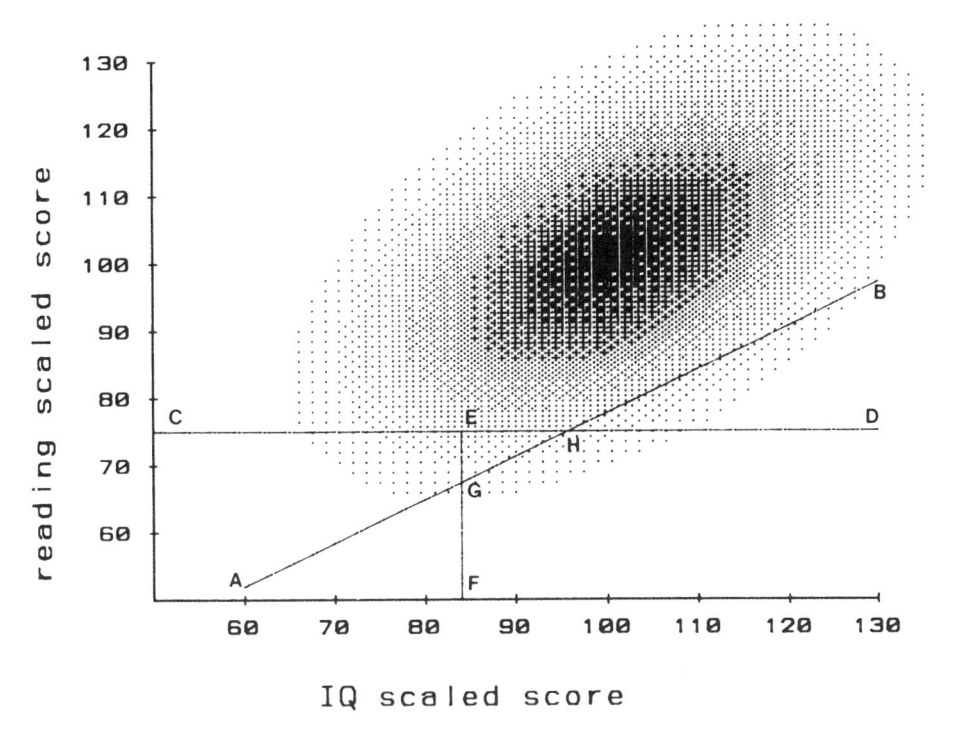

Fig. 11.1. Scatter plot of theoretical bivariate normal distribution of reading and IQ. Subjects falling below line AB have reading scores significantly below the level predicted on the basis of IQ ('specific reading retardation'). Those below line CD obtain low reading scores irrespective of IQ ('backward readers'). Line EF divides the sample into subjects with low IQ scores and the remainder. The area bounded by FED contains subjects who would be defined as having specific learning disability by the conventional cut-off approach. (Reprinted from Bishop 1989*b*, p. 342.)

measurement of handedness (see Chapter 5) but also with variability in the definition of dyslexia. The bulk of research has adopted a double cut-off approach, as in Figure 11.1, without attempting to subclassify children who fit the selection criteria. There is tremendous variability in the cut-offs used, particularly as regards reading level, which may range from a lag of six months to two years or more below age level. A complicating factor is that the abnormality of a given lag in reading attainment can vary with age. For instance, on a popular British reading test, 22 per cent of 12-year-olds, but only 3 per cent of 8-year-olds, are expected to have a reading age 24 months below age level (Elliott *et al.* 1978). This complication can be avoided if reading impairment is defined statistically in terms of standard scores rather than in terms of discrepancy between age equivalent score and chronological age (Bishop 1989*b*), but this practice is not commonly followed.

Despite the confusion over criteria and definitions, the term 'developmental dyslexia' will be used here as a convenient shorthand to refer to children whose severe reading problems appear disproportionate to their other mental abilities.

However, my use of this term should not be taken to imply that I accept the validity of a distinctive syndrome.

Early explanations in terms of cerebral dominance: Orton's theory
Orton was one of the first to suggest a link between laterality and specific reading problems. The most detailed account of his views was given in the 1936 Salmon Lectures delivered to the New York Academy of Medicine and published in 1937 under the title 'Reading, writing and speech problems in children'. Orton (1925) coined the term 'strephosymbolia', meaning 'twisted symbols'. He explained specific reading problems by arguing that delayed neurological development leads to a lack of a dominant cerebral hemisphere which in turn results in confusion between the visual images processed by the two halves of the brain, so that mirror images (such as b and d) are not distinguished. Orton proposed that the lack of cerebral dominance was also evident in a failure to develop a clear hand preference and in lack of agreement between hand and eye dominance. He did not, however, regard left-handedness as having adverse significance:

. . there is no real reason to consider the straight left-handed individual in any way inferior to the right-handed except by reason of those inconveniences which are forced upon him by the custom and usage of the right-handed majority. It is only those in whom the tendency toward some measure of left-sidedness is present, but not in sufficient strength to assure complete unilateral superiority of the right hemisphere of the brain, in whom trouble may ensue and who form a fertile soil for the disturbing effects of misguided training. (p. 130)

Orton's theories were developed on the basis of his extensive clinical experience, but he presented little in the way of hard data. Before turning to evaluate the experimental evidence gathered by others, it is worth considering some theoretical objections to his claims.

A criticism that has been frequently advanced is that there can be no meaningful relationship between eyedness, as measured by sighting preference, and cerebral lateralization, since each eye projects to both cerebral hemispheres (see Fig. 2.2). In fact, however, Orton did not subscribe to the view that one eye was perceptually dominant. Rather, he saw eyedness as primarily a function of motor control of the extraocular muscles. The notion of a dominant eye in this sense does not contravene any established neurophysiological principles.

A second logical problem concerns Orton's exclusion of strong left-handers from those at risk for reading problems. At the time he was writing, there was a widespread view that whereas right-handers had left hemisphere language representation, left-handers had the opposite pattern. Orton took this a stage further in assuming that individuals without a strong hand preference would lack clear cerebral lateralization. We now know that there is no such direct correspondence between handedness and language laterality, and that many left-handers do have some degree of bilateral language representation (see Chapter 2). If lack of strong cerebral lateralization were a factor causing reading difficulties, then we should expect left-handers as well as those with mixed hand preferences to be at risk for such problems.

The strongest objection to Orton's original account is empirical rather than theoretical: there is little support for a link between crossed eye–hand dominance and reading problems. Bishop (1983) listed 16 studies comparing the frequency of crossed dominance in reading-retarded and normal children, only two of which obtained marginally significant differences in the predicted direction. These studies confirmed not only the lack of association between hand–eye laterality and reading status, but also the high frequency of crossed dominance in normal individuals (between 30 and 40 per cent in most studies). This is in agreement with population studies which have indicated that eyedness and handedness are only weakly related in the general population (*e.g.* Douglas *et al.* 1967, Porac and Coren 1981).

Although Orton's original theory cannot be sustained, it has been influential, and belief in a link between crossed dominance and dyslexia has proved impervious to contrary evidence. One reason for this may be that many of those who work in this field assess hand–eye dominance only in disordered children, so they obtain regular confirmation that many dyslexic children have crossed dominance, without ever recognizing that the frequency is just as high in normal readers.

Even among those who recognize the limitations of Orton's claims, his influence continues to be strong and theories that retain certain elements of his original formulation continue to be popular. Specific instances of these will now be reviewed.

An alternative conceptualization of eye dominance: Dunlop's reference eye test
Dunlop *et al.* (1973) proposed a new method of measuring eye dominance. Noting that the central foveal strip of the visual field projects to both cerebral hemispheres, they argued that a neurophysiologically meaningful measure of eye dominance can be obtained if one can discover which of the duplicated foveal representations is dominant. Their technique involved presenting foveal stimuli separately to the two eyes to yield a fused image, and then slowly separating these to see which image remained stable, this defining the 'reference eye'. They claimed that dyslexic children were more likely than normal readers to have the reference eye contralateral to the preferred hand. However, this result was not confirmed in three studies by other investigators (Bishop *et al.* 1979, Newman *et al.* 1985, Stein *et al.* 1986). Stein and Fowler (1981) argued that although 'crossed reference' is not characteristic of reading-retarded children, inconsistent performance on this test was related to reading problems, and they interpreted this as indicating unstable control of vergence eye movements, rather than in terms of cerebral lateralization. However, inconsistent performance on Dunlop's test is found in many children with average or superior reading skills (Bishop *et al.* 1979, Newman *et al.* 1985), and claims for a link between unestablished reference eye and reading difficulties have been criticized on methodological grounds (Bishop 1989c).

Unestablished language lateralization
In recent years, there has been increasing awareness of the fact that many dyslexic children have a range of verbal deficits involving spoken as well as written language. Although the possibility remains that a subset of dyslexics may have underlying visual perceptual disturbances, in general the emphasis has moved away

from looking for a visual basis for dyslexia, to regarding it as a form of language disorder (Vellutino 1979). At the same time, interest has shifted from relationships between hand and eye dominance to concern with cerebral lateralization for language. Orton's theory requires only minor modification to make it fit in with current views, by substituting lack of lateralization of language processes rather than confusion between visual images as the basis for reading difficulties. The notion that dyslexics have weak cerebral lateralization has been extremely popular. Some have gone so far as to propose that by encouraging consistent motor laterality in children, we can improve neurological organization and so help reading problems (Delacato 1963).

Many people, however, would not subscribe to such a view, but would accept the postulate that non-right-handedness is an index of cerebral lateralization that is linked with dyslexia. Zangwill (1960, 1962), for instance, proposed that left-handedness, or more especially inconsistent hand preference, could be an indicator of imperfect cerebral lateralization which makes the individual vulnerable to developmental disorders of reading and language, especially if subjected to such stresses as minimal brain injury at birth. The view that atypical language laterality puts the individual at risk for reading and other learning disabilities is a cornerstone of two recent and influential theories, Annett's (1985) right shift theory (see pp. 40–46) and the hormonal theory of Geschwind and Galaburda (1985*a,b,c*). These theories make additional distinct and specific proposals about the origins of dyslexia and the features associated with it, which will be discussed later in this chapter and in Chapter 14. For the present, however, attention will be focused on the evidence for abnormal language lateralization in dyslexic children.

We know that most individuals who do not have language strongly lateralized to the left hemisphere are non-right-handers (*e.g.* see Table 2.I). If, then, lack of strong left hemisphere language representation were the major cause of dyslexia, we would expect a *substantial* increase in the proportion of non-right-handers in this population. The lack of evidence for reading deficits in non-right-handers reviewed in Chapter 6 seems difficult to reconcile with a theory that relates developmental reading difficulties to cerebral lateralization. It could, however, be argued that such studies do not provide a valid test because they fail to distinguish between developmental dyslexia and poor readers of low IQ. If most individuals with low reading ability are not dyslexic, then any relationship between handedness and dyslexia will be obscured when comparing average reading scores of left- and right-handers. It is therefore important to consider the evidence from studies that do look separately at those with *specific* reading disabilities.

Overview of studies of handedness in dyslexia

In view of the problems inherent in defining dyslexia, it seems advisable to adopt stringent criteria, to avoid the possibility that genuine relationships with dyslexia might be diluted by the inclusion of other types of poor reader. In reviewing this literature, I have excluded reports which did not give information about reading level or IQ, or which looked at 'poor readers' regardless of IQ. (This led to the omission of some studies included in a summary table in Bishop 1983, *e.g.* that by

Belmont and Birch 1965.) Also omitted were studies which adopted a criterion of reading disability so generous that it included children with very mild difficulties, *e.g.* those scoring six months below age level on a reading test. There had to be some indication that reading level was well below mental age as well as chronological age. Assessment of handedness of dyslexics by self-report is unsatisfactory, not least because problems in telling left from right are especially frequent in poor readers (Rutter *et al.* 1970*b*), so only studies that used objective assessment were included. Finally, studies with no control data were omitted. A search was conducted for studies fitting these criteria. Provided that handedness was not used as a selection criterion, papers were included even if handedness was reported as an incidental finding rather than the main focus of the article: it was hoped that this would redress to some extent the bias that can arise from selective publication of positive findings.

The experimental evidence gathered in this manner is summarized in Table 11.I. One problem encountered in compiling this table was that there was a tendency for studies that found no significant differences in handedness to report statistical test results only, without providing data (and hence leading to their omission from the table, *e.g.* Sparrow and Satz 1970, Dalby and Gibson 1981, Swanson and Mullen 1983).

Hunter *et al.* (1982) noted that the usual approach to reviewing such data is to do a 'vote count' of significant and non-significant findings; if we do so here we find that only two out of 25 comparisons reach significance at the 0.05 level (Hallgren's 1950 clinic sample, and Harris's 1957 sample of 7-year-olds)—hardly an impressive result. Hunter *et al.*, however, questioned this approach, pointing out that it is preferable to combine data from different studies to obtain a more accurate estimate of the true value of the statistic of interest. The problem here is that varied criteria were used to classify handedness, giving widely differing estimates of left- and mixed-handers in control groups. The best we can do is to select for each study a cut-off for non-right-handedness so that around 10 per cent of control children fall into this category. This gives an overall rate of left-handedness of 11.3 per cent in dyslexics and 10.6 per cent in controls, a non-significant difference. The sceptic's conclusion would be that there is no real difference in handedness between dyslexic and control children.

Having considered the most negative view of the data, is there any justification for adopting a more positive interpretation? One reason for being uncomfortable about summing data across all studies is that this gives tremendous weight to the negative data from the National Child Development Study (Bishop 1984), which makes a substantial contribution because of the large sample size. One could argue that the identification of cases of specific reading retardation from an unselected population using objective test results alone makes this a particularly valuable study, as it will be uninfluenced by clinical selection biases. (Specific reading retardation was defined in terms of a reading test score that was more than two standard deviations below the level expected on the basis of a non-verbal test score.) However, massive surveys also have drawbacks. Undoubtedly, in a study of this kind where data are collected by many different examiners there is a greater

TABLE 11.I
Review of studies of handedness in individuals with specific reading retardation

Study	R-handed %	Mixed-handed %	L-handed %
Monroe (1932)			
155 retarded readers	91	—	9
101 controls	89	—	11
Gates and Bond (1936)			
64 retarded readers	91	6	3
64 controls	89	8	3
Schonell (1941)			
73 backward readers	86	—	14
75 controls	93	—	7
Wolfe (1941)			
18 retarded readers	72	6	22
18 controls	89	0	11
Hallgren (1950)			
38 dyslexics (school sample)	82	—	18
173 controls for school sample	91	—	9
144 dyslexics (clinic sample)	82	—	18
103 unaffected sibs	93	—	7
Smith (1950)			
50 retarded readers	92	—	8
50 controls	86	—	14
Harris (1957)			
20 retarded readers, aged 7 yrs.	25	70	5
61 controls, aged 7 yrs.	53	39	8
68 retarded readers, aged 9 yrs.	49	42	9
184 controls, aged 9 yrs.	53	45	2
Malmquist (1960)			
34 specific reading disabled	91	—	9
286 average readers	93	—	7
Bettman et al. (1967)			
47 retarded readers	85	2	13
58 controls	88	2	10
Doehring (1968)			
39 reading retarded boys	87	—	13
39 controls	82	—	18
Rutter et al. (1970b)			
107 retarded readers	71	19	10
125 controls	81	15	4
Wussler and Barclay (1970)			
25 retarded readers	88	—	12
25 controls	96	—	4
Naidoo (1972)			
54 dyslexics	50	41	9
56 controls for dyslexics	75	20	5
41 spelling retarded	59	29	12
42 controls for spelling retarded	81	14	5
Gross et al. (1978)			
14 reading disabled	79	—	21
14 controls	100	—	0
Schevill (1980)			
75 retarded readers	80	4	16
40 controls	83	0	18
Prior et al. (1983)			
10 specific reading retarded	70	20	10
10 controls	80	20	0

TABLE 11.I
(continued)

Study	R-handed %	Mixed-handed %	L-handed %
Annett and Kilshaw (1984)			
109 dyslexic boys	50	44	6
617 control males	65	33	3
20 dyslexic girls	45	45	10
863 control females	61	35	4
Bishop (1984)			
195 specific reading retarded	88	—	12
9427 remainder of sample	88	—	12
Pennington et al. (1987)			
64 dyslexics	77	22	2
75 relatives of dyslexics	80	17	3
Wolf and Goodglass (1986)			
14 retarded readers	100	—	0
75 controls	91	—	9
Felton et al. (1987)			
45 retarded readers	89	—	11
53 controls	87	—	13

chance of error in data scoring and coding than in small-scale studies. If we use these arguments to justify removing the NCDS data, then the overall rate of left-handedness in the remaining studies is 11.2 per cent in dyslexics compared with 5.8 per cent in controls, a significant difference. We may conclude that, on the most optimistic interpretation, the rate of left-handedness in dyslexics is twice that of controls. This has important methodological implications for future research, because to detect an effect of this size one would need a sample size of nearly 400 (half dyslexic and half control). Note that Rutter et al. (1970b), whose results are close to these overall estimates of left-handedness for affected and unaffected children respectively, concluded that there was no association between specific reading retardation and handedness, because the difference between their groups did not reach significance. However, despite including 107 reading-retarded children and 125 controls, their study would not have been powerful enough to distinguish between a genuine doubling in the rate of left-handedness and a difference due to sampling error.

A second, theoretical, point is that even if we accept that there is a significant excess of non-right-handedness in dyslexia, the percentage is well below that which would be expected if weak cerebral lateralization were the major cause of dyslexia. All the evidence reviewed in Chapter 2 indicated that bilateral language representation is virtually never found except in non-right-handers. On the basis of handedness studies alone, then, the notion that dyslexia is a consequence of atypical language laterality seems implausible, even if we adopt the most liberal interpretation of the available data.

Dichotic listening indices of cerebral lateralization in dyslexia
Handedness is not the only source of evidence for the hypothesis of atypical

cerebral lateralization in dyslexia. There have been numerous studies of dyslexic individuals using techniques such as dichotic listening. Bryden (1988a) tabulated the evidence, concluding that there were 14 studies finding no evidence of any difference between retarded readers and controls, 30 showing poor readers to be less lateralized than controls, and seven in which poor readers were more strongly lateralized. Although the typical finding of a right ear advantage of reduced magnitude could indicate more bilaterality of language mediation, Bryden cautioned that there are other explanations. Dyslexic children are usually less accurate overall than controls on verbal dichotic tests. In this situation, whether or not differences in strength of lateralization are obtained will depend on whether lateralization measures are corrected for level of performance (see p. 26). Bryden recommended that to disentangle effects of overall performance and degree of lateralization, we need studies comparing performance of dyslexic children with younger normal children at a similar level of performance.

Another problematic feature of many studies is that they typically exclude non-right-handers. This convention derives from research using procedures such as dichotic listening to investigate cerebral lateralization of mental processes in normal individuals, where it makes sense to exclude cases where there is a strong likelihood that the pattern of cerebral lateralization is atypical. However, the logic of applying the same selection criteria to the study of disordered populations is questionable. Here the hypothesis of interest is that the disordered group is characterized by atypical lateralization. To exclude those who, by virtue of non-right-handedness, are known to be likely to have atypical lateralization is to bias the study against finding the effect of interest.

At present, the evidence from dichotic studies is inconclusive. It is possible that clearer results would emerge if some coherent subclassification of subjects could be achieved. However, to date, studies trying this approach have been largely unsuccessful in bringing any more regularity to data on cerebral lateralization (Aylward 1984).

Morphological brain asymmetries
There is some evidence that normal patterns of morphological brain asymmetry are not found in dyslexics. A claim by Hier *et al.* (1978) that dyslexics were unusually likely to have reversed occipital asymmetry on CT scan has not been replicated, but a reduction in the usual extent of asymmetry (see pp. 27–31) has been found in more than one study (Haslam *et al.* 1981, Rumsey *et al.* 1986).

Does this mean that bilateral or right hemisphere language representation is characteristic of dyslexics? A second study by Rumsey *et al.* (1987) suggested a very different answer. Regional cerebral blood flow was monitored in 14 dyslexic men* as they performed a range of mental tasks. Relative to a control group, the dyslexics showed an *increased* asymmetry of cerebral blood flow (left greater than right) whilst carrying out a verbal task. This study suggests that dyslexics, like other

*Most of these subjects had participated in the previous study finding reduced morphological asymmetry (Rumsey, *personal communication*).

individuals, use the left hemisphere for language processing, but that this hemisphere operates inefficiently.

Reading ability in individuals known to have atypical cerebral lateralization
A final point to note is that if bilateral language representation were disadvantageous for learning to read, one might have expected to find evidence of this in individuals whose cerebral dominance had been assessed using the Wada test, and who were known to have atypical cerebral lateralization in the absence of early brain damage. No such evidence has been reported, although in fairness it must be said that there are few published data on the psychometric characteristics of such individuals.

Before moving on from this kind of explanation, we need to consider a modified theory that proposes a rather different set of relationships between cerebral lateralization and developmental reading problems.

The right shift theory and developmental reading problems

Annett's (1975, 1985) right shift theory (see Chapter 3) leads to much more precise predictions than other theories concerned with cerebral lateralization, because handedness is treated as a continuous variable that can be measured in terms of relative proficiency of the two hands. According to this theory, handedness is determined by environmental factors interacting with genotype. Individuals who are homozygous for the right shift allele (rs++) will be very likely to show both left hemisphere language representation and right-handedness, because this genotype strongly boosts early left hemisphere development. Those who are homozygous for the rs– allele have no bias to either side, so are equally likely to be left- or right-handed, except that environmental pressures make right-handedness slightly more probable. Bilateral language representation would presumably be common in this population, although chance biases favouring development of one hemisphere may result in some having language represented in the left hemisphere and others in the right. The majority of individuals will have the heterozygous genotype (rs+–), which results in a moderate boost to left hemisphere development, so that most heterozygotes will have left hemisphere language representation and be right-handed, but the probability of this pattern will be less strong than for rs++ homozygotes.

In her initial account of developmental disorders, Annett suggested that rs– – homozygotes were at particular risk for language and reading problems because they lacked the normal boost to left hemisphere development. Hand preference data from Annett and Kilshaw's (1984) study of 129 dyslexic children are included in Table 11.I. As well as examining hand preference, these authors also collected data on relative skill of the two sides. They predicted that dyslexics would show less 'right shift' than other individuals, with a higher rate of left-handedness, and a smaller skill difference between hands, consistent with the notion that this group contained a higher proportion of rs– – individuals. However, although there was a significant excess of left-handed writers among the dyslexics in their sample, an overall comparison of dyslexic and control groups did not reveal a significant difference in relative hand skill. One problem with this study was that although the control group was impressive in terms of size, it was not closely matched to the dyslexic group but was formed by combining data from a series of previous studies of adults and children, some conducted up to 20 years before the study of dyslexics. The significant excess of left-handed writers in the dyslexic group could reflect secular trends for increasing left-handedness, rather than a true relationship with reading status.

On closer inspection of their data, Annett and Kilshaw found that hand difference scores for right-handed dyslexics were more extreme than those of controls. This finding led them to reformulate the theory to propose that both types of homozygote, rs−− and rs++, are at risk for learning disabilities. Annett's original account suggested that overcommitment to left hemisphere language processing (in rs++ individuals) might result in selective impairment of right hemisphere *visuospatial* skills. However, the dyslexia study of Annett and Kilshaw and a later study of intellectual development by Annett and Manning (1989) indicated that verbal as well as visuospatial development tends to be poor in those who are very strongly right-handed. Annett has argued that the disadvantages in intellectual development associated with both types of homozygote can explain why the rs− gene is maintained in the population.

However, it could be argued that the link between extreme right-handedness and cognitive deficit reflects no more than the fact that dyslexia is associated with general neuromotor deficits and that these will be particularly obvious when an unpractised hand is used. The procedure used by Annett and Manning of converting all hand scores to scaled scores relative to the right hand will magnify any deficit of the left side, given that the variance in control left hand scores is greater than for the right (see Bishop 1990*b*). Other studies using performance measures with dyslexic children have not found an excess of strongly right-handed individuals compared to controls (Harris 1957).

In summary, the theory advanced by Annett and Kilshaw is ingenious but still highly speculative. It is important to replicate the more extreme difference in hand skill in right-handed dyslexics, which was an unpredicted finding of the Annett and Kilshaw study. Annett and Manning's study indicated that extreme right-handedness is not a specific correlate of dyslexia, but is associated with general cognitive deficits. One needs to be cautious about inferring pattern of cerebral specialization from a consideration of relative skill of the two hands, especially when the overall skill level is below average. The data presented to date are compatible with simpler explanations in terms of general motor impairment. What would give greater credence to Annett's genetic theory of dyslexia would be a demonstration that strongly right-handed and non-right-handed dyslexics had different types of reading problem.

Handedness and maturational lag
Although atypical cerebral dominance seems unlikely as a cause of dyslexia, the related idea of a neuromaturational lag is more attractive. On this view, lack of strong handedness is not a sign of bilateral language mediation, but of neurological

immaturity. Unfortunately, reliance on handedness inventories in the majority of studies makes it difficult to test this notion against published data. As argued in Chapter 5, inventories confound cases where there is delay in establishing hand preference and those where there is a stable mixed or left hand preference. It may be that by failing to distinguish these different subgroups of non-right-hander, links between handedness and developmental dyslexia have been obscured. If dyslexia reflects neurodevelopmental immaturity, then it is only unstable hand preference that is relevant. Although his sample size was small, Harris's (1957) finding of excess mixed-handedness among 7-year-old but not 9-year-old poor readers is compatible with the notion that a lag in establishing hand preference may be an indicator of neuromotor immaturity in dyslexics.

This explanation for moderate increases in non-right-handedness in dyslexics generates a number of testable predictions. First, we should expect to find poorer motor performance overall in dyslexics compared to controls. There are several studies that confirm this prediction (Rutter *et al.* 1970*a*, Naidoo 1972, Wolff *et al.* 1984). Second, we would expect to confirm Harris's observation of more evidence of non-right-handedness in younger than in older samples of dyslexics. Third, the excess of non-right-handedness should take the form of within-task inconsistency of hand preference rather than stable mixed preference. Finally, the higher the rate of motor impairment in a dyslexic sample, the more evidence of unestablished hand preference should be apparent.

Overview
Taking all the lines of evidence together, there is little support for the theory that individual differences in the direction and degree of laterality of language representation are the basis for developmental dyslexia. If this were the major explanation for dyslexia we would expect to find a much higher rate of non-right-handedness, and much clearer evidence from dichotic listening studies for atypical language laterality. What we can say is that in most cases of developmental dyslexia language functions are weakly developed. It seems plausible that the dyslexic is characterized by the normal pattern of cerebral lateralization, but that the left hemisphere is poorly developed and provides an inadequate substrate for development of competence in verbally-based skills. Dyslexics typically have poor motor skills, and this could be a consequence of underlying neurological immaturity. However, the notion of a lateralized motor impairment in developmental dyslexia remains questionable.

12
SPECIFIC DEVELOPMENTAL DISORDERS OF SPEECH AND LANGUAGE

Definitions and terminology
When we turn to consider developmental language disorders, we find problems of definition even more complex than those encountered in the study of developmental dyslexia. The fact that some children have impairments of language development that cannot be explained in terms of intellectual retardation or hearing loss has been recognized for many years, and a variety of terms has been used to refer to this type of problem. As with reading problems, there has been a borrowing of terminology from adult neurology which has been criticized as being misleading on two counts: first, terms such as 'developmental dysphasia' or 'congenital aphasia' imply underlying brain damage as the cause of disorder, and second, they encourage one to think in terms of a well-defined syndrome when this is not justified (Bishop and Rosenbloom 1987). In fact, there is no direct evidence of left hemisphere damage in the vast majority of children with specific language problems (Bishop 1987), and the heterogeneity of disorders encountered suggests that we are dealing with a range of different conditions. To give just a few examples, the traditional diagnosis by exclusion encompasses such diverse problems as (i) specific phonological impairment (traditionally termed 'functional articulation disorder'), where the problem is largely restricted to difficulty in producing speech sounds; (ii) severe grammatical difficulties, evident in very restricted sentence structure and deficits in understanding complex constructions; (iii) problems in using and understanding language appropriately, coupled with relatively intact phonological and grammatical skills.

While it is easy to criticize conventional medically based terminology and to stress the heterogeneity of language disorders in children, there has been little consensus about classification and so the researcher is often forced back into using diagnosis by exclusion, which results in a group that contains a wide variety of types of language difficulty.

Relationship between developmental disorders of spoken and written language
One point to note is that there is overlap between developmental language disorder and specific reading problems. Many dyslexic children show some impairment on tests involving spoken language (Vellutino 1979), and in some cases there is clear evidence of language disorder even without formal testing. Most children whose verbal impairments are pronounced enough to merit a diagnosis of developmental language disorder will have difficulty in learning to read (Tallal and Katz 1989). Thus there is some justification for regarding developmental language disorder as on a continuum with developmental dyslexia, although the heterogeneity in

manifestations of both conditions suggests this might not be appropriate in all cases (see Bishop and Adams 1990).

In so far as developmental language disorder represents a more extreme form of the same condition as developmental dyslexia, we would expect similar associations to hold between laterality and disorder.

Theories linking non-right-handedness with developmental language disorders

It is possible to distinguish at least three theories that predict an increase in the rate of non-right-handedness in children with developmental language disorders.

We may start with the theory of *atypical cerebral lateralization*, first proposed by Orton, and discussed at length in Chapter 11 in relation to specific reading difficulties. This theory maintains that adequate language functioning depends on verbal operations being predominantly mediated by the left cerebral hemisphere. Non-right-handedness is seen as an indirect manifestation of atypical cerebral lateralization, and so should be unusually common in language-impaired children. Annett's right shift theory, also reviewed in Chapter 11, may be regarded as a variant of this theory. According to Annett and Kilshaw (1984) we would expect children who lack the right shift factor (who do not have strong left hemisphere language superiority, and do not show large skill differences between the hands) to be at particular risk for developmental language disorders. The theory also predicts that extreme right-handedness (where weak left hand skills are indicative of poor right hemisphere functioning) might be common in this group.

The second theory to consider is that of *pathological left-handedness*. At first glance, it seems plausible that specific language difficulties in children, like acquired aphasia in adults, might arise as a consequence of a focal lesion of the left cerebral hemisphere. Such a lesion might also impinge on brain areas concerned with motor function, so raising the probability that a naturally right-handed individual will shift to become left-handed.

The third possibility is that children with specific language disorders may show *increased randomness* in their hand preferences. The notion of increased randomness was first introduced in Chapter 9 in the context of mental impairment. According to this theory, reliable and consistent hand preference for an activity is a function of motor skill, which will depend both on practice and on neurological status. Increased randomness might be predicted in children with specific developmental disorders as well as in those with more global mental impairment, in so far as these disorders are associated with neuromotor immaturity.

Handedness in children with speech and language disorders

In evaluating these theories, the first point to establish is how strong the association is between handedness and developmental language disorders. It is advisable, as with the analysis of the dyslexia literature, to look carefully at the criteria used to select cases. Because language difficulties are a frequent concomitant of mental impairment, one must be cautious in evaluating studies which talk simply of 'language difficulties', 'speech problems' or 'need for speech therapy' without distinguishing specific from more general delays.

An early study by Johnson and House (1937) compared handedness in 41 children (aged 6 to 12 years) with functional articulation defects and 33 matched controls of similar intelligence. Full data were not presented so interpretation is unclear, but the impression is that while the two groups did not differ in manifest hand preference, those with articulation disorders showed significantly stronger tendencies to non-right-handedness on a performance test.

A link between articulation problems and left-handedness was also indicated in a study by McAllister (1937). Her report is confusing because she uses the term 'stammering' to refer to 'disability in making the necessary articulations and muscular adjustments for speech', but it is clear from the case descriptions that this refers to problems that would nowadays be classified as phonological disorders (rather than cases of dysfluency). 11 out of 35 'stammering' subjects were left-handed. Although no controls were included, this does seem to be a remarkably high rate of left-handedness, particularly when one considers the date of the study. However, we should note that the majority of these children had IQs below 80 and most had evident motor problems.

Ingram (1959) studied laterality in 80 children who had been diagnosed as suffering from 'specific developmental disorders of speech', *i.e.* retarded development of the ability to articulate speech sounds accurately, not due to mental impairment or physical disease. Many of these also had retardation of language development and difficulties in learning to read and write. Most were aged under 5 years. Handedness was defined as left, ambidextrous or right, on the basis of four activities (throwing a ball, catching a ball, turning a door handle, breaking a stick), each observed three times. Handedness was regarded as lateralized if the child used the same hand on nine or more out of the 12 tests. Ingram reported that 46 per cent were right-handed, 4 per cent left-handed, and the remainder not strongly lateralized. He noted that this was very different from figures obtained with 200 control children aged from 4 to 7 years who were hospitalized for other conditions, where 60 per cent were right-handed and 13 per cent left-handed, with 28 per cent showing no strong hand preference. Unfortunately, evaluation of this report is hampered by lack of detail. The account of the handedness assessment is unclear. Ingram did not state how he classified handedness in a child who could not catch a ball in one hand, although one would expect that many of his sample would have fallen into this category. The precise age at which handedness was assessed, and the extent of age-matching between control and speech-disordered children were not stated. Since the control children were aged between 4 and 7 years, whereas the speech-disordered group included 32 who were referred below the age of 4 years, inability of young children to perform unimanual tasks could have seriously biased the findings. Furthermore, it was not made explicit whether the 200 control children had handedness assessed in exactly the same way, or whether it was categorized by self-report (as was the case for siblings of affected children). It is difficult to judge whether the difference reported by Ingram was important, or whether it reflected lack of comparability between samples and assessment procedures.

Morley (1972) reported data on laterality of hand, foot and eye for children with a wide variety of speech and language disorders, but, in this study also, the control group were not well matched in terms of either age or ability. The mildest type of disorder considered was 'dyslalia', defined as persistence of faulty articulation in children whose language otherwise developed normally and in whom there was no physical basis for the disorder. This would include such problems as lisping. In a sample of 115 such children, 91 per cent were right-handed, a slightly *higher* frequency than in the control group. In a sample of 33 children diagnosed as having 'developmental aphasia', 76 per cent were right-handed, compared with 86 per cent of controls, a non-significant difference.

More recently, four further controlled studies have been conducted in this field, and all have reported no increase in the frequency of non-right-handedness among children with developmental language disorders.

Fundudis *et al.* (1979) found equal numbers of right-handers among children with a history of language delay and a control group. However, their language-delayed group, who had been identified because of poor language development at 3 years of age, did not in general have major language difficulties at the time of assessment, although low scores were obtained on a range of verbal tests.

The children studied by Johnston *et al.* (1981) appear to have had rather more severe problems, because all were receiving speech or language therapy when referred at the age of 5 to 8 years. These children, who were on average 15 months below chronological age in receptive language and 24 months below in expressive language, were compared with a normal control group matched on performance IQ, socioeconomic status and age. Preference for hand, leg and eye was assessed on a set of performance tasks. Percentages of non-right-handers were not reported, but it was stated that there was no significant difference between the groups in hand, leg or eye preference.

Neils and Aram (1986) compared 75 children aged 4 to 5 years with specific language impairment and 36 normal controls on measures of hand preference and proficiency. No significant handedness differences were found between the two groups.

A similar null result was reported by Bishop (1990*b*) for a group of over 80 language-impaired children studied longitudinally between the ages of 4 and 8 years. These children did not differ from normal controls on either hand preference or relative skill of the two hands as assessed on Annett's (1985) peg-moving task.

Overall, then, there is little support for the view that developmental language disorders are linked with non-right-handedness. However, there is one important qualification that must be made. It is possible that there are certain subtypes of developmental language disorder in which the prevalence of non-right-handedness is raised, but that such relationships are masked by the tendency to treat all language-impaired children as a homogeneous group.

Is there an increase of left-handedness in certain subtypes of disorder?
As well as investigating children with specific language disorders ('developmental aphasia'), Morley (1972) also considered what she referred to as 'developmental disorders of articulation'. She described rare cases of 'isolated developmental

dysarthria' and 'developmental articulatory apraxia' where problems in controlling the articulatory apparatus occurred in the absence of other neurological signs, often as familial disorders. Delayed language development, expressive language difficulties and clumsiness were common accompaniments of such disorders. Left-handedness was reported in 10 out of 29 subjects (34 per cent) with 'isolated dysarthria' and lack of hand preference in a further two subjects (7 per cent), giving an overall incidence of non-right-handedness significantly in excess of that reported for the control group (14 per cent). A similar excess was found among 67 subjects with 'articulatory apraxia', 22 per cent being left-handed and 17 per cent showing no hand preference.

Many researchers would not have distinguished the subgroups of children identified by Morley, but would have treated as one group all children with low language attainment coupled with normal non-verbal ability. Her classification, however, suggests that an excess of non-right-handedness may be characteristic only of those children with some evidence of motor involvement in their expressive difficulties. This would explain why the earlier studies by Johnson and House (1937), McAllister (1937) and Ingram (1959) all reported high rates of non-right-handedness: in each case the sample was composed of children with problems of speech sound production.

The study by Neils and Aram (1986) emphasized that relationships between handedness and developmental language disorder might be obscured by treating language-impaired children as a single group. Although the overall comparison between language-impaired and control children did not reveal significant differences, when the language-impaired children were divided into six subgroups according to severity of semantic and phonological impairments, handedness differences were apparent. Children with severe impairments in both semantic and auditory perceptual/phonological skills were significantly more likely to be left-handed than other subgroups. These were the most severely affected children, and also the youngest and the lowest in terms of IQ, but the authors showed that the latter two factors could not explain this difference. This study stressed the possible importance of identifying subtypes of developmental language disorder, but in evaluating the results one should bear in mind that the division of children into subgroups was apparently made *post hoc* on the basis of inspection of scatterplots of language scores, and statistical analysis involved use of analysis of variance when sample sizes were small and departures from normality were pronounced.

Altogether, the literature offers some support for a link between severe phonological problems and left-handedness. Morley's study suggested that children with severe phonological problems but normal comprehension are the most likely to be non-right-handed, whereas the Neils and Aram study found that it was children with severe phonological problems plus other language impairments who had the highest frequency of non-right-handedness. However, I have been unable to confirm either finding in a longitudinal study of language-impaired children seen between the ages of 4 and 8 years (Bishop 1990*b*). These children were assessed for hand preference and given Annett's peg-moving task. The sample was divided into three groups: children with moderate-to-severe phonological problems and normal comprehension, children with moderate-to-severe phonological problems and impaired comprehension, and the remainder. No relationship was found between phonological impairment and left-handedness, regardless of whether language comprehension was impaired.

Hypothesis 1: atypical cerebral lateralization
A supposed link between left- or mixed handedness and developmental language disorders provided the rationale for formulating an explanation in terms of disturbed cerebral dominance. Yet, as we have seen, the evidence for a link between laterality and disorder is inconsistent, with little evidence of an association in the most recent studies, where clear diagnostic criteria were used with reasonably large samples. Supporters of the cerebral lateralization hypothesis may, nevertheless, argue that handedness is in any case a very indirect indicator of cerebral lateralization. This raises the question of whether clearer results can be obtained with more direct measures of laterality of brain function.

Dichotic listening studies
As with dyslexic children, dichotic listening has been used to investigate cerebral lateralization in language-impaired children. Slorach and Noehr (1973) found that 'dyslalic' children showed a normal right ear advantage in a free recall condition but not when asked for ordered recall. This study is hard to evaluate: apart from the inconsistent results, no details are given about the nature or severity of the language problems in the dyslalic group. Sommers *et al.* (1976) compared children who had severely defective articulation with others who had normal or mildly impaired articulation on tests of laterality and dichotic listening. There was no difference between groups on handedness, but sample sizes were small (15 per group). Ear differences did not reach significance on the dichotic test for the group with severe articulation problems, whereas they did for the other children, but the trend was for a right ear advantage and the lack of difference may simply have been a consequence of the brevity of the dichotic test (36 items). Overall, this study was inconclusive. Springer and Eisenson (1977) used a much longer dichotic test with 10 language-disordered children, and found that, although accuracy on this test was low for this sample, their laterality coefficients did not differ from those of a control group. However, Springer and Eisenson noted that while children with 'reading problems only' had a stronger right ear advantage than controls, those with expressive or receptive language problems had significantly lower ear advantages than matched controls. This subclassification is questionable, though, given that the two children in the 'reading problems only' subgroup who had the largest right ear advantages both had verbal IQs two standard deviations or more below the mean.

Two recent studies (Isaacs and Haynes 1984, Edly *et al.* 1986) found no differences between children with severe articulation impairments and a control group on a dichotic listening task in which the child responded by pointing to a picture: both groups showed a right ear advantage.

Morphological asymmetries
Physical asymmetry of the two hemispheres of the brain has also been investigated in language-impaired children. Here the results are similar to those obtained for developmental dyslexia (see Chapter 11), with some evidence for reduced morphological asymmetry in affected children. Rosenberger and Hier (1980) studied CT scans from a group of learning-disabled individuals, many of whom had a history of delayed language development and large discrepancies between verbal and performance IQ. A substantial proportion of subjects showed a reversal of the normal pattern of morphological asymmetry in the occipital region and this reversal was associated with low verbal IQ and a history of delayed speech. It was not associated with hand preference: only one of the eight left-handers had the reversed pattern of asymmetry. While understandable, it is unfortunate that the CT scan was not administered or analysed blind, as there is a real possibility of artefactual error using this type of procedure (see p. 113). Nevertheless, this result is exciting in providing some physical indication of a link between cerebral lateralization and developmental language disorder. A recent study reported by Tallal and Katz (1989) obtained similar findings using magnetic resonance imaging: children with specific language impairments were less likely than control children to have the left posterior region of the brain larger than the right.

The studies on lateralization of motor and language functions in this population caution against equating morphological brain symmetry with lack of language lateralization. Rather, just as with dyslexic children, it seems likely that language-impaired children have verbal functions lateralized to the left hemisphere, but this hemisphere is not sufficiently well-developed to process language adequately.

We may sum up by saying that neither handedness data nor dichotic listening studies offer strong support for the view that functional cerebral lateralization is abnormal in children with specific language disorders.

Hypothesis 2: pathological left-handedness
At first glance, it seems plausible that children with language disorders should be strong candidates for pathological left-handedness. The underlying lesion responsible for pathological left-handedness will involve the left hemisphere, which has primary responsibility for language functions. Furthermore, as noted in Chapter 7, a theory of pathological left-handedness predicts only modest increases in the frequency of left-handedness in an affected population, so the lack of a significantly increased prevalence of left-handedness in relatively small samples is not necessarily damaging to the theory.

When looked at more carefully, however, the theory is less attractive. Satz *et al.* (1985) noted that when an early lesion of the left hemisphere language areas is sustained, the usual consequence is that language develops in the right hemisphere instead. Studies of individuals with early focal brain damage indicate that when this occurs, the impact on language development is minimal, whereas the development of the visuospatial functions normally mediated by the right hemisphere suffers. Language functions appear to take priority over other types of processing (Bishop

1981). Accordingly, Satz *et al.* argued that, far from being associated with language impairment, pathological left-handedness caused by an early left hemisphere lesion should be associated with relatively *intact* language functions but impaired visuospatial skills. They presented case histories of 12 left-handed individuals with early left hemisphere damage, several of whom had verified bilateral or right hemisphere speech representation. In general, language skills were relatively normal, but visuospatial skills were depressed. Vargha-Khadem *et al.* (1985) produced data consistent with this view. They found that in children with left cerebral lesions, naming ability was positively correlated with strength of left-handedness, and they concluded that their results contradicted the general view that 'pathological left-handedness' is associated with verbal impairments: on the contrary, left-handers who had suffered early left hemisphere injury had relatively good language skills.

Further negative evidence comes from a study by Bergström *et al.* (1984), in which 109 children with 'minor neurodevelopmental disorders' underwent cranial computed tomography (CT scan). 30 of these children had severe developmental language disorders, and a further 46 had mild language disorders. However, language status was unrelated to laterality of CT scan abnormalities: children with pathology restricted to the left hemisphere were no more likely than others in this study to have language disorders. Furthermore, although the overall rate of left-handedness in this population was high (18 per cent), there was no association between presence or laterality of CT scan abnormality and handedness. Thus, focal left hemisphere lesions could explain neither the presence of developmental language disorder nor the high rate of left-handedness.

In general, then, it seems unlikely that pathological left-handedness should be a correlate of developmental language disorders. Nevertheless, some evidence for a link between speech difficulties and pathological left-handedness was found in a study based on the National Child Development Study (Bishop 1984). Data on language functions were extremely limited, but one of the items recorded in this survey was 'unintelligible speech', as judged by the medical officer examining the child at 7 years of age. This item was coded as present in 75 children (0.6 per cent) in the study (after excluding cases of known neurological or mental impairment). Although the proportion of left-handedness in this subgroup (20 per cent) was not significantly higher than the frequency in control children from the same population (12.3 per cent), it agreed well with predictions made by the pathological left-handedness model (see Chapter 7), and, in line with predictions from the model, there was a particularly high rate of left-handedness among those children who were unusually clumsy with the non-preferred hand (three out of six in this subgroup were left-handed). The numbers of speech-impaired children were too small to prove a convincing test of the model, but the overall pattern of results suggested that pathological left-handedness was a plausible explanation for the relatively high rate of left-handedness observed in speech-impaired children in this study. In line with the literature reviewed above, where a link between disorder and handedness was found, it was for children with marked difficulty in speech output.

Abnormalities of early neurological development
In discussing links between left-handedness and language problems, the contrast has been drawn between pathological left-handedness, where there is shift from natural hand preference as a response to underlying cerebral injury, and normal variations in handedness linked to variability in cerebral lateralization. This dichotomy may, however, be too sharp. The work of Geschwind and Galaburda (1987) has emphasized the need to be aware of a further possibility: the brain may develop abnormally, not because of early injury, but in response to the intrauterine environment. The particular hypothesis proposed by these authors, which regards hormonal influences as an important factor affecting prenatal neurological developmental, is evaluated in Chapter 14 and found to be inadequate in a number of respects. Nevertheless, the general point, that external influences may disturb brain development without producing obvious lesions, is an important one. There is as yet no direct evidence of cytoarchitectonic abnormalities in the brains of language-impaired children, although these have been reported in the brains of dyslexic individuals (Galaburda *et al.* 1985). It is to be hoped that this exciting line of work will be extended to other diagnostic groups, using blind evaluation of brains of control and affected children.

Some circumstantial evidence of lateralized disturbances to developmental processes is provided in an intriguing study by Dlugosz *et al.* (1988). These authors investigated school performance in 80 children who were born with one forearm and hand missing. Such upper limb reduction defects are found in two to eight per 10,000 births, but, despite much speculation, the cause is not known. Dlugosz *et al.* found a laterality effect: learning difficulties, including speech delay and reading problems, were especially prevalent among those with right limb defects, despite the fact that they did not differ from those with left limb defects on overall IQ. One can only speculate as to the cause of this association, but it raises the possibility that a lateralized abnormality affecting embryological development of the limb might also affect development of the central nervous system, leading to specific cognitive deficits.

Hypothesis 3: poor motor skills lead to increased randomness
It was suggested in Chapter 9 that where a child has poor motor skills, clear hand preference may not be observed: instead the child's lateral preferences for given activities will be relatively unstable. Conventional handedness assessments fail to distinguish such children from those with stable preferences within activities but left-sided or inconsistent preferences between activities. This raises the possibility that such links as do exist between language impairment and handedness may reflect poor motor skills in language-impaired children, rather than being linked in any more direct sense with the language disorder itself.

What makes this hypothesis plausible is the widespread finding of motor deficits in children with specific language disorders (Robinson 1987). Johnston *et al.* (1981) used a range of neurological tests concerned with sensory and motor function. This battery differentiated language-impaired from control children, especially in those tasks involving rate of movement, control of involuntary movements, perception of bilateral haptic stimuli and left–right identification. The authors concluded that neurological deficits in children with specific language impairment are in general bilateral and symmetrical. They further noted that performance on many of their tasks was dependent on age, implying that one should be cautious about assuming that neurological injury was the cause of impaired performance. This agrees with the views of Bishop and Edmundson (1987) who noted that slow performance on a peg-moving task was correlated with severity of language impairment, not only between children, but also within individuals: as the language disorder improved over time, so did the motor performance. The conclusion was that poor peg-moving is an indication of neuromotor immaturity rather than brain injury.

In this regard it is noteworthy that where excess non-right-handedness has been reported in language-impaired children it is typically in those with severe articulation problems, where motor clumsiness is often apparent.

Following this line of reasoning, one might predict that non-right-handedness, especially in the form of lack of lateral differentiation, would be particularly common in language-impaired children with poor motor scores. However, data from my own study offered no support to this interpretation (Bishop 1990*b*): normal rates of right-handedness were found in all language-impaired children, regardless of motor status.

Concluding comment

Motor function appears to be immature in language-impaired children, but there is little evidence of abnormal lateralization in this population. Theories that attribute developmental language disorders to constitutional variation in cerebral lateralization, whether determined by genetic factors (Annett 1985) or intrauterine hormonal environment (Geschwind and Galaburda 1987) are offered little support by handedness studies. The only type of disorder for which there is any suggestion of an increase in non-right-handedness is that where phonological disorders with a possible motor component are involved, and even here, the evidence is contradictory. If this link does exist, it could reflect the contribution of children with random hand preference for actions at which they are unskilled. One way of testing this hypothesis would be to compare handedness in children with specific language disorders with that found in children with developmental clumsiness but no language disorder. The prediction would be that it is motor rather than language status that is linked with handedness.

13
STUTTERING

It has been a notable and constant feature of the cerebral dominance theory of stuttering for nearly fifty years that every time it is given up for dead it twitches. (Bloodstein 1981, p. 139)

Stuttering refers to repetitions, hesitations and other dysfluencies that interfere with the free flow of speech and impede communication. Although most people feel that they know what is meant by stuttering, this disorder suffers from the same problems of definition as do the other disorders of spoken and written language. There is no agreement on a formal definition, the boundary between normal dysfluency and stuttering is not a sharp one, and it is unclear whether stuttering is a single condition that may be manifest in rather different ways, or whether there are several distinct varieties of stuttering, each with its own aetiology and mechanism. Most people use 'stuttering' and 'stammering' as synonyms, although these terms are sometimes used contrastively to distinguish between speech blocks (stammering) and repetitions (stuttering). There is also the question of whether stuttering and cluttering are the same thing, and how far stuttering is associated with other language difficulties (Homzie and Lindsay 1984).

Enforced right-handedness and confused cerebral dominance

Stuttering raises questions of particular interest in relation to handedness, as it has been claimed that attempts to alter hand preference from left to right can cause stuttering. One of the earliest attempts to study this question systematically was by Ballard (1912), who in his position as schools inspector was well-equipped to obtain information on handedness and stuttering in large numbers of children. On the basis of questionnaires sent out to head teachers he obtained information on 13,189 children, and reported that whereas the prevalence of stuttering was 1.1 per cent among those whose hand preference had not been interfered with, it rose to 4.3 per cent among natural left-handers who were forced to write with the right hand. In such a large sample, an increase of this size is highly statistically significant. Even more dramatic results were reported for mentally handicapped children, in whom the rate of stuttering rose from 1.5 per cent among those whose handedness was allowed to develop naturally, to 19 per cent in those with forcibly shifted hand preference. Ballard went on to do a further study of personally observed cases, and reported an even stronger link between stuttering and enforced right-handedness. Confirmatory reports from other investigators soon followed. Fagan (1931) noted that 27 per cent of the stutterers in his survey had had their handedness changed. Apparently untrammelled by the strictures of an ethics committee, a certain Mr Lewis of Lingfield Colony Special Schools (cited by Oates 1929) demonstrated that training right-handed children of low intelligence to write left-handed induced stuttering in nearly half of them. Luckily, the effect was transient and fluent speech reappeared when the training was reversed. Orton (1927) proposed an explanatory mechanism, arguing that if the child was not allowed to develop a strong lateral preference, there would be confusion of cerebral dominance which could result in stuttering. Speech involves the coordination of both sides of the brain, so it was proposed that lack of complete dominance would lead to the incoordination of the articulatory muscles.

After Ballard's pioneering work, much of the early work on this topic was done by Bryngelson and his associates in the 1930s. They found that a shift from left- to right-handedness was strongly associated with stuttering (Bryngelson and Rutherford 1937, Bryngelson 1939). Subjects for their studies were child or adult stutterers attending the authors' clinic, and the reported association between shifted handedness and stuttering was dramatic. In a study comparing 74 child stutterers with 74 matched controls, it was reported that 72 per cent of stutterers compared with 9 per cent of controls were forcibly shifted sinistrals, and among 78 adult stutterers, the rate of shifted sinistrality was 58 per cent, compared to 1 per cent in matched controls. Many stutterers also showed signs of ambidexterity, this being observed in 34 per cent of child stutterers and 29 per cent of adult stutterers, but in only 8 per cent of child controls and none of the adult controls. Unfortunately, Bryngelson did not give details as to how handedness was assessed in these studies.

Decline of interest in cerebral lateralization
Over the next few decades, fashions swung dramatically from tolerance of left-handedness (coupled with a belief that anyone interfering with handedness ran a serious risk of causing stuttering) to advocacy of right-handedness for all. Burt (1937) noted that in the majority of children, enforced right-handedness did not lead to stuttering, and he suggested that previously reported relationships arose simply because of the unsympathetic techniques that teachers had adopted to shift handedness. Thus, it was suggested, stuttering was more a consequence of general stress than of confused cerebral dominance. Several studies subsequently appeared reporting little or no relationship between stuttering and handedness (McAllister 1937, Van Dusen 1939, Daniels 1940, Spadino 1941, Johnson and King 1942, Johnson et al. 1942). It was noted that even in those studies reporting a high rate of non-right-handedness in stutterers, the great majority were fully right-handed (Meyer 1945). Attempts to manipulate cerebral dominance were found to have no effect on stuttering. Travis (1978) carried out a study in which stuttering students (including two eminent researchers in this field, Wendell Johnson and Charles van Riper) had their right forearms and hands encased in plaster for one year to force them to use the left hand. No beneficial effect was observed.

The decline in enthusiasm for explanations of stuttering in terms of cerebral lateralization occurred at a time when there was a dramatic swing away from physiological to psychogenic accounts of aetiology. What made this trend particularly influential was the fact that the two researchers who were eloquent advocates of psychogenic theories, Travis and Johnson, had previously been staunch proponents of explanations in terms of cerebral lateralization (Travis and

Johnson 1934). Meyer (1945) summed up the prevailing attitude of the time: 'Stuttering is the result of a "squabble", but one in which the contestants are not organic masses of brain substance but antagonistic emotional impulses' (p. 137).

Recent studies on stuttering and laterality
By 1986, however, the fashion had swung full circle and Travis published a paper in which he reaffirmed his belief in abnormal cerebral lateralization as the constitutional basis for stuttering. He did not abandon his psychoanalytic notions, but argued that they accounted for the consequences rather than the causes of the speech impediment, stating: '. . stuttering is not caused by repressed thoughts and feelings expressed on the couch; instead, they are caused by the stuttering, which results from a lack of the two cerebral hemispheres cooperating sufficiently in managing the bilaterally innervated peripheral speech mechanism' (Travis 1986, p. 121).

What caused this change of emphasis? Surprisingly, it does not appear to have been new data on handedness. The bulk of studies appearing since 1940 have found little or no evidence for an excess of non-right-handedness in stutterers (Spadino 1941, Johnson and King 1942, Andrews and Harris 1964, Records et al. 1977, Porfert and Rosenfield 1978, Bishop 1986, Webster and Poulos 1987; but cf. Chrysanthis 1947).

Studies using techniques such as dichotic listening to investigate cerebral lateralization more directly generated inconsistent results (see reviews by Bloodstein 1981, van Riper 1982). A promising early report of an absence of the normal dichotic right ear advantage in stutterers (Curry and Gregory 1969) was not replicated in larger studies that followed (Quinn 1972, Slorach and Noehr 1973). Sussman and MacNeilage (1975) argued for a distinction between lateralization of speech perception and production. Their stuttering subjects showed the usual right ear advantage on dichotic listening, but a lack of lateralization in an auditory tracking task in which the subject had to control the pitch of a tone by movement of an articulator. However, inspection of their data indicates that the laterality of the stuttering group on this task did not differ significantly from that of a normal group studied in an earlier experiment. Blood (1985) cautioned that stutterers did not give uniform results on dichotic testing and the average result of a group may not be typical of all members. Quinn (1972), for instance, found no overall difference between stutterers and control subjects, but there was a significant excess of stutterers showing a reversal of the usual ear advantage. Likewise, Rosenfield and Goodglass (1980) found no effect of group on size of dichotic ear advantage, but significantly more stutterers than controls failed to show the normal right ear advantage. However, a recent study by Blood and Blood (1989*a*) found a quite different pattern of results: the proportions showing a right ear advantage were similar for stutterers and controls, but the size of the ear advantage was significantly reduced in stutterers.

Research using dichotic listening to investigate cerebral lateralization in stutterers suffers from the same defects as studies of children with reading and language problems, namely: (i) problems in deciding on the best index of cerebral lateralization, especially bearing in mind that groups may differ in overall level of performance (Blood and Blood 1989*b*); (ii) introduction of bias in studies by restricting consideration to right-handers (see p. 126); and (iii) general agreement that the population is heterogeneous, but no consensus as to how to handle this.

One study that created great excitement in this field was that of Jones (1966). Four adult stutterers (three of whom were left-handed) were given the Wada test before undergoing surgery for neurological disease unconnected with the stuttering. All four had bilateral speech representation. Remarkably, all ceased to stutter after surgery on one cerebral hemisphere, and postoperative Wada testing indicated that speech was now unilaterally represented in the unoperated hemisphere. Jones concluded that competition between the two hemispheres was responsible for stuttering. However, two studies that attempted to replicate this result with stutterers who had no brain pathology but who volunteered for the Wada test failed to find significant departures from the normal pattern of left hemisphere language representation (Andrews *et al.* 1972, Luessenhop *et al.* 1973).

Can the inconsistent findings be explained?
As with other developmental disorders of speech and language, the literature on stuttering presents a confusing picture with some claiming strong links with handedness and others denying that these exist. On the whole, those studies that find an increase of non-right-handedness among stutterers are the earlier ones, whereas studies conducted during the last 10 years or so obtain null results. One possible explanation is that inadequate methodology in early studies gave spurious associations. Haefner's (1929) study reporting dysfluency in 10 out of 46 enforced right-handers is often cited as supporting a link between handedness shift and stuttering, yet he must have used a very liberal definition of dysfluency, since 13 to 14 per cent of unshifted right-handed children were categorized as dysfluent. In fact Haefner himself was appropriately cautious in interpreting these results, which do not, in any case, show significant links between dysfluency and handedness.

Bloodstein (1981), in a comprehensive review, pointed out that early researchers usually failed to appreciate that a degree of non-right-handedness was common in the normal population, so interpreted any signs of left-sidedness as aberrant. Once properly controlled studies were conducted, people began to realize that it is an unusual person who does not show some signs of left-sidedness on a lengthy handedness battery. Early studies are further open to the criticism that preconceptions of observers might affect their results: if we believe that enforced right-handedness is a major cause of stuttering, then we will enquire about the writing experience of stutterers, but take less notice of whether or not normal speakers have had their handedness shifted. Clearly, use of control groups and standard procedures for obtaining handedness information can overcome such biases to a large extent, but when one is relying on retrospective report, remembrance of past events may be influenced by preconceived ideas. Thus the stutterer may be more likely than the non-stutterer to remember being forced to write right-handedly precisely because everyone has subsequently attributed the stuttering to that experience.

However, we should not dismiss all the significant results reported from early studies as artefacts, without considering the possibility that there may have been genuine changes over this century in factors associated with stuttering. Tolerance of left-handedness in Western cultures has increased markedly over the past 80 years. Shifting a left-handed writer to right-handedness typically results in an individual who remains left-handed for untaught actions (Teng *et al.* 1976), and so this practice will lead to an increase in the proportion of individuals categorized as mixed handers. If the shift does play a causal role in stuttering (either by affecting cerebral lateralization or by acting as a general stressor), we would expect a negative correlation between the frequency of stuttering in a population and the proportion of left-handed writers, with a secular decline in stuttering as overt left-handedness increased. Furthermore, it would be expected that as enforced handedness declined as a factor responsible for stuttering, we would move from a position where there was a positive association between mixed handedness and stuttering to one in which there was no association. If, on the contrary, atypical cerebral lateralization rather than a shift of handedness were linked to stuttering, then we would expect the prevalence of stuttering to remain relatively constant despite changing attitudes to handedness. As more and more individuals are allowed to retain their natural handedness, the link between non-right-handedness and stuttering should become clearer.

Unfortunately, we lack the epidemiological studies that would allow us to test these ideas conclusively: van Riper's (1982) review of what he describes as the 'miserable' literature on this topic makes it clear that there is so much variability of definition and reliance on questionnaire identification of cases that it would be hazardous to compare a study conducted at one time and place with another. The experimental literature reviewed so far suggests that there has been a weakening rather than a strengthening of the relationship between non-right-handedness and stuttering over the decades of this century. However, there is little evidence of a decline in the overall prevalence of stuttering over this period, and similar figures, generally hovering around 1 per cent, are reported for cultures with negative attitudes towards left-handedness (*e.g.* Germany in 1955) and for more liberal societies (*e.g.* USA in 1971). Nevertheless, van Riper's personal impression, based on years of experience of working in this field, was that the prevalence of stuttering was declining, and he reported data from an unpublished study by Jackson that agreed with this view.

Another factor that needs to be taken into account when assessing secular trends is the possible contribution of pathological left-handedness. Ballard (1912) reported a striking increase in the relationship between handedness shift and stuttering for his population of mentally handicapped children compared to a normal group. Although he attributed the association to the effects of handedness shift, an alternative view would be that the mentally handicapped group contained many individuals who had suffered left hemisphere lesions which resulted both in left-handedness and stuttering. The secular decline in the association between stuttering and handedness might then reflect a reduction in the numbers of individuals to whom such pathological processes applied, as obstetric and paediatric health care improved. (Note, however, that one could make a case for the proposition that improved neonatal care will lead to increased pathological left-handedness as more high risk infants survive—Harris and Carlson 1988.)

A study published by Gordon in 1920 agrees with the view that language functions of mentally handicapped people may vary depending on whether or not pathological left-handedness is implicated. From the tables presented by Gordon one can compute that out of 4620 children attending schools for the mentally handicapped, 843 (18 per cent) were left-handed, of whom 129 (15 per cent) had speech defects. In contrast, only 110 of the 3777 right-handers (3 per cent) had speech defects. The nature of the speech defects was not specified, but it is likely that stuttering accounted for at least some of these cases. A tendency for stuttering and left-handedness to be associated in epileptic patients was reported by Bolin (1953), although this was an unusual sample in which the majority of patients were psychotic. It is possible that variations from one study to another in the associations reported between stuttering and left-handedness might be a function of the proportion of brain-damaged individuals included in the sample.

Concluding comment

Of all the conditions we have considered, stuttering is perhaps the one where a theoretical explanation in terms of disordered laterality seems most plausible. Brain (1945) and, more recently, Peters (1976) have suggested that lateralization of motor control became necessary when humans developed speech and so needed to programme finely graded bilateral symmetrical movements of the articulators. It follows that if this unilateral motor control were not established, one might expect to see problems in the timing and synchronization of articulation. Attractive although this explanation seems, the evidence, as for so many disorders, is not so much weak as wildly inconsistent. The suggestion by Sussman and MacNeilage (1975) that we should concentrate on lateralization of speech output rather than on receptive language (or indeed handedness) seems worth pursuing. Maybe techniques such as positron emission tomography, which would allow one to monitor brain activity during speech, will provide clearer insights into the lateralization of speech control in stutterers. However, optimism seems incautious, given the multitude of cherished theories that have been broken on the rack of stuttering research.

14
HANDEDNESS, HORMONES AND DEVELOPMENTAL DISORDERS

In recent years, a theory linking handedness, developmental dyslexia and immune disorders has aroused considerable excitement. This theory, which originally appeared in a series of articles in *Archives of Neurology* (Geschwind and Galaburda 1985*a,b,c*), was subsequently published as a book (Geschwind and Galaburda 1987). Formulation of the theory was stimulated by evidence for a four-way association between male gender, left-handedness, developmental disorders such as dyslexia, stuttering and autism, and high visuospatial ability. The theory sought to account for this pattern of associations within a single framework.

Geschwind and Galaburda proposed that fetal testosterone affects the relative rate of maturation of the two cerebral hemispheres by retarding development of the left side. According to their theory, it is normal for the right hemisphere to develop ahead of the left. However, excessive testosterone will delay left hemisphere maturation to such an extent that the probability of both left-handedness and developmental disorders such as dyslexia will be increased. Since males have higher levels of testosterone than females, the risk is particularly high for boys. It was further argued that delayed development of the left brain will lead to enhanced development of homologous areas of the right hemisphere, boosting visuospatial skills. In addition, it was postulated that testosterone affects maturation of the thymus, in extreme cases retarding development so much that the individual would be predisposed to immune disorders in later life.

Evaluation of the theory is complex, because it contains many postulates, including some which Geschwind and Galaburda admit are highly speculative. The major steps of their argument will now be considered in turn.

A three-way relationship between gender, handedness and learning disabilities
The claim of a link between gender and developmental disorders involving language is uncontroversial. There is plentiful evidence in support of the claim that males are more likely than females to be affected by developmental dyslexia, stuttering, developmental language disorders and autism (Eme 1979). Furthermore, no aetiological theory to date has provided a satisfactory explanation for the sex difference in the prevalence of these disorders.

A link between gender and handedness is widely though not universally accepted. Annett's (1985) review of the literature confirmed that, although some studies have failed to find sex differences, most large-scale investigations do report a slight preponderance of males among non-right-handers. Her own work using peg-moving to assess relative skill of the two sides found that, on average, females show a more pronounced superiority of the right hand over the left than do males.

It has been argued, however, that sex differences may reflect greater social conformity in females, rather than biological factors (Porac *et al.* 1986).

The most controversial link in the postulated three-way relationship is that between handedness and learning disabilities. Geschwind and Galaburda (1985*b*) stated: 'We believe that the majority, and possibly nearly all LD [learning disordered] children are drawn from the AD [anomalous dominance] population' (p. 538). Note that by 'anomalous dominance' they refer to any departure from the normal pattern of cerebral lateralization. Thus this term is not synonymous with 'ambiguous handedness', as defined in Chapter 9 (pp. 106–107), and nor is it equivalent to left-handedness. It is assumed that most left-handers have anomalous dominance, but so too will many right-handers.

The evidence for an association between handedness and developmental disorders of speech, language and reading was presented in Chapters 11 to 13. A comprehensive look at the literature on this topic shows that if such a link does exist it is only weak, and many would deny the existence of any association at all. Autistic children have been found to be more likely than normal controls to be non-right-handed, but they do not differ from mentally handicapped individuals of similar intellectual level (see Chapter 10). A recent large-scale and well-controlled study of Tourette syndrome found no association with left-handedness (Comings and Comings 1987).

Geschwind and his co-workers have largely ignored the extensive literature on this topic, preferring to rely on data from their own studies. In the first of these (Geschwind and Behan 1982), strongly left-handed individuals were recruited from a specialist supply shop for left-handers in London and asked to report whether or not they suffered from learning disorders such as dyslexia or stuttering. 24 out of 253 left-handers (9.5 per cent) but only two right-handers (0.8 per cent) described themselves as having a learning disorder. However, this survey may be criticized on the grounds that the right-handers and left-handers were recruited from different populations. In a second survey (ibid.) this drawback was overcome, with all subjects being recruited from a range of settings in Glasgow. In this sample 10.9 per cent of left-handers and 1.2 per cent of right-handers described themselves as dyslexics or stutterers. Geschwind and Behan (1984) carried out a similar study comparing 440 strongly left- and 652 strongly right-handed subjects, but again these were apparently self-selected and recruited from different sources. Dyslexia was reported by 7 per cent of left-handers but only 0.3 per cent of right-handers, and stuttering by 4.5 per cent of left-handers and 0.9 per cent of right-handers, both differences being statistically significant.

The main problem with these studies is that the results obtained are totally discrepant with those reported by other workers, indicating a six- to 10-fold increase in the proportion of left-handers among learning-disordered individuals. The only other studies in the literature reporting effects approaching this magnitude also identified learning disability by self-report using a written questionnaire (van Strien *et al.* 1987). Subjects' perception of themselves as dyslexic may be affected by pre-existing beliefs about links between handedness and dyslexia. Popular texts on dyslexia frequently mention left-handedness as a symptom. Thus individuals who do not read easily and who are left-handed will be more likely to perceive themselves as dyslexic than those who read just as poorly but are right-handed. The same argument applies to a recent study in which Schachter *et al.* (1987) mailed handedness questionnaires to 2700 professionals who were also asked whether they had any history of learning disability 'including dyslexia, hyperactivity, delayed speech, difficulty learning mathematics, autism and Tourette syndrome'. It is surprising that the authors gave no breakdown of the type of learning disabilities reported by their respondents, given that the hormonal theory makes opposite predictions about the frequencies of left-handedness expected in those with language-related disorders and those with 'difficulty learning mathematics' (according to the theory, *superior* mathematical skills go with left-handedness—see below). Although a significant association between non-right-handedness and learning disability was found, the response rate of 41 per cent was poor enough to cast serious doubt on this result. In general, people who respond to questionnaires are those who have something positive to report, so spurious associations can be generated where response rates are low. Furthermore, while Geschwind and Behan had found a link between learning disability and handedness only when extreme left-handers were selected, Schachter *et al.* found the highest rates for those with laterality quotients between 0 and 70, *i.e.* those who were predominantly but not strongly right-handed. In total contrast to Annett and Kilshaw's (1984) sample, strong right-handers had the lowest reported rates of learning disability. In short, the studies cited by Geschwind and associates as demonstrating links between learning disabilities and handedness have innumerable methodological weaknesses, the most serious being that subjects were self-selected, identification of learning disability (itself a multifarious category) was by self-report, and handedness of putative dyslexics was assessed by written questionnaire.

Relative maturation of the left and right hemispheres
The question of whether one hemisphere matures before the other has been a matter of considerable debate, and the discussion of this issue by Geschwind and Galaburda (1985*a*) is rather confusing. On the one hand they point to neuroanatomical studies showing that the right planum temporale develops around the 30th week of gestation, a full week to 10 days before the left (Chi *et al.* 1977). On the other hand, they also cite evidence that a longer Sylvian fissure is present on the left side as early as 16 weeks gestation. Note that the claim that the right hemisphere develops ahead of the left is diametrically opposed to the views of Annett (1985) and Morgan and Corballis (1978) (see Chapter 3), and indeed of Broca (see Chapter 2). A possible resolution is suggested in a review by Best (1988), who stressed the complexity of maturational differences between left and right. According to her model, there is no general factor favouring left or right hemisphere development: rather there is a three-dimensional growth vector that has the effect of imposing a counterclockwise torque on the shape of the developing brain, twisting the left hemisphere rearward and dorsal, and the right hemisphere forward and ventral. The impact of this growth vector will vary not only from one

region of the brain to another, but also from one cortical layer to another. Best argued that while Heschl's gyrus and primary auditory cortex develop on the right side first, this is not so for the formation of Wernicke's association area, which is concerned with receptive language.

Relationship between left and right hemisphere development
Another confusing aspect of Geschwind and Galaburda's account concerns the influence of the left and right hemispheres upon one another. They were impressed by evidence from animal experiments that, after brain lesions, more extensive connections develop in other brain areas, both those surrounding the damaged area, and homologous areas in the opposite hemisphere. They suggested that if development of certain areas of the left hemisphere were delayed by hormonal influences, then similar consequences would ensue: the right hemisphere would grow correspondingly faster and develop a richer pattern of neural connections. According to Geschwind and Galaburda (1987): 'A delay in development of some cortical regions on the left side should . . . favor growth of cortical regions on the opposite side and of unaffected regions on the same side' (p. 12). If this were so, however, it is hard to see how the left planum temporale could end up larger in most people if, as they claim, it develops after the right. Later on they state that 'it appears to be the case that regions on the left side that will be larger in the mature brain develop more slowly than the corresponding areas on the right' (p. 41), but no explanation is given for the apparent contradiction.

Furthermore, if the right hemisphere were to grow unusually fast, it is unclear what the consequences for intellectual development would be. Geschwind and Galaburda (1985*a*) state that growth retardation of left hemisphere regions leads to 'a greater degree of shift to right-hemisphere participation in handedness and language and . . . augmented right-hemisphere skills' (p. 432). They appear to be arguing that the right hemisphere will simultaneously mediate functions that it would not usually control, and also achieve superiority in those functions which it normally mediates. Note that this contrasts sharply with Levy's (1976) suggestion that use of the right hemisphere for language processing will limit the capacity for visuospatial functions. Implicit in Levy's formulation is the notion of a fixed capacity in the right hemisphere, so that there will be a trade-off between the amount of neural power that can be dedicated to verbal and visuospatial functions. No such limit is envisaged in Geschwind and Galaburda's account. We do not know which formulation is correct. It is clear, however, that until we gain a better understanding of functional division of labour within each hemisphere, we cannot make clear predictions about how cerebral lateralization of function will affect intellectual profile.

Finally, if one accepts the simple underlying ideas that (i) the growth of the two hemispheres is inversely related, and (ii) level of mental function is directly related to the rate of growth of the hemisphere mediating that function, then one would predict that for the population as a whole there should be an inverse relationship between language and visuospatial skills: the lower the language, the better the visuospatial skills, and vice versa. In practice, this is not found: on the contrary, language and visuospatial functions tend to be positively correlated. Geschwind and Galaburda cited a paper by Gordon (1980) showing that dyslexics have superior visuospatial skills, but this result can be explained as a consequence of the way in which dyslexia is defined. In order to be regarded as dyslexic, one has to have severe reading problems in the context of normal intelligence. Since intelligence is typically measured as a composite of verbal and non-verbal skills, and verbal functions are usually compromised in poor readers, it follows that individuals meeting the criteria for dyslexia tend to be those who have strong non-verbal abilities (Bishop and Butterworth 1980). There are plenty of poor readers who do not have such abilities: however, they would be regarded as generally backward rather than dyslexic. We may note in passing that only one of the 12 dyslexics studied by Gordon was left-handed (no handedness data were reported for controls).

Overall, the neurological basis for cerebral lateralization proposed by Geschwind and Galaburda is one of the most confusing parts of their theory. Much of the confusion could be resolved if the postulate of earlier right hemisphere development were abandoned. According to Best's analysis, this postulate is in any case inaccurate as regards Wernicke's area. If we were to assume, rather, that the language areas of the left hemisphere usually mature earlier, unless retarded by hormonal influences, we could explain why in most brains the left planum temporale is larger than the right. Other aspects of the theory have come into question in the light of a recent study by Galaburda *et al.* (1987), who measured the size of planum temporale asymmetry in the series of brains originally studied by Geschwind and Levitsky (1968) and correlated this with size of the two plana. Symmetry resulted more from an increase in the size of the right side than from a decrease in the size of the left, and the combined area of the two plana was somewhat larger for those with symmetrical brains. On the basis of this result, Galaburda *et al.* suggested that asymmetry and symmetry may 'not reflect issues of distribution or sharing of a given amount of language substrate between the hemispheres, but rather changes essentially limited to one side' (p. 862), *i.e.* the modified claim is that asymmetry is normally achieved by neuronal loss in the right hemisphere.

The effect of testosterone on left hemisphere development
Geschwind and Galaburda suggested that the majority of humans are predisposed to left hemisphere language representation, but that hormonal influences can diminish this innate bias and lead to random dominance for handedness and language. Unlike Annett, who regards a bias to left hemisphere language representation as a variable factor dependent on genetic influences, they believe that this bias is present in nearly all people but that its expression can be modified by hormone levels *in utero* which are only partly under genetic control.

Since fetal testosterone levels are higher in males, the theory predicts slower neurological maturation in males than in females. Behavioural data lend support to this view, although neuroanatomical studies have failed to find predicted sex differences in relative rate of maturation of the two cerebral hemispheres (Chi *et al.*

1977). Geschwind and Galaburda cite a paper by Taylor (1969) who inferred sex differences in maturation of the cerebral hemispheres on the basis of data concerning age at onset of temporal lobe epilepsy. Temporal lobe epilepsy can develop as a secondary consequence of febrile convulsions in infancy which result in anoxic cerebral damage and sclerosis of mesial structures. In general, onset of epilepsy associated with such lesions is most probable when the brain is most immature, *i.e.* in the first two or three years of life, but the age at onset varies as a function of laterality of lesion. In boys the inception rate falls away gradually with increasing age, but in girls the decline is more precipitate. If, as Taylor suggested, vulnerability to epilepsy is an indicator of immaturity, then this result indicates that girls mature more rapidly than boys, consistent with what we know about cognitive development early in life. Where the left hemisphere is affected, the age of onset is typically within the first two years of life. However, where a right hemisphere lesion is involved, onset is often later in childhood. Following the logic developed so far, this result suggests that the right hemisphere remains immature, and hence vulnerable to develop seizures, longer than the left. Note that this is contrary to Geschwind and Galaburda's theory which maintains that it is the left hemisphere which develops more slowly.

The role of testosterone in retarding left hemisphere growth has been questioned by Pennington *et al.* (1987). These authors noted that verbal IQ is normal in individuals with adrenogenital syndrome, who have extremely high levels of prenatal testosterone. Furthermore, Cappa *et al.* (1988) found no effect on handedness or functional cerebral lateralization in individuals with congenital androgen deficiency, who would be expected to have unusually strong left hemisphere development relative to the right.

Delayed maturation as a cause of left-handedness

In vivo imaging of rate of brain maturation has only recently become a reality, so evidence for this postulate is necessarily indirect.

Again there seems to be some inconsistency in the arguments put forward by Geschwind and Galaburda. They claim that the likelihood of a hemisphere mediating language and hand preference is dependent on its rate of maturation, yet they regard earlier right hemisphere maturation as the norm. This would seem to entail that left-handedness and right hemisphere language representation should be the normal state of affairs, which clearly is not the case.

There are, however, several strands of evidence linking non-right-handedness with maturation, especially development of language functions. For a start we know that males are on average slower to learn to talk, and more likely to be left-handed than females. Although there is as yet no neuroanatomical support for this view, a plausible explanation is in terms of the left hemisphere developing more slowly in males.

A second factor that has been associated with both increased non-right-handedness and delayed language acquisition is twinning (see Chapter 3). The language delay is most pronounced in males (Hay *et al.* 1987). Annett (1985) was the first to relate increased left-handedness and language delay by a single explanation in terms of delayed maturation *in utero* (which she saw as reducing the expression of the right shift factor).

Another group providing relevant data is males with an extra X chromosome (Klinefelter syndrome: 47,XXY). Individuals with this syndrome usually perform quite normally on tests of non-verbal ability, but typically are impaired on language tests (Netley and Rovet 1982*a*). Netley and Rovet (1982*b*) reported a rate of 24 per cent left-handedness in 33 individuals with Klinefelter syndrome, which was significantly above the frequency in age-matched controls. Similarly, Thielgaard (1981) reported that XXY males were much more likely than XYY males to be ambidextrous (although the criterion for ambidexterity was not defined). Netley and Rovet (1984) noted that there is evidence for slowed development in XXY males, both fetally and in early childhood. They interpreted their findings in terms of delayed maturation of the left hemisphere. To this extent, the syndrome is consistent with Geschwind and Galaburda's theory. However, there is one major flaw in the hormonal explanation of these findings: Netley and Rovet (1988) reported that males with Klinefelter syndrome do not have abnormally high levels of testosterone during fetal life—if anything, their levels are unusually low. Thus, while left-handedness and language delay may be signs of slow maturation in this syndrome, there is no evidence that fetal testosterone plays a causal role.

A final piece of evidence linking non-right-handedness with immaturity comes from Coren *et al.* (1986), who obtained questionnaire data on handedness and retrospective reports of age at puberty from a sample of 1180 university students. There was a significant association between left-handedness and late puberty in both sexes. In evaluating this study it should be noted that both handedness and age at puberty were assessed by self-report. There is a possibility that a correlation between two unusual characteristics may arise because of individual variation in the extent to which people are ready to represent themselves as in some way abnormal. To rule out this kind of explanation, we need a study of maturity and handedness in a sample where both characteristics are measured directly rather than by self-report. If this result were confirmed, it would fit in with the idea that there is a subgroup of 'late developers' who are characterized both by late puberty and delayed neurological maturation in early life. Coren *et al.* proposed a more general explanation in terms of left-handedness as a 'readily visible behavioral marker that is probabilistically related to a syndrome caused by a set of minor abnormalities in neurological development' (p. 21).

Left hemisphere impairment in dyslexia
The neurological basis of developmental dyslexia has puzzled investigators for many years. Techniques such as brain scanning seldom reveal any sign of focal brain damage. Increasing evidence of a genetic link in dyslexia suggests that abnormality of neuronal development rather than damage by disease or trauma is the most plausible basis.

Post-mortem studies of dyslexic brains are understandably rare. Galaburda *et al.* (1985) carried out post-mortem studies on the brains of four individuals known to be dyslexic and found areas of cytoarchitectonic abnormalities, mainly around the Sylvian fissure and predominantly in the left hemisphere. These included nests of medium-sized neurons in cortical layer I (which is normally free of such cells) and excessive numbers of large cells ('architectonic dysplasias') which disrupted the normal laminar and columnar organization of the cortex. Geschwind and Galaburda (1985a) argued that these abnormalities arose when neuronal migration in the left hemisphere was disrupted during fetal development.

The significance of the abnormalities described by Galaburda and his colleagues has been questioned, on the grounds that there were no controls. Architectonic anomalies of this kind were first remarked on during routine post-mortems, and it could be argued that if any brain is examined in sufficient detail some misplaced neurons will be detected. Furthermore, the first patient studied by Galaburda was epileptic as well as dyslexic and another had paroxysmal slowing of the EEG, raising the possibility that the reported abnormalities may be more a correlate of epilepsy than of dyslexia. Geschwind and Galaburda (1985a) countered this objection by arguing that too little is known about the presence of minor forms of learning disability or psychiatric disturbance in individuals who undergo post-mortem neuroanatomical studies. It is possible that those who show similar migrational abnormalities would prove to have learning disabilities if this were properly studied. Furthermore, Kaufmann and Galaburda (1989), in a study of a series of brains of dyslexic and non-dyslexic individuals, showed that cytoarchitectonic anomalies affected only a minority of the control brains and when they were found they were much less extensive than was the case in the brains of the dyslexics. However, none of these neuroanatomical studies was conducted blind to the status of the individual whose brain was being examined.

Studies measuring the relative sizes of the two hemispheres (reviewed in Chapter 11) lend some support to the notion that dyslexics tend to have brains that are more symmetrical than is usual. However, it seems that this physical symmetry does not necessarily indicate functional symmetry: rather it is likely that dyslexics, like other individuals, rely on the left hemisphere for language processing, but the left hemisphere is poorly developed and so provides a rather inadequate basis for verbally based operations.

Fetal testosterone and development of the thymus
Those proficient in this field appear sceptical of the proposed physiological basis linking fetal testosterone with impairment of the immune system (Wofsy 1984). As with those aspects of theory dealing with laterality, it seems that while Geschwind and Galaburda can point to studies consistent with their position, a less selective review of the literature indicates little consensus over key postulates, *e.g.* that fetal testosterone levels affect maturation of the thymus.

One might suppose that the hormonal theory would have problems in coping with the fact that most immune disorders are more common in females than males. However, Geschwind and Behan accounted for this by arguing that after puberty the presence of testosterone exerts a protective influence against immune disorders. Thus the theory predicts a male preponderance of immune disorders only in prepubertal children.

A three-way association between left-handedness, immune disorders and learning disabilities

A particularly original aspect of the hormonal theory is that it predicts a link between immune disorders and left-handedness.

Preliminary data on this question were presented by Geschwind and Behan (1982). In an initial study they reported a significant increase in the incidence of immune diseases in left-handers compared to right-handers. 27 out of 253 left-handers (10.7 per cent) compared to 10 out of 253 right-handers (4.0 per cent) suffered from one of the following immune disorders: coeliac disease, dermatomyositis, diabetes, Hashimoto's thyroiditis, myxoedema, regional ileitis, rheumatoid arthritis, thyrotoxicosis, ulcerative colitis and uveitis. However, left- and right-handers were not recruited from the same sources so this difference could be attributable to population differences. A second study with better matching of left- and right-handers obtained less impressive though still significant results: 13 out of 247 left-handers (5.3 per cent) compared to 15 out of 647 right-handers (2.3 per cent) suffered from immune diseases. A third study by these authors compared the frequency of left-handedness among patients referred to neurological clinics in Glasgow because of migraine or immune disorders. A significant increase in left-handedness was reported for migraine and myasthenia gravis, but no association was found for rheumatoid arthritis, mixed collagen vascular disease or multiple sclerosis. However, the effects were small: Satz and Soper (1986) noted that reassignment of a single left-handed subject with immune disease to the right-handed group would have meant that the result would have fallen short of statistical significance. More seriously, the cut-offs for left-handedness (assessed by questionnaire) were varied from one disease to another, apparently in order to maximize differences between groups. Bishop (1990a) used a computer simulation to demonstrate that *post hoc* selection of cut-off points could raise the odds of obtaining a 'significant' result as high as 2:3.

Geschwind and Behan (1984) reported a further study in which 652 strongly right-handed and 440 strongly left-handed individuals were compared on personal and familial medical history as assessed by questionnaire. Subjects came either from Scotland or from a shop for left-handed people in London. A raised frequency of certain disorders was found in the left-handers. Significant differences were reported in the incidence of migraine (15 per cent of left-handers vs. 7 per cent of right-handers), allergies (7 per cent vs. 0.6 per cent), skeletal malformations (2 per cent vs. 0.6 per cent) and thyroid disorders (3 per cent vs. 1 per cent). As with the previous studies by these authors, the fact that the left- and right-handers were not drawn from the same population and subjects were largely self-selected makes interpretation problematic. The most convincing data relating handedness to autoimmune disease were reported in a second study of hospital patients (Geschwind and Behan 1984). 304 patients who were treated in hospital clinics for autoimmune diseases were given a handedness questionnaire. With the criterion for left-handedness set at a laterality quotient less than zero, a statistically significant increase was found in Crohn's disease, coeliac disease, thyroid disorders, ulcerative colitis and myasthenia gravis, but not in rheumatoid arthritis, diabetes mellitus or polymyositis.

Since these initial reports there have been several studies by other investigators testing for a link between autoimmune disorder and handedness. Results have been very mixed. Van Strien *et al.* (1987), relying on self-report of disease in volunteers, found no association between handedness and autoimmune disorders. Smith (1987) found an elevated prevalence of left-handedness among patients attending an allergy clinic compared with a control group recruited at a railway station. Bishop (1986), however, found no link between allergy and handedness in the epidemiological sample of over 10,000 children from the National Child Development Survey (NCDS). Eczema, psoriasis and asthma were also unassociated with handedness.

Systemic lupus erythematosus (SLE) is a multisystemic autoimmune disease that usually affects women of childbearing age. Two studies, one of them controlled, looked at laterality in patients with this disease and found no association with left-handedness (Salcedo *et al.* 1985, Schur 1986).

In Bishop's (1986) analysis of the NCDS data set, there was a non-significant trend for an association between type I (insulin dependent) diabetes and left-handedness in males but not in females, although the sample size was very small. Searleman and Fugagli (1987) recruited diabetic subjects from regional diabetic associations and found a significantly elevated frequency of left-handedness in males but not females with type I diabetes relative to those with type II diabetes. This result is in line with prediction from the hormonal theory, because only type I diabetes is thought to be an autoimmune disorder. However, when compared to a normal control group, males with type I diabetes did not have a particularly high rate of left-handedness: rather, those with type II diabetes had a very low rate.

More impressive results from the Searleman and Fugagli study were obtained for inflammatory bowel disorders (ulcerative colitis and Crohn's disease), where the frequency of left-handedness was 27 per cent for males and 28 per cent for females, well above control levels and in line with findings reported by Geschwind and Behan.

Pennington *et al.* (1987) studied 173 members of 14 three-generation kindreds in which there was a high frequency of developmental dyslexia with apparent autosomal transmission. No association was found between handedness and dyslexia (see Table 11.I), but there was an increased frequency of allergies and autoimmune disorders in dyslexic individuals, consistent with the theory.

Urion (1988) compared relatives of 100 language-disabled boys with those of 100 control boys. Data on handedness of the probands were not presented, but the two groups of relatives did not differ with respect to either handedness or autoimmune diseases. Urion went on to divide the language-disabled sample into two groups, with a high, or low, proportion of non-dextral relatives. The first group had a much higher incidence of autoimmune diseases in their relatives, leading Urion to suggest that there may be one familial subtype of language disorder linked with non-dextrality and autoimmune disorder. This is an interesting notion but requires further study given that (a) division of language-impaired boys into subgroups was made *post hoc* after inspecting the data, (b) criteria for placing subjects in one group rather than the other were not specified, (c) potential confounding variables such as number, age and sex of relatives were apparently not controlled, and (d) there was no evidence of any phenotypic differences in the nature of the language difficulties of children in the two subgroups.

Hansen *et al.* (1987) did not report data on handedness, but they found a familial association between specific dyslexia and type I diabetes. In their account they did not consider an hormonal theory, favouring a genetic explanation. Linkage analysis has suggested that a gene on chromosome 15 is important in one form of dyslexia. This chromosome also carries a gene that is important both in protein synthesis for testosterone and in the structuring of the autoimmune system. Rather than assuming that testosterone directly affects brain development to cause dyslexia, Hansen *et al.* suggested that autoimmune disorders and dyslexia may co-occur because the genes determining these conditions are closely located on the chromosome and so are inherited together.

Left-handedness and superior right hemisphere skills
According to Geschwind and Galaburda, the same factors that retard left hemisphere growth and depress verbal abilities will enable the right hemisphere to grow with a concomitant boost to visuospatial abilities. Left-handers are thus expected to be over-represented among those who excel in activities that demand good right hemisphere skills. We may note that this prediction is diametrically opposed to the position adopted by Levy (1969), who regarded left-handers as selectively impaired in visuospatial functions (see Chapter 6).

Handedness patterns in sports champions are often cited as providing evidence for a link between visuospatial aptitude and non-right-handedness. Annett and Kilshaw (1982) noted that 20 per cent of the top tennis professionals of both sexes in 1981 were left-handed, and left-handers were common also among fencing champions and cricketers. An excess of left-handers is reliably found among champion baseball players (McLean and Ciurczak 1982). Such findings appear robust enough to be taken seriously, but their interpretation is controversial. One obvious factor that must be taken into account is the tactical advantage of left-handedness in any sport that is played face-to-face against an opponent. Success in baseball, tennis or cricket depends not only on one's own ability to predict where a ball might appear and act accordingly, but also on the opponent's ability to position the ball to make this task as difficult as possible. Because right-handers are more common than left-handers, the typical opponent will have had many years of practice against right-handed players and will have learned to place the ball in positions they find difficult. This skill will be less useful when competing with a left-hander. In tennis, for instance, shots that would force a right-handed opponent to play a backhanded return can be played forehand by a left-hander. In short, the advantage for left-handers may be not so much that they have special skills, but that their opponents will have less experience of competing against left-handers than right-handers. [Professor Max Hammerton has drawn my attention to an ancient Aztec practice which may be explained in similar terms. A left-handed warrior was kept in reserve to confront any sacrificial victim who had succeeded in conquering four right-handers (Roberts 1937).]

The *New England Journal of Medicine* has featured a lively correspondence on the topic of handedness in baseball players. McLean and Ciurczak claimed that a tactical advantage for left-handers could not explain their results because players who batted and pitched the ball left-handed obtained significantly higher batting averages than those who threw right-handed but batted left-handed, whose averages resembled those of consistent right-handers. Unfortunately, some error appears to have crept into the data analysis (the degrees of freedom and probability levels seem inaccurate), clouding interpretation of this result. In any case, Hemenway (1983) criticized this study on logical grounds. He noted that the sample was not random, but consisted of all hired professionals. If left-handedness were associated with superior batting, and batting average were the major criterion determining who was selected for a team, then one would expect to find over-representation of left-handers in a selected sample, but one would not expect any difference in batting score between left- and right-handers who had been selected. Hemenway argued that the higher batting average of left-handers only made sense if selection criteria other than batting were operational. He suggested that left-handedness gives a tactical advantage when batting, but is a severe disadvantage when fielding. A left-hander is likely to be selected only if his batting average is unusually good, thereby compensating for his weakness in fielding.

It would be of considerable interest to investigate handedness of champions in sports that demand high levels of visuospatial competence but where an opponent's handedness has no influence on an individual's performance, *e.g.* archery, golf, darts or snooker.

Another group with superior visuospatial skills is artists. Michaelangelo is thought to have been left-handed, and other famous artists have shown remarkable facility in using both hands. Leonardo da Vinci produced fluent mirror-writing with his left hand, Landseer could paint a background with one hand while completing a detail with the other, and Escher used his right hand to write but the left for engraving and drawing. Anecdotal snippets such as these can, of course, mislead by focusing attention on the abnormal, leading us to disregard the numerous talented artists who are right-handed. What is needed is a systematic comparison of a clearly defined group of artists and a control group. Such a study was conducted by Mebert and Michel (1980) who gave Annett's handedness questionnaire to 204 students, half of whom were studying fine arts. They found a significant excess of non-right-handers among the artists (21 per cent left-handed and 28 per cent mixed-handed, compared with figures of 7 per cent and 15 per cent respectively for the control group). However, this finding was not replicated in a study of university faculty members in architecture, art, law and psychology, which found no hint of a higher rate of left-handedness in the former two groups (Shettel-Neuber and O'Reilly 1983). Furthermore, a study of 1045 students by Peterson (1979), which is widely quoted as showing excess left-handedness in students of art and architecture, in fact gives a non-significant result when all 10 subject groupings are compared using the chi-squared test. The significant result reported by the author was only achieved by the dubious procedure of selecting the group with one of the lowest rates of left-handedness (scientists; 4.35 per cent left-handed) for comparison with the artists (12.24 per cent left-handed). However, if business administrators (9.54 per cent left-handed), engineers (10.67 per cent left-handed) and 'others' (14.66 per cent left-handed) are taken into consideration, it is clear that the rates of left-handedness in those studying art-related subjects are quite unremarkable. A further negative result was reported by Schlichting (1982), who found no differences in handedness between Navy sonar operators (who need good visuospatial skills) and other Navy staff.

Geschwind and Galaburda cited a study by Peterson and Lansky (1974) that reported a high rate of non-right-handedness among architects, and superior maze-design abilities in left-handed architecture students. The major problem with this study was the lack of controls: 79 out of 484 students (16.3 per cent) checked the statement 'I use either hand equally' or 'I am totally left-handed' in preference to the statement 'I am totally right-handed'. In the absence of a control group we have no idea how other student groups would react to being forced to classify themselves into one of these three alternatives, none of which is suitable for the person who is biased to prefer one side but sometimes uses the other. When we look at the skill difference between left- and right-handed architects reported by these authors we discover that the anticipated difference (in maze-solving ability) was not found, but a *post hoc* analysis of mazes designed by students revealed that the left-handers were more likely to comply with instructions accurately. Hardly compelling evidence for a link between superior visuo-spatial skills and left-handedness!

A third type of talent that has been linked with left-handedness is mathematical ability. Geschwind and Galaburda are not the only authors to propose such an association. Annett and Kilshaw (1982) had previously suggested that it might be advantageous for mathematical thinking to have a brain without extreme bias to left hemisphere language representation. They predicted a raised frequency of left-handedness and decreased difference between the skill of the two hands among mathematicians compared to non-mathematicians. Data inconsistent with this prediction had been presented by Douglas *et al.* (1967), who found no evidence that good mathematical ability was linked with non-right-handedness: in a large national sample, the top 15 per cent on a maths attainment test resembled those of moderate ability in their handedness, whereas there was a significant tendency for those with the lowest attainment to have mixed hand preference. Negative results were also obtained by Jones and Bell (1980), who compared the handedness distribution from a group of engineering students selected for strong mathematical skills with that from a less selected group of psychology students. The handedness distributions were close to general population estimates, with the engineering students showing slightly less left-handedness than the psychologists. Peterson's (1979) finding of a non-significant trend towards *low* rates of left-handedness in science students has already been commented upon. Annett and Kilshaw, however, presented evidence for a specific link with mathematical skills from a variety of samples. The strongest support came from two samples of undergraduates who completed handedness questionnnaires, both of which showed a significant increase in the proportion of left-handers among male, but not female,

TABLE 14.I

Handedness in mathematicians (Annett and Kilshaw 1982)

Sample	N	L-handed writers %	L-handed any activity %
Volunteer samples			
(50% response rate)			
I. Undergraduates responding to mailed eight-item questionnaire			
Mathematics			
Male	28	28.6	42.9
Female	8	12.5	50.0
Other subjects			
Male	435	11.0	23.2
Female	239	10.5	34.7
III. Undergraduates responding to mailed 12-item questionnaire			
Mathematics			
Male	41	21.9	58.5
Female	31	6.4	25.8
Other subjects			
Male	40	10.0	32.5
Female	106	4.7	30.2
Complete samples			
II. Schoolgirls			
Mathematics	24	16.7	37.5
Non-mathematics	134	7.5	44.0
IV. Miscellaneous completing 12-item inventory			
Mathematics			
Male	17	5.9	11.8
Female	31	12.9	41.9
V. Lecturers and teachers examined on 12-item inventory			
Mathematics			
Male	97	11.3	36.1
Female	27	7.4	44.4
Non-mathematics			
Male	50	12.0	28.0
Female	20	0.0	45.0

mathematics students when compared to other students (Table 14.I). One drawback of these samples was that about half of those who were sent the questionnaire failed to return it. However, although this could introduce response bias if, for instance, left-handers were more likely to return the questionnaire, it is hard to see how it could explain the association between area of study and hand preference, unless students were aware of the specific hypothesis under investigation. Furthermore, the rate of left-handedness reported by the non-mathematicians was not appreciably different from that found in non-volunteer groups of schoolchildren and students, going against the notion that handedness affected likelihood of completing the questionnaire.

Direct investigation of hand preference in more complete samples of mathematicians, however, gave less impressive results. For samples II, IV and V (see table) almost all members of each population were directly examined on a 12-item inventory. No comparisons between mathematicians and non-mathematicians of the same sex were significant, nor was the overall comparison when these three groups were summed to give a larger sample. This does make one wonder whether the results from the less complete samples arose through sampling error. However, Annett and Kilshaw noted two further points about their data. When the sample V mathematicians were divided according to whether they specialized in pure mathematics or some other discipline (*e.g.* computer science), then for males a significant difference emerged, with 18.2 per cent of pure mathematicians writing left-handed compared to 7.8 per cent of other mathematicians. While intriguing, this difference was not predicted in advance, and so one needs to be cautious in interpreting the reported significance levels (see Bishop 1990*a*). A replication of this study is needed. Also reported were data on hand differences in peg-moving times, as measured by a stopwatch, where the group V sample of mathematicians showed significantly less shift to the right than a normative population, this result holding up independently for both male and female samples. The size of the difference between groups was small (around 200 msec.), and only just reached statistical significance at the 0.05 level on a one-tailed test. Also, the hand difference for mathematicians was significantly different from zero so one cannot conclude that most mathemicians lack the right shift factor, but simply that they are less strongly shifted to the right than non-mathematicians. It would be of interest to replicate this study, ideally using automated timing, restricting consideration to pure mathematicians and combining hand difference measures with dichotic listening tests.

Benbow (1986) argued that while superior mathematical skills were not usually found to relate to handedness, if one restricted consideration to exceptionally talented individuals, relationships with handedness emerged. Benbow studied 416 individuals, identified in a talent search covering the whole USA as being in the top 0.01 per cent of their age-group on mathematical and/or verbal reasoning. For the control group, she selected 230 students whose achievement scores were in the top 5 per cent of the population, but who did poorly on the scholastic aptitude test used in the talent search. The Edinburgh Handedness Inventory (see Appendix) was used to assess handedness, taking a laterality quotient of less than zero as the criterion of left-handedness. Benbow reported that the frequency of left-handedness in the mathematically precocious group (15.1 per cent) was significantly higher than that for the control group (10.2 per cent). However, in the precocious group males outnumbered females by almost three to one (a result which has stirred up a lively debate—see Benbow 1988). As there are small but reliable sex differences in handedness, this bias needs to be taken into account when comparing groups. Among the precocious males, 37 out of 226 (16.3 per cent) were left-handed, compared with nine out of 86 control males (10.5 per cent), a difference that does not reach significance on chi-squared test. The precocious group included some who were selected for outstanding performance on a test of verbal reasoning. However, if we restrict attention only to males with extremely high mathematics scores, we find that 25 out of 175 (14.2 per cent) are left-handed, a frequency that is again not significantly different from that of the comparison group.

Benbow's conclusion from this study was that there is a high frequency of left- or mixed handedness among extremely mathematically and/or verbally gifted students, a result that was interpreted as supporting the hormonal theory. However, this conclusion does not seem justified by the data. When same-sex groups are compared on handedness, the mathematically precocious did *not* have higher rates of left-handedness than controls, irrespective of whether those with verbal precocity are included in the comparison. The only same-sex comparison to approach conventional levels of statistical significance was that between the subgroup of males who were *verbally* (but not mathematically) precocious, 12 out of 51 (23.5 per cent) of whom were left-handed. Now, if asked *a priori* to predict, on the basis of the Geschwind and Galaburda theory, what the handedness distribution of this group should be like, the answer would be that they should be *less* likely to be left-handed, since left-handedness is supposed to be associated with retarded left hemisphere development and a relative impairment of verbal skills. To this extent, then, these results go directly against the predictions of Geschwind and Galaburda. Benbow (1988) countered this argument by noting that the test used was one of verbal *reasoning*, which may depend on right hemisphere processing. However, the evidence cited to support this claim is indirect and unconvincing. Indeed, one could make a strong case for arguing just the opposite, *i.e.* that both the mathematical and the verbal tests were assessing left hemisphere function (Bryden 1988*b*).

Other evidence produced by Benbow, on comparisons between handedness of intellectually precocious individuals and their relatives, is difficult to interpret because of the age differences in samples. Higher rates of left-handedness in offspring than in their parents are regularly reported in normal samples, and a similar finding in the intellectually precocious cannot be regarded as indicating anything other than a secular trend.

Benbow's sample is the most extremely selected in terms of ability ever to have been tested. If an increase in left-handedness cannot be clearly demonstrated for this group, one wonders whether the link between handedness and mathematical ability really exists. Furthermore, Benbow's study did find evidence for an excess of left-handers in those with superior verbal abilities, which would seem to pose a problem for the hormonal theory. However, Geschwind and Galaburda (1985*b*) have an answer: 'It could be the case that although growth of the left hemisphere is slowed to a greater extent in sinistrals than dextrals, it may attain a greater final size in sinistrals. This could occur when the growth period is prolonged, e.g. when the duration of pregnancy exceeds the average or when puberty is late, which would allow for further development in childhood' (p. 521).

Appraisal of the theory

Geschwind and Galaburda's theory has been extremely influential. In the short period since Geschwind and Behan's first report, numerous papers have appeared citing this work. Does it deserve the attention it has received? One reason it has generated such excitement is that it proposes a mechanism which could explain the sex differences that are observed in developmental disorders of spoken and written language. No other theory has adequately accounted for this major finding. However, the foundations of the hormonal theory are decidedly wobbly. Geschwind and Galaburda (1985*a,b,c*) stressed that much of the theory is speculative, but this does not justify their highly selective citation of relevant evidence. Small-scale studies and even anecdotal reports consistent with their position are given prominence, while substantial bodies of contrary work are ignored. When we are told that 'Left-handers of both sexes . . . often exhibit superior right-hemisphere functions' (p. 431), it is as if the large-scale studies reviewed in Chapter 6 never existed. In arguing for a link between learning disorders and handedness, the authors cite the studies by Geschwind and Behan (1982) and Schachter *et al.* (1987) to support their case, but fail to mention the extensive literature reviewed in Chapters 10 to 13. In comparison to other investigations, the studies that are cited are notably weak in terms of sampling and criteria used to identify dyslexia. The unprecedented finding by Geschwind and Behan of a rate of dyslexia 15 times higher in left-handers than in right-handers is so discrepant with other studies that it does more to cast doubt on the validity of their study than to convince one that an association exists.

Another problem with the hormonal theory is that it is hard to see what would constitute disproof. We have seen that the theory has been used to predict that left-handers will have both inferior and superior verbal abilities. Because the precise outcome depends on testosterone levels, sensitivity of target tissues to testosterone, timing and duration of hormonal influences, duration of pregnancy and age at puberty, almost any pattern of cognitive abilities can be explained in terms of the theory (see *e.g.* Geschwind and Galaburda 1985*b*, pp. 521–523).

15
CONCLUSIONS AND CLINICAL IMPLICATIONS

There is almost no pattern of cerebral lateralization or handedness that has not at some time been mooted as the cause or correlate of one kind of developmental disorder. Orton (1925) and Zangwill (1960) popularized the view that lack of strong cerebral lateralization was a factor in reading problems, whereas according to Levy (1976), bilateral language representation leads to good or average verbal skills but depressed non-verbal abilities. Dyslexia has in its time been thought to be characterized by mixed handedness (Orton 1937, Harris 1957), strong left-handedness (Geschwind and Behan 1982), strong right-handedness (Annett and Kilshaw 1984), and lack of strong right-handedness (Schachter et al. 1987).

I would like to suggest three ways in which some of this confusion could be resolved: (1) by being aware of methodological problems that bedevil handedness research and lead to spurious associations; (2) by adopting a theoretical perspective that distinguishes different reasons why handedness and disorder might be linked; and (3) by using assessment procedures that can distinguish between theories.

Methodological issues
Findings of excess non-right-handedness are robust for conditions in which there is evidence of underlying neurological damage: mental impairment, infantile autism and, to a lesser extent, epilepsy. When we turn to developmental disorders in which brain damage is not typically found, we find that despite the plethora of theories linking handedness and disorder, the evidence is weak and inconsistent.

The difficult but crucial issue for neuropsychologists to come to terms with is whether we are just misleading ourselves in holding on to the idea that laterality and the more specific developmental disorders, such as dyslexia or stuttering, are somehow linked. Those of a sceptical disposition will argue that we should follow the advice that Zeman (1967) gave about dyslexia 20 years ago: stop the relentless pursuit of statistical significance, and accept that a resoundingly negative answer has been given to the question of whether handedness and disorder are linked. Those with higher levels of credulity will argue that there are genuine links between disorder and handedness, but these are obscured by reliance on inappropriate ways of measuring handedness, and failure to distinguish subtypes of disorder.

Let us first consider the point of view of the sceptic. Occasional significant associations have been reported and need to be accounted for. Hardyck et al. (1976) blamed biased sampling in clinical studies. More recently, Soper et al. (1988) discussed the role of two further factors: publication bias, and spurious associations arising when samples are small and non-conservative statistical procedures are used.

Publication bias simply refers to the tendency of journals to favour papers that report significant rather than null results. Could it be that for every published paper reporting a significant difference at the 0.05 level, 19 studies that have found no difference go unpublished? If such a reporting bias operates, then techniques such as meta-analysis, which combine results from several published studies to test a hypothesis with a larger sample, will only make matters worse. Of course, publication bias is not specific to handedness research, but there is reason to believe that it might have an unduly strong effect in this field. Because left-handedness is rare relative to right-handedness, one needs large samples to estimate accurately the percentage of left-handers in a disordered group. If, despite having a small sample, we find a statistically significant excess of non-right-handers in a disordered group, we are likely to publish this finding, arguing that if the effect can be detected in such a small group, then it must be a real one. If, however, we obtain a null result with a small sample, we are more likely to be aware of the possibility of making a type II error (accepting the null hypothesis when a real difference exists), so the result goes unreported. A further factor which could enhance bias is the fact that handedness assessment by inventory is quick and inexpensive, so there is a tendency to include hand preference as a bonus factor in neuropsychological studies of disorder, even if it is not the major focus of interest. When data collection has involved little effort, null results are especially likely to be given little emphasis.

The second point raised by Soper *et al.* was that the odds of spurious association are high when contingency analysis is used with small samples, especially if subdivision of subjects into handedness groups is made *post hoc*. There is no agreed convention as to where cut-off points should be placed when dividing the continuum of handedness quotients into ranges. Suppose we had a five-item inventory, simply scored in terms of the number of items performed with the right hand. We could make a case for dividing the sample into strong right-handers (scoring 5) and the remainder (0 to 4), or for distinguishing the right-biased (scoring 3 to 5) from the left-biased (0 to 2), or for treating mixed handers (scoring 1 to 4) as a separate group, and so on. Indeed, there are few ways of dividing a distribution of laterality quotients into ranges that do not have some precedent in the literature. The problem is that the lack of an *a priori* rationale makes it easy to fall into the trap of deciding on cut-off selection only after scrutiny of the data. Indeed, some investigators are quite open about adopting this procedure, and it seems probable that in many studies cut-offs are determined by a trial and error procedure, even where this is not explicitly stated. However, to analyse data in this way is to contravene the underlying assumptions of statistical tests and makes interpretation of significance levels impossible because one is capitalizing on chance. This may sound like a purist's quibble, but the effects can be dramatic. To demonstrate this point, I simulated hand preference data from two groups sampled from populations with identical handedness distributions, and then scrutinized the distributions and placed cut-offs to form handedness categories that maximally differentiated the groups (Bishop 1990*a*). Given that there were no real differences between groups, by chance we should find that the odds of obtaining a significant association at the 0.05 level on a one-tailed test should be 1:9. In fact, with *post hoc* selection of cut-offs, and a simulated sample size of 50 per group, it was possible to increase this to 1:3 for a five-item inventory, and 2:3 for a nine-item inventory. This simulation demonstrated that we adopt *post hoc* classification procedures at our peril. Failure to recognize this is probably the single most important source of non-replicable findings in this field.

We can see, then, that the sceptic has a strong armamentarium in support of the view that reported links between handedness and specific developmental disorder are spurious. Is there anything to be said in favour of continuing to search for meaningful relationships? There is no doubt that there is considerable reluctance to abandon theories linking laterality and developmental disorder. Although in part this perseverance may simply be a function of human perversity, the fact remains that there are such limitations to our diagnostic procedures and assessment methods that we cannot be said to have adequately evaluated all the theoretical possibilities. Research has been limited by undue emphasis on cerebral lateralization processes and gross categorization of disorders.

A further problem is that many studies that are carried out are so designed that they could not detect an effect of interest even if it were there. Left-handers are a minority: as Galaburda (1987) pointed out, unless a disorder is associated with a dramatic increase in the frequency of left-handedness, large samples will be needed to detect effects of interest. The necessary sample size to demonstrate an effect of a given magnitude can easily be calculated (Cohen 1977), but this is seldom done. Indeed, it is unusual for investigators to attempt to estimate the size of effect that would be predicted from their theory. Before concluding that a null result indicates a lack of association, we do need to check whether with a given sample size the statistical test was powerful enough to have detected an association had one existed. For example, where links between abnormal conditions and handedness have been claimed, it is unusual to find more than a two-fold increase in the proportion of left-handers. Assuming a rate of 10 per cent left-handedness in a control group and 20 per cent in a disordered group, we can use Cohen's power tables to show that we would need a sample of around 435 subjects to have a three in four chance of rejecting the null hypothesis at the 0.05 level.

Theoretical perspective

If an increase in non-right-handedness is suspected in a disordered population, then there are at least three possibilities to be considered. (1) Hand preference may be an indication of a constitutional pattern of cerebral lateralization that is disadvantageous for the development of certain abilities. (2) Focal brain pathology may have caused impaired function of one side, leading to an increased rate of pathological left-handedness. (3) Hand preference may be random. This could correspond to an extreme developmental delay, or might be a deviant phenomenon arising as a consequence of brain damage, not corresponding to any normal stage of development.

Orton's influence has been so powerful that research in this field has concentrated overwhelmingly on the first of these possibilities. Yet, the literature reviewed in Chapters 10 to 13 shows that there is little empirical support for atypical cerebral lateralization as a factor causing learning disabilities. Only over the past 10 years have studies been carried out which indicate that where non-right-handedness is associated with disorder (*i.e.* in autistic and mentally handicapped individuals), the second two explanations are likely to be far more important. They should also be considered in less extreme cases.

Assessment procedures
In practice, handedness inventories—or even binary categorization (left/right) of handedness for writing—have been the measures used in research studies and clinical practice when investigating developmental disorders. The disadvantages of such methods were reviewed in Chapter 5. The most severe drawback of an inventory is that it does not provide information that allows us to distinguish between different theoretical explanations of disorder.

It is common to find the paediatric neurologist or psychologist recording hand preference in the course of an examination, but it is unclear what is gained by this exercise. We assess a child and find he or she has a specific reading problem and is left-handed. How does this latter piece of information affect our diagnosis or management? The answer is not at all. There is no good reason for basing diagnostic or treatment decisions on a child's handedness. The only clinical situation that I can think of where information about an individual's hand preference should be taken into account is when contemplating neurosurgery, where left- or mixed handedness is an indication that atypical cerebral lateralization may be expected, and a Wada test may be advisable to establish the localization of language functions before surgery. In other cases, it may be of some use to keep a record of hand preference for research purposes, but this information on its own serves little purpose in clinical evaluation of the individual.

Supplementing observation of writing hand with longer preference inventories, or with information about familial handedness or writing posture, is not, in my opinion, the way forward. Much more useful would be the inclusion of measures of within-task stability of hand preference, and hand proficiency.

Assessment of within-task stability of preference is essential for identifying ambiguous as opposed to mixed handedness. As discussed in Chapters 4 and 5, most studies measure only between-task consistency of hand preferences on a single occasion, and so confound stable, mature mixed handedness with random preference that alters from one occasion to another. The work of Soper and his colleagues, discussed in Chapters 7 and 10, attests to the importance of assessing within-task stability of preference and has helped clarify findings on hand preference in mentally retarded and autistic children. This work needs to be extended to take into account the possibility of ambiguous handedness in other disordered groups, and to document the normal developmental progression from ambiguous handedness to stable hand preference.

Until more normative data are available, the assessment procedures used by Soper *et al.* provide the best method we have for evaluating ambiguous handedness. Details of these are given in the Appendix.

Quantitative assessment of hand function is necessary to establish whether there is general motor impairment, lateralized impairment, or normal function. General motor impairment can be found when there are no hard neurological signs. Poor performance on motor tasks is a common observation in children with specific disorders of written and spoken language and appears to be more a sign of neurodevelopmental immaturity than of brain damage (Johnston *et al.* 1981, Bishop and Edmundson 1987). In contrast, when focal pathological processes affect handedness we expect to find disproportionate impairment of the non-preferred hand. Use of this approach in the study of developmental disorders has been discussed in detail in Chapters 7 and 12.

Clinical application of these research findings is in its infancy. We still have a long way to go before we have adequate normative developmental data to apply the results of such studies to the assessment of individual children. However, a start has been made. The Henderson Revision of the Test of Motor Impairment (Stott *et al.* 1984) is a recently standardized procedure for 5- to 11-year-olds, specifically designed to identify impairment (rather than to quantify the whole range of performance). It includes such activities as bead-threading, pegboard dexterity and drawing between guidelines, depending on the age of the child. The main drawbacks to using this test are practical. The space requirements for the gross motor items can be difficult to meet, it takes time to prepare the room (by applying masking tape to the floor at carefully measured intervals), and the test is not cheap. In contrast, the motor coordination tests described by Denckla (1974) require little apparatus and are quick and easy to apply in clinical settings. Normative data on these tasks are reproduced in the Appendix.

Although we need more validation studies, speeded tasks appear to be the most useful for detecting neuromotor immaturity (Johnston *et al.* 1981). Bishop (1984) found that there were differences between motor tasks in their ability to show evidence of pathological left-handedness in a population, but the reasons for this were unclear. Norms are not available on experimental tests such as the square-tracing task used by Bishop (1980*b*), except for a very restricted age range. However, the Test for Motor Impairment (Henderson Revision) contains some manual dexterity tests which specify the normal range of performance for both preferred and non-preferred hands, which could prove useful for investigating lateralized impairment.

Peters (1988) has argued persuasively in favour of including measures of foot performance in neuropsychological assessment. He contends that there are two features which make foot performance a particularly useful measure. First, it gives an index of motor laterality that is relatively uncontaminated by practice. Second, the lower limb, he argues, is more readily affected by neurological impairment than the upper limb, and so foot performance can provide a particularly sensitive index of minor degrees of neurological impairment. His evidence for this latter point is somewhat anecdotal (including the observation that when drunk one can play the piano but not walk in a straight line), but this is an interesting suggestion which seems worth pursuing. We have few normative data on foot proficiency in children or adults, but Denckla has provided some results which are given in the Appendix.

Unlike Zeman (1967), I do not feel that research on laterality and developmental disorders should be abandoned. However, more headway might be made if we started out by formulating a theoretical model of the types of relationships we might expect to find, using this to guide the measures we adopt. For instance, rather than asking, 'Is left-handedness associated with reading problems?' and then brooding over how to measure handedness, we should consider, 'Why might left-handedness be associated with reading problems?' When we adopt this approach we find that there are several different reasons why we might predict such a link, and these can then be distinguished by different measurement techniques.

APPENDIX

A SELECTION OF ASSESSMENT PROCEDURES

Hand preference inventories
Hand preference can indicate whether an individual is likely to have atypical cerebral language lateralization. However, the relationship between handedness and cerebral lateralization is complex (see Chapter 2), and hand preference alone is unlikely to provide important clinical information in individual cases, except where neurosurgery is contemplated. Furthermore, relationships between atypical hand preference and developmental disorders are weak (see Chapter 15). Nevertheless, it is worth recording hand preference systematically, as this information may be of use in group studies. The three hand-preference inventories given here (Figs. A.1–A.3) are those most commonly used in research studies. When used with adults, they are given as questionnaires. Children with a mental age below 9 years may have difficulty in reading the instructions and/or in distinguishing left and right. In such cases, the child should be observed carrying out or miming each activity. Other inventories, designed specifically with children in mind, have been published by Harris (1958) and Auzias (1984).

Measures of inter-item stability of hand preference
Ambiguous handedness, *i.e.* a tendency to shift hand preference *within* a given activity, has been shown to be common in cases of mental impairment and autism (see Chapters 9 and 10), although it remains unclear whether this represents a form of developmental delay, or whether it is a pathological condition.

The distinction between ambiguous handedness and mixed handedness is seldom made clinically. Systematic normative studies of intra-item stability of hand preference have yet to be conducted, so we are forced to rely on limited research data to give guidelines for identifying children who are abnormal in changing hand preference from trial to trial on a given activity.

Bruml (1972) reported data on children, aged 5, 8 and 10 years, given a set of unimanual tasks twice within one session and twice again one week later. Retesting after such an interval is seldom practical in clinical settings, but it is reasonable to assume that a child should be at least as consistent as Bruml's subjects if given four trials (separated by other activities) within one session. Results may then be interpreted relative to Table A.I.

TEST FOR HANDEDNESS

Answer the following questions carefully. Imagine yourself performing the activity described before answering each question. Answer by drawing a circle around the appropriate set of letters appearing to the left of each question whose meaning is:

Ra = right hand always   Lm = left hand most of the time
Rm = right hand most of the time   La = left hand always
E = both hands equally often   X = do not know which hand

(1) Ra Rm E Lm La X: is used to write with
(2) Ra Rm E Lm La X: to hold nail when hammering
(3) Ra Rm E Lm La X: to throw a ball
(4) Ra Rm E Lm La X: to hold bottle when removing top
(5) Ra Rm E Lm La X: is used to draw with
(6) Ra Rm E Lm La X: to hold potato when peeling
(7) Ra Rm E Lm La X: to hold pitcher when pouring out of it
(8) Ra Rm E Lm La X: to hold scissors when cutting
(9) Ra Rm E Lm La X: to hold knife when cutting food
(10) Ra Rm E Lm La X: to hold needle when threading
(11) Ra Rm E Lm La X: to hold glass when drinking
(12) Ra Rm E Lm La X: to hold toothbrush when brushing teeth
(13) Ra Rm E Lm La X: to hold dish when wiping
(14) Ra Rm E Lm La X: holds tennis racket when playing

Fig. A.1. Crovitz and Zener (1962) test for handedness.
Every item is scored on a five-point scale. On items 1, 3, 5, 7, 8, 9, 11, 12 and 14, Ra is scored '1'; Rm, '2'; E, '3'; Lm, '4'; and La, '5'. All other items (2, 4, 6, 10, 13) are scored in the reverse fashion. Items marked X are prorated. The highest possible right-handed score is 14, and the highest left-handed score is 70.

HANDEDNESS RESEARCH

Name .... Age ...... Sex ......

Were you one of twins (or triplets, etc.) at birth or were you single born?
....

*Please indicate which hand you habitually use for each of the following activities by writing R (for right), L (for left), E (for either).

Which hand do you use:
1. To write a letter legibly?
2. To throw a ball to hit a target?
3. To hold a racket in tennis, squash or badminton?
4. To hold a match whilst striking it?
5. To cut with scissors?
6. To guide a thread through the eye of a needle (or guide needle on to thread)?
7. At the top of a broom while sweeping?
8. At the top of a shovel when moving sand?
9. To deal playing cards?
10. To hammer a nail into wood?
11. To hold a toothbrush while cleaning your teeth?
12. To unscrew the lid of a jar?

If you use the *right hand for all of these actions*, are there any one-handed actions for which you use the *left hand*? Please record them here ....
....
If you use the *left hand for all of these actions*, are there any one-handed actions for which you use the *right hand*? Please record them here ....
....

*To discourage 'E' responses, this sentence may be omitted.

Fig. A.2. Handedness research questionnaire of Annett (1970a).

EDINBURGH HANDEDNESS INVENTORY

Surname . . . .   Given Names . . . .

Date of Birth . . . .   Sex . . . .

Please indicate your preferences in the use of hands in the following activities *by putting + in the appropriate column*. Where the preference is so strong that you would never try to use the other hand unless absolutely forced to, *put ++*. If in any case you are really indifferent, *put + in both columns*.

Some of the activities require both hands. In these cases the part of the task, or object, for which hand preference is wanted is indicated in brackets.

Please try to answer all the questions, and only leave a blank if you have no experience at all of the object or task.

		Left	Right
1	Writing		
2	Drawing		
3	Throwing		
4	Scissors		
5	Toothbrush		
6	Knife (without fork)		
7	Spoon		
8	Broom (upper hand)		
9	Striking match (match)		
10	Opening box (lid)		
i	Which foot do you prefer to kick with?		
ii	Which eye do you use when using only one?		

Fig. A.3. Edinburgh Handedness Inventory (adapted from Oldfield 1971).

TABLE A.1
Age by which 90 per cent of children show consistent hand preference on four trials*

Task	Age
Drawing	5 years
Hand-clasping	5 years
Snapping fingers	5 years
Throwing a ball	8 years
Eating with fingers	10 years
Clapping examiner's palm	10 years
Pointing	10 years

*Based on data from Bruml (1972).

Soper *et al.* (1987) used a handedness test in which eight items were administered three times, giving a total of 24 responses. Each stimulus was presented with both hands along the midline, with minimal use of speech. The items were: (a) eating with a spoon; (b) drinking from a cup, at least one quarter full of water; (c) brushing the teeth with a toothbrush; (d) drawing with a crayon on a piece of paper; (e) throwing a ball; (f) hammering the table with a plastic hammer; (g) picking up a sweet; and (h) picking up a coin (dime). To minimize perseverative responding, items were presented in quasi-random order. The index of interest is to what extent the child is inconsistent within a test item, *i.e.* responding with the left hand on some trials and with the right hand on others. Soper *et al.* noted that only two out of 47 normal 5-year-olds were inconsistent in hand preference on three items, and none was inconsistent for more items than this. Thus, in children aged 5 years or over, if there are three or more items where hand preference changes from trial to trial, this may be regarded as abnormal.

Measures of absolute hand/foot skill
A measure of absolute level of motor skill can help identify the child whose motor development is generally delayed, with poor performance on both sides, and is also useful in providing evidence of lateralized impairment (see Chapter 7).

Motor coordination tests
The data reported here are taken from Denckla's (1973, 1974) study of speeded performance by right-handed 5- to 10-year-old children on a range of motor coordination tests commonly used by neurologists. Rudel *et al.* (1984) subsequently showed that performance of the preferred and non-preferred hands by left-handed children is comparable to that seen in right-handers; thus data are given here for preferred and non-preferred hands and can be applied to either right- or left-handers. Only those tests found to have acceptable levels of test–retest reliability will be considered here.

GENERAL INSTRUCTIONS
The only equipment required is a stopwatch. The child is seated, facing the

TABLE A.II
Time (secs.) to perform 20 repetitive finger movements*

Age	Boys Preferred Mean	SD	Boys Non-preferred Mean	SD	Girls Preferred Mean	SD	Girls Non-preferred Mean	SD
5 years	7.30	1.08	7.95	1.00	7.85	1.78	8.56	1.86
6 years	6.69	0.82	7.44	0.91	6.51	1.01	7.15	0.97
7 years	5.94	0.81	6.60	0.83	5.99	0.70	6.83	0.82
8 years	5.99	0.98	6.31	0.64	5.50	0.80	6.14	0.88
9 years	5.97	0.72	6.35	1.23	5.84	1.25	6.43	0.90
10 years	5.55	1.22	6.09	1.11	5.77	1.38	6.27	1.79

*Data from Denckla (1973).

TABLE A.III
Time (secs.) to perform 20 successive finger movements*

Age	Boys Preferred Mean	SD	Boys Non-preferred Mean	SD	Girls Preferred Mean	SD	Girls Non-preferred Mean	SD
5 years	16.70	4.08	16.86	5.32	14.40	2.94	14.33	2.20
6 years	14.48	3.23	14.26	2.66	13.13	2.61	13.18	3.21
7 years	12.22	2.92	12.60	3.05	11.29	3.18	11.68	3.30
8 years	10.41	2.03	10.84	2.70	9.25	2.69	9.89	2.76
9 years	10.45	2.95	10.94	3.82	9.59	2.10	9.84	2.20
10 years	10.22	2.74	10.19	2.65	8.41	2.37	7.99	2.11

*Data from Denckla (1973).

examiner. Brief practice is allowed, untimed, and without specifying which side the child should try first. No effort is made during practice or timed trials to control whether the child looks at the performing limb, or whether vocalization or counting is engaged in. After practice with each side, the examiner instructs the child to begin the task and to keep repeating it as fast as possible until told to stop. The child performs first with the preferred side and then with the non-preferred side, and the time taken to perform 20 movements is recorded for each side.

REPETITIVE FINGER MOVEMENTS

The child is told, 'When I say "go", tap your pointer (index finger) and thumb together as fast as you can till I stop you'. The stopwatch is started on the second movement (not from "go"), and thus 21 taps are performed per trial. The normative data are shown in Table A.II.

Reliability. Denckla (1973) retested 20 right-handed children (10 boys, 10 girls) after a three-week interval, and obtained a correlation of 0.69 for the right hand and 0.68 for the left.

TABLE A.IV
Time (secs.) to perform 20 arm pronation–supination movements*

Age	Boys				Girls			
	Preferred		Non-preferred		Preferred		Non-preferred	
	Mean	SD	Mean	SD	Mean	SD	Mean	SD
5 years	9.32	1.67	9.35	1.64	9.57	1.56	10.28	1.61
6 years	8.37	1.47	8.76	1.17	9.38	1.51	9.02	1.26
7 years	8.59	1.90	8.87	1.93	7.69	0.88	7.54	1.01
8 years	6.84	1.43	7.27	1.08	7.29	1.33	7.69	1.15
9 years	7.59	1.91	7.66	1.76	6.76	1.30	7.05	1.19
10 years	7.09	1.54	7.41	1.73	7.05	1.36	7.04	1.55

*Data from Denckla (1973).

TABLE A.V
Time (secs.) to perform 20 heel–toe alternating movements*

Age	Boys				Girls			
	Preferred		Non-preferred		Preferred		Non-preferred	
	Mean	SD	Mean	SD	Mean	SD	Mean	SD
5 years	15.03	3.75	14.50	3.40	12.71	4.07	13.16	3.94
6 years	12.16	1.49	12.93	3.45	11.75	3.44	12.36	4.11
7 years	10.23	2.27	11.70	2.90	9.22	3.00	9.71	3.14
8 years	9.44	2.36	10.14	2.74	8.71	2.06	8.43	1.72
9 years	9.21	1.84	9.84	2.25	7.44	1.02	8.11	2.33
10 years	8.07	1.56	8.61	1.57	6.90	1.57	7.00	1.49

*Data from Denckla (1973).

SUCCESSIVE FINGER MOVEMENTS

The examiner demonstrates opposition of each finger to the thumb in the sequence: index, middle, ring, little finger. The instruction is given, 'When I say "go", make each finger march past the thumb and tap it in turn; don't go backwards, keep marching from pointer to "pinkie" (little finger) till I stop you'. The 20 movements that are timed comprise five repeats of this sequence; again, the stopwatch is started from the second set, and so six sets of successive taps are performed. Normative data are shown in Table A.III.

Reliability. Correlations at retest were 0.78 (right hand) and 0.81 (left hand).

ARM PRONATION–SUPINATION

This test involves alternating hand (with arm) pronation–supination. Normative data are given in Table A.IV.

Reliability. Denckla (1974) retested 60 right-handed children (30 boys, 30 girls) after a three- to five-week interval, obtaining correlations of 0.64 for the right arm and 0.68 for the left.

HEEL–TOE ALTERNATING MOVEMENTS

The heel and toes alternately make contact with the floor in a rocking motion. Normative data are given in Table A.V.

Reliability. Correlations obtained after retesting as above were 0.65 for the right foot and 0.57 for the left.

The Purdue pegboard*

This test was originally designed for the selection of factory workers, but has been found useful in the assessment of motor coordination in children.

The pegboard consists of two parallel rows of 25 holes. The child is given practice in taking pegs from a cup in the top of the board and placing them as rapidly as possible into one of the rows. Once the child demonstrates understanding, the examiner explains that on the word "begin" the child should place as many pegs as possible into one of the rows in the allotted time. Only one peg should be picked up at a time. If a peg is dropped, it should be ignored and the child should return to the cup for another. A stopwatch is used and the total number of pegs placed in the holes during a 30-second period is recorded. The trial is restarted if the child picks up two pegs at once. The pegs are allowed to remain in the holes and the same procedure is repeated with the non-preferred hand. (There are two further stages to the test, in which the child is required to (i) place pegs in the pegboard using both hands together, and (ii) assemble pegs with washers and collars. These will not be considered here.)

The normative data given in Table A.VI are taken from a report by Gardner and Broman (1979). They calculated means and standard deviations for children grouped in six-month age-bands. Here, statistics have been recomputed for one-year age-bands to give more reliable estimates.

Measures of relative hand skill

Annett has used difference in peg-moving time for the two hands as an indirect index of underlying genotype in studies of genetic aspects of handedness (see Chapter 3) and to look at handedness correlates of intellectual aptitude and disability (see Chapters 11 and 14). Relative hand skill is unlikely to be of use in clinical assessment of *individuals*, because the relationship with postulated genotype is not strong enough for accurate classification of individuals. However, relative hand skill can be important when comparing different clinical *groups*.

Annett's peg-moving task
APPARATUS

The peg-moving apparatus (see Fig. 5.6, p. 80) is not commercially available, but is easily constructed. Figure A.4 shows the dimensions of the peg-board. The holes

---

*Suppliers: UK—Campden Instruments Ltd., 186 Campden Hill Road, London W8 7TH (Tel: 071 727 3437; Fax: 071 229 3442). USA—Lafayette Instrument Co., P.O. Box 5729, 3700 Sagamore Parkway North, Lafayette, IN 47903 (Tel: 317 423 1509; Fax: 317 423 4111).

TABLE A.VI
Number of pegs moved on the Purdue pegboard (unimanual trials)*

| Age | \multicolumn{5}{c}{Boys} | \multicolumn{5}{c}{Girls} |
	N	Preferred Mean	SD	Non-preferred Mean	SD	N	Preferred Mean	SD	Non-preferred Mean	SD
5 years	60	9.63	1.65	8.62	1.63	60	9.65	1.62	8.82	1.47
6 years	60	10.67	1.72	9.65	2.02	60	11.65	1.49	10.35	1.41
7 years	60	11.87	1.78	11.12	1.65	60	12.25	1.56	10.98	1.96
8 years	60	13.30	1.96	12.37	1.65	60	13.42	1.70	12.17	1.30
9 years	60	13.60	1.73	12.65	1.80	60	13.88	1.69	12.43	1.95
10 years	60	14.38	1.70	13.38	1.81	60	15.30	1.50	13.42	1.32
11 years	60	14.88	1.69	13.97	1.75	60	15.30	1.81	13.92	1.89
12 years	60	15.10	2.30	13.83	2.15	60	15.48	1.76	14.13	1.65
13 years	70	15.02	1.80	13.99	1.75	72	15.47	1.61	14.13	1.52
14 years	60	15.18	1.51	14.37	1.56	60	16.18	1.71	14.88	1.67
15 years	53	15.36	1.52	14.62	1.52	59	16.54	1.64	15.10	1.73

*Data from Gardner and Broman (1979).

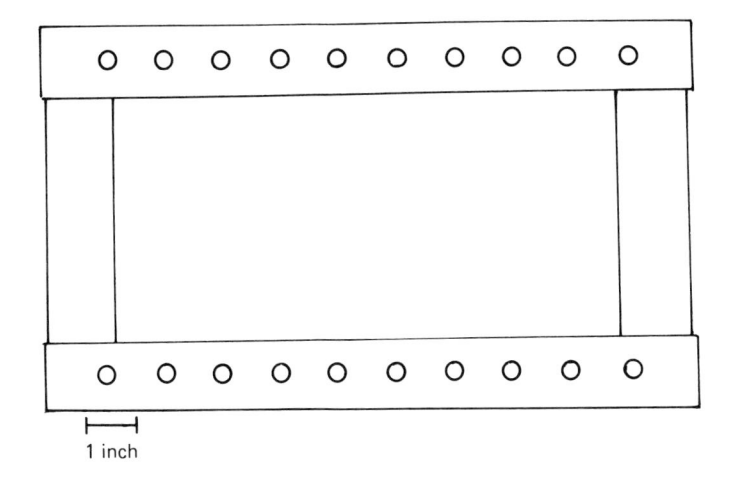

Fig. A.4. Dimensions of Annett's peg-moving apparatus (see Fig. 5.6, p. 80) (1 inch ≈ 2.5cm). (Reprinted from Annett 1985, p. 209.)

are ½ inch (1.3cm) in diameter, ⅞ inch (2.2cm) deep and 1 inch (2.5cm) apart. The 10 pegs are made from ⅜ inch (1.0cm) dowelling rod, and are 2 inches (5.1cm) long.

PROCEDURE

The pegboard is placed on a table of convenient height for the standing subject. The pegs are always moved from right to left by the right hand, and from left to right by the left hand. They are picked up and placed one by one. If the subject grasps two at once or drops a peg the trial must be restarted. The apparatus is

TABLE A.VII
Left–right peg-moving time (secs.)*

Sample	Males			Females		
	N	Mean	SD	N	Mean	SD
Schoolchildren aged from 6 to 15 years	122	0.71	1.31	156	1.20	1.27
Secondary schoolchildren and adults	617	0.64	0.84	863	0.79	0.88

*Data from Annett and Kilshaw (1983).

constructed so that the examiner can hold on to the recessed side of the pegboard to steady it while the subject moves the pegs.

The trial consists of moving the 10 pegs from the back row to the front. Performance is timed (using a stopwatch) from touching the first peg to releasing the last. Trials are made by the two hands alternately. Annett's norms are based on the mean of five trials per hand, except for very young children who are given three trials per hand.

NORMATIVE DATA

Absolute level of performance by the two hands increases steadily with age (see Annett 1970*b*), but the difference between the two hands, as reported by Annett and Kilshaw (1983) and shown in Table A.VII, is relatively constant.

Reliability. Annett *et al.* (1974) reported data on test–retest reliability for 53 adult students: the correlation between mean peg-moving times, measured on two occasions separated by an interval of six to 18 months, was 0.69.

Other tests of relative motor skill
Denckla (1974) reported data on left–right differences on the motor coordination tasks described above. However, it is not recommended that these be used as normative data because her sample was selected for both ability and handedness.

Tapley and Bryden (1985) described a group test that could be used to assess relative performance of the two hands. However, it has the disadvantage that it requires subjects to hold a pen or stylus, so that differential performance of the two sides is likely to be strongly influenced by practice in writing.

REFERENCES

Ajersch, M.K., Milner, B. (1983) 'Handwriting posture as related to cerebral speech lateralization, sex, and writing hand.' *Human Neurobiology*, **2**, 143–145.

Albrecht, H., Dunnett, S.C. (1971) *Chimpanzees in Western Africa*. Munich: Piper.

Alekoumbides, A. (1978) 'Hemispheric dominance for language: quantitative aspects.' *Acta Neurologica Scandinavica*, **57**, 97–140.

Anderson, E.M., Spain, B. (1977) *The Child with Spina Bifida*. London: Methuen.

Andrews, G., Harris, M. (1964) *The Syndrome of Stuttering. Clinics in Developmental Medicine, No. 17*. London: The Spastics Society with Heinemann Medical.

—— Quinn, P.T., Sorby, W.A. (1972) 'Stuttering: an investigation into cerebral dominance for speech.' *Journal of Neurology, Neurosurgery and Psychiatry*, **35**, 414–418.

Annett, M. (1970a) 'A classification of hand preference by association analysis.' *British Journal of Psychology*, **61**, 303–321.

—— (1970b) 'The growth of manual preference and speed.' *British Journal of Psychology*, **61**, 545–558.

—— (1975) 'Hand preference and the laterality of cerebral speech.' *Cortex*, **11**, 305–328.

—— (1976) 'A co-ordination of hand preference and skill replicated.' *British Journal of Psychology*, **67**, 587–592.

—— (1978) 'Genetic and nongenetic influences on handedness.' *Behaviour Genetics*, **8**, 227–249.

—— (1985) *Left, Right, Hand and Brain: the Right Shift Theory*. Hillsdale, NJ: Erlbaum.

—— (1987) 'Comments on Tambs, Magnus, and Berg: Twinning and the right-shift theory of handedness.' *Perceptual and Motor Skills*, **64**, 201–202.

—— Kilshaw, D. (1982) 'Mathematical ability and lateral asymmetry.' *Cortex*, **18**, 547–568.

—— —— (1983) 'Right and left hand skill. II: Estimating the parameters of the distribution of L-R differences in males and females.' *British Journal of Psychology*, **74**, 269–283.

—— —— (1984) 'Lateral preference and skill in dyslexics: implications of the right shift theory.' *Journal of Child Psychology and Psychiatry*, **25**, 357–377.

—— Manning, M. (1989) 'The disadvantages of dextrality for intelligence.' *British Journal of Psychology*, **80**, 213–226.

—— Turner, A. (1974) 'Laterality and the growth of intellectual abilities.' *British Journal of Educational Psychology*, **44**, 37–46.

—— Hudson, P.T., Turner, A. (1974) 'The reliability of differences between the hands in motor skill.' *Neuropsychologia*, **12**, 527–531.

Aram, D.M., Ekelman, B.L., Satz, P. (1986) 'Trophic changes following early unilateral injury to the brain.' *Developmental Medicine and Child Neurology*, **28**, 165–170.

Ardila, A., Ardila, O., Bryden, M.P., Ostrosky, F., Rosselli, M., Steenhuis, R. (1989) 'Effects of cultural background and education on handedness.' *Neuropsychologia*, **27**, 893–897.

Auzias, M. (1984) *Enfants Gauchers, Enfants Droitiers*. 2nd Edn. Neuchatel: Delachaux et Niestle.

Aylward, E.H. (1984) 'Lateral asymmetry in subgroups of dyslexic children.' *Brain and Language*, **22**, 221–231.

Baddeley, A.D., Logie, R.H., Ellis, N.C. (1988) 'Characteristics of developmental dyslexia.' *Cognition*, **2**, 191–228.

Bailey, R.E. (1972) *Maye's Midwifery, 8th Edn*. London: Baillière Tindall.

Baird, H.W., Gordon, E.C. (Eds.) (1983) *Neurological Evaluation of Infants and Children*. London: S.I.M.P. with Heinemann Medical; Philadelphia: J.B. Lippincott.

Bakan, P. (1971) 'Left-handedness and birth order.' *Nature*, **229**, 195.

—— Dibb, G., Reed, P. (1973) 'Handedness and birth stress.' *Neuropsychologia*, **11**, 363–366.

Bakare, C.G.M. (1974) 'The development of laterality and right–left discrimination in Nigerian children.' *In*: Dawson, J.L.M., Lonner, W.J. (Eds.) *Readings in Cross-Cultural Psychology*. Hong Kong: Hong Kong University Press. (pp. 150–166)

Ballard, P.B. (1911–2) 'Sinistrality and speech.' *Journal of Experimental Pedagogy*, **1**, 298–310.

Balow, I.H. (1963) 'Lateral dominance characteristics and reading achievement in the first grade.' *Journal of Psychology*, **55**, 323–328.

Barnsley, R.H., Rabinovitch, M.S. (1970) 'Handedness: proficiency versus stated preference.' *Perceptual and Motor Skills*, **30**, 343–362.

Barry, R.J., James, A.L. (1978) 'Handedness in autistics, retardates, and normals of a wide age range.' *Journal of Autism and Childhood Schizophrenia*, **8**, 314–323.

Bates, E., O'Connell, B., Vaid, J., Sledge, P., Oakes, L. (1986) 'Language and hand preference in early development.' *Developmental Neuropsychology*, **2**, 1–15.
Batheja, M., McManus, I.C. (1985) 'Handedness in the mentally handicapped.' *Developmental Medicine and Child Neurology*, **27**, 63–68.
Beckman, L., Elston, R. (1962) 'Data on bilateral variation in man: handedness, hand clasping and arm folding in Swedes.' *Human Biology*, **34**, 99–103.
Beecher, M.D., Petersen, M.R., Zoloth, S.R., Moody, D.B., Stebbins, W.C. (1979) 'Perception of conspecific vocalizations by Japanese macaques: evidence for selective attention and neural lateralization.' *Brain, Behavior and Evolution*, **16**, 443–460.
Belmont, L., Birch, H.G. (1963) 'Lateral dominance and right–left awareness in normal children.' *Child Development*, **34**, 257–270.
—— —— (1965) 'Lateral dominance, lateral awareness, and reading disability.' *Child Development*, **36**, 57–72.
Benbow, C.P. (1986) 'Physiological correlates of extreme intellectual precocity.' *Neuropsychologia*, **24**, 719–725.
—— (1988) 'Sex differences in mathematical reasoning ability in intellectually talented preadolescents: their nature, effects, and possible causes.' *Behavioral and Brain Sciences*, **11**, 169–232.
Benson, R.C. (1983) *Handbook of Obstetrics and Gynecology*. Los Altos, CA: Lange Medical.
Bergström, K., Bille, B., Rasmussen, F. (1984) 'Computed tomography of the brain in children with minor neurodevelopmental disorders.' *Neuropediatrics*, **15**, 115–119.
Berker, E.A., Berker, A.H., Smith, A. (1986) 'Translation of Broca's 1865 report.' *Archives of Neurology*, **43**, 1065–1072.
Berlin, C.I. (1977) 'Hemispheric asymmetry in auditory tasks.' *In:* Harnad, S., Doty, R., Goldstein, L., Jaynes, J., Krauthamer, G. (Eds.) *Lateralization in the Nervous System*. New York: Academic Press. (pp. 303–323)
Best, C.T. (1988) 'The emergence of cerebral asymmetries in early human development: a literature review and a neuroembryological model.' *In:* Molfese, D.L., Segalowitz, S.J. (Eds.) *Brain Lateralization in Children: Developmental Implications*. New York: Guilford Press. (pp. 5–34)
Bettman, J.W., Stern, E.L., Whitsell, L.J., Gofman, H.F. (1967) 'Cerebral dominance in developmental dyslexia.' *Archives of Ophthalmology*, **78**, 722–729.
Bingley-Wennström, T. (1958) 'Mental symptoms in temporal lobe epilepsy and temporal lobe gliomas: with reference to laterality of lesion and the relationship between handedness and brainedness.' *Acta Psychiatrica et Neurologica Scandinavica*, Suppl. 120.
Bishop, D.V.M. (1980a) 'Measuring familial sinistrality.' *Cortex*, **16**, 311–313.
—— (1980b) 'Handedness, clumsiness and cognitive ability.' *Developmental Medicine and Child Neurology*, **22**, 569–579.
—— (1981) 'Plasticity and specificity of language localization in the developing brain.' *Developmental Medicine and Child Neurology*, **23**, 251–255.
—— (1983) 'How sinister is sinistrality?' *Journal of the Royal College of Physicians of London*, **17**, 161–172.
—— (1984) 'Using non-preferred hand skill to investigate pathological left-handedness in an unselected population.' *Developmental Medicine and Child Neurology*, **26**, 214–226.
—— (1986) 'Is there a link between handedness and hypersensitivity?' *Cortex*, **22**, 289–296.
—— (1987) 'The causes of specific developmental language disorder ("developmental dysphasia").' *Journal of Child Psychology and Psychiatry*, **28**, 1–8.
—— (1988) 'Language development after focal brain damage.' *In:* Bishop, D.V.M., Mogford, K. (Eds.) *Language Development in Exceptional Circumstances*. Edinburgh: Churchill Livingstone. (pp. 203–219)
—— (1989a) 'Does hand proficiency determine hand preference?' *British Journal of Psychology*, **80**, 191–199.
—— (1989b) 'Quantitative aspects of specific developmental language disorders.' *In:* Munsat, T. (Ed.) *Quantification of Neurologic Deficit*. Boston: Butterworths. (pp. 327–344.)
—— (1989c) 'Unfixed reference, monocular occlusion, and developmental dyslexia—a critique.' *British Journal of Ophthalmology*, **73**, 209–215.
—— (1990a) 'How to increase your chances of obtaining a significant association between handedness and disorder.' *Journal of Clinical and Experimental Neuropsychology*, **12**, 786–790.
—— (1990b) 'Handedness, clumsiness and developmental language disorders.' *Neuropsychologia*, **28**, 681–690.
—— (1990c) 'On the futility of using familial sinistrality to subclassify handedness groups.' *Cortex*, **26**, 153–155.

—— Adams, C. (1990) 'A prospective study of the relationship between specific language impairment, phonological disorders and reading retardation.' *Journal of Child Psychology and Psychiatry*. (*In press*.)
—— Butterworth, G.E. (1980) 'Verbal-performance discrepancies: relationship to birth risk and specific reading retardation.' *Cortex*, **16**, 375–390.
—— Edmundson, A. (1987) 'Specific language impairment as a maturational lag: evidence from longitudinal data on language and motor development.' *Developmental Medicine and Child Neurology*, **29**, 442–459.
—— Rosenbloom, L. (1987) 'Classification of childhood language disorders.' *In:* Yule, W., Rutter, M. (Eds.) *Language Development and Disorders. Clinics in Developmental Medicine No. 101/102.* London: Mac Keith Press with Blackwell Scientific; Philadelphia: Lippincott. (pp. 16–41.)
—— Jancey, C., Steel, A.M. (1979) 'Orthoptic status and reading disability.' *Cortex*, **15**, 659–666.
Blau, A. (1946) *The Master Hand. American Orthopsychiatric Association Research Monographs, No. 5.* New York: A.O.A.
Blood, G.W. (1985) 'Laterality differences in child stutterers: heterogeneity, severity, and statistical differences.' *Journal of Speech and Hearing Disorders*, **50**, 66–72.
—— Blood, I.M. (1989a) 'Laterality preferences in adult female and male stutterers.' *Journal of Fluency Disorders*, **14**, 1–10.
—— —— (1989b) 'Multiple data analyses of dichotic listening advantages of stutterers.' *Journal of Fluency Disorders*, **14**, 97–107.
Bloodstein, O. (1981) *A Handbook on Stuttering, 3rd Edn.* Chicago: National Easter Seal Society.
Blumstein, S., Goodglass, H., Tartter, V. (1975) 'The reliability of ear advantage in dichotic listening.' *Brain and Language*, **2**, 226–236.
Boder, E. (1973) 'Developmental dyslexia: a diagnostic approach based on three atypical reading–spelling patterns.' *Developmental Medicine and Child Neurology*, **15**, 663–687.
Boklage, C.E. (1977) 'Schizophrenia, brain asymmetry development and twinning: cellular relationship with etiological and possibly prognostic implications.' *Biological Psychiatry*, **12**, 19–35.
—— (1980) 'The sinistral blastocyst: an embryonic perspective on the development of brain function asymmetries.' *In:* Herron, J. (Ed.) *The Neuropsychology of Left-Handedness.* New York: Academic Press. (pp. 115–137)
—— (1981) 'On the distribution of nonrighthandedness among twins and their families.' *Acta Geneticae Medicae et Gemellologiae*, **30**, 167–187.
Bolin, B.J. (1953) 'Left-handedness and stuttering as signs diagnostic of epileptics.' *Journal of Mental Science*, **99**, 483–488.
Bolser, L.A., Runfeldt, S., Morris, R.A. (1988) 'Handedness in language-trained chimpanzees (*Pan troglodytes*) in daily activities and assessment tasks.' *Journal of Clinical and Experimental Neuropsychology*, **10**, 40–41.
Boucher, J. (1977) 'Hand preference in autistic children and their parents.' *Journal of Autism and Childhood Schizophrenia*, **7**, 177–187.
Brackenridge, C.J. (1981) 'Secular variation in handedness over ninety years.' *Neuropsychologia*, **19**, 459–462.
Bradshaw-McAnulty, G., Hicks, R.E., Kinsbourne, M. (1984) 'Pathological left-handedness and familial sinistrality in relation to degree of mental retardation.' *Brain and Cognition*, **3**, 349–356.
Brain, W.R. (1945) 'Speech and handedness.' *Lancet*, **2**, 837–842.
Briggs, G.G., Nebes, R.D., Kinsbourne, M. (1976) 'Intellectual differences in relation to personal and family handedness.' *Quarterly Journal of Experimental Psychology*, **28**, 591–601.
Broca, P. (1865) 'Sur le siège de la faculté du langage articulé.' *Bulletin de la Société d'Anthropologie*, **6**, 377–393. (For translation, *see* Berker *et al.* 1986.)
Broman, S., Nichols, P.L., Shaughnessy, P., Kennedy, W. (1987) *Retardation in Young Children: a Developmental Study of Cognitive Deficit.* Hillsdale, NJ: Erlbaum.
Brooker, R.J., Lehman, R.A.W., Heimbuch, R.C., Kidd, K.K. (1981) 'Hand usage in a colony of bonnett monkeys *Macaca radiata*.' *Behavior Genetics*, **11**, 49–56.
Bruml, H. (1972) 'Age changes in preference and skill measures of handedness.' *Perceptual and Motor Skills*, **34**, 3–14.
Bryant, P., Impey, L. (1986) 'The similarities between normal readers and developmental and acquired dyslexics.' *Cognition*, **24**, 121–137.
Bryden, M.P. (1965) 'Tachistoscopic recognition, handedness and cerebral dominance.' *Neuropsychologia*, **3**, 1–8.
—— (1977) 'Measuring handedness with questionnaires.' *Neuropsychologia*, **15**, 617–624.
—— (1988a) 'Does laterality make any difference? Thoughts on the relation between cerebral

asymmetry and reading.' *In:* Molfese, D., Segalowitz, S. (Eds.) *Brain Lateralization in Children: Developmental Implications.* New York: Guilford Press. (pp. 509–525)
—— (1988*b*) 'Cerebral organization and mathematical ability.' *Behavioral and Brain Sciences*, **11**, 186–187.
—— Hecaen, H., DeAgostini, M. (1983) 'Patterns of cerebral organization.' *Brain and Language*, **20**, 249–262.
Brynleson, B. (1939) 'A study of laterality of stutterers and normal speakers.' *Journal of Speech Disorders*, **4**, 231–234.
—— Rutherford, B. (1937) 'A comparative study of laterality of stutterers and non-stutterers.' *Journal of Speech Disorders*, **2**, 15–16.
Bryson, S., Mononen, L.J., Yu, L. (1980) 'Procedural constraints on the measurement of laterality in young children.' *Neuropsychologia*, **18**, 243–246.
Burt, C. (1937) *The Backward Child.* London: University of London Press.
Butterworth, G., Hopkins, B. (1988) 'Hand–mouth coordination in the new-born baby.' *British Journal of Developmental Psychology*, **6**, 303–314.
Buxton, C.E. (1937) 'A comparison of preference and motor-learning measures of handedness.' *Journal of Experimental Psychology*, **21**, 464–469.
Calnan, M., Richardson, K. (1976) 'Developmental correlates of handedness in a national sample of 11-year-olds.' *Annals of Human Biology*, **3**, 329–342.
Caparulo, B.K., Cohen, D.J., Rothman, S.L., Young, J.G., Katz, J.D., Shaywitz, S.E., Shaywitz, B.A. (1981) 'Computed tomographic brain scanning in children with developmental neuropsychiatric disorders.' *Journal of the American Academy of Child Psychiatry*, **20**, 338–357.
Caplan, P.J., Kinsbourne, M. (1976) 'Baby drops the rattle: asymmetry of duration of grasp by infants.' *Child Development*, **47**, 532–534.
Cappa, S.F., Guariglia, C., Papagno, C., Pizzamiglio, L., Vallar, G., Zoccolotti, P., Ambrosi, B., Santiemma, V. (1988). 'Patterns of lateralization and performance levels for verbal and spatial tasks in congenital androgen deficiency.' *Behavioural Brain Research*, **31**, 177–183.
Carter-Saltzman, L. (1980) 'Biological and sociocultural effects on handedness: comparison between biological and adoptive families.' *Science*, **209**, 1263–1265.
—— Scarr-Salpatek, S., Barker, W.B., Katz, S. (1976) 'Left-handedness in twins: incidence and pattern of performance in an adolescent sample.' *Behaviour Genetics*, **6**, 189–203.
Chamberlain, H.D. (1928) 'The inheritance of left-handedness.' *Journal of Heredity*, **19**, 557–559.
Chi, J.G., Dooling, E.C., Gilles, F.H. (1977) 'Left–right asymmetries of the temporal speech areas of the human fetus.' *Archives of Neurology*, **34**, 346–348.
Christian, J.C., Hunter, D.S., Evans, M.M., Standeford, S. (1980) 'Association of handedness and birth order in monozygotic twins.' *Acta Geneticae et Medicae Gemellologiae*, **28**, 67–68.
Chrysanthis, K. (1947) 'Stammering and handedness.' *Lancet*, **1**, 270–271.
Chui, H.C., Damasio, A.R. (1980) 'Human cerebral asymmetries evaluated by computerized tomography.' *Journal of Neurology, Neurosurgery and Psychiatry*, **43**, 873–878.
Churchill, J.A., Igna, E., Senf, R. (1962) 'The association of position at birth and handedness.' *Pediatrics*, **29**, 307–309.
Clymer, P.E., Silva, P.A. (1985) 'Laterality, cognitive ability and motor performance in a sample of seven year olds.' *Journal of Human Movement Studies*, **11**, 59–68.
Cobb, K., Goodwin, R., Saelens, E. (1966) 'Spontaneous hand positions of newborn infants.' *Journal of Genetic Psychology*, **108**, 225–237.
Cohen, A.I. (1966) 'Hand preference and developmental status of infants.' *Journal of Genetic Psychology*, **108**, 337–345.
Cohen, J. (1977) *Statistical Power Analysis for the Behavioral Sciences.* New York: Academic Press.
Colbourn, C. (1981) 'What can laterality measures tell us about hemisphere function during childhood development?' *In:* Lebrun, Y., Zangwill, O. (Eds.) *Lateralisation of Language in the Child.* Lisse: Swets & Zeitlinger. (pp. 91–102)
Colby, K.M., Parkison, C. (1977) 'Handedness in autistic children.' *Journal of Autism and Childhood Schizophrenia*, **7**, 3–9.
Coleman, M., Gillberg, C. (1985) *The Biology of the Autistic Syndromes.* New York: Praeger.
Collins, R.L. (1970) 'The sound of one paw clapping: an inquiry into the origin of left-handedness.' *In:* Lindzey, G., Thiessen, D.D. (Eds.), *Contributions to Behavior-Genetic Analysis.* New York: Appleton Century Crofts. (pp. 115–136)
Comings, D.E., Comings, B.G. (1987) 'A controlled study of Tourette syndrome. VI. Early development, sleep problems, allergies, and handedness.' *American Journal of Human Genetics*, **41**, 822–838.

Connolly, K., Elliott, J. (1972) 'The evolution and ontogeny of hand function.' *In:* Jones, N.B. (Ed.) *Ethological Studies of Child Behaviour.* New York: Cambridge University Press. (pp. 329–379)
—— Stratton, P. (1968) 'Developmental changes in associated movements.' *Developmental Medicine and Child Neurology,* **10,** 49–56.
Conrad, K. (1949) 'Über aphasische Sprachstörungen bei hirnverletzten Linkshändern.' *Nervenarzt,* **20,** 148–154.
Corballis, M.C., Beale, I.L. (1976) *The Psychology of Left and Right.* Hillsdale, NJ: Erlbaum.
Coren, S., Porac, C. (1977) 'Fifty centuries of right-handedness: the historical record.' *Science,* **198,** 631–632.
—— —— (1978) 'The validity and reliability of self-report items for the measurement of lateral preference.' *British Journal of Psychology,* **69,** 207–211.
—— —— Duncan, P. (1981) 'Lateral preference behaviors in preschool children and young adults.' *Child Development,* **52,** 443–450.
—— Searleman, A., Porac, C. (1986) 'Rate of physical maturation and handedness.' *Developmental Neuropsychology,* **2,** 17–23.
Coryell, J.F. (1985) 'Infant rightward asymmetries predict right-handedness in childhood.' *Neuropsychologia,* **23,** 269–271.
—— Michel, G.F. (1978) 'How supine postural preferences of infants can contribute toward the development of handedness.' *Infant Behavior and Development,* **1,** 245–257.
Critchley, M. (1970) *The Dyslexic Child.* London: Heinemann Medical.
—— Critchley, E.A. (1978) *Dyslexia Defined.* London: Heinemann Medical.
Crovitz, H.F., Zener, K. (1962) 'A group-test for assessing hand- and eye-dominance.' *American Journal of Psychology,* **75,** 271–276.
Curry, F.K.W. (1967) 'A comparison of left-handed and right-handed subjects on verbal and non-verbal dichotic listening tasks.' *Cortex,* **3,** 343–352.
—— Gregory, H.H. (1969) 'The performance of stutterers on dichotic listening tasks thought to reflect cerebral dominance.' *Journal of Speech and Hearing Research,* **12,** 73–82.
—— Rutherford, D.R. (1967) 'Recognition and recall of dichotically presented verbal stimuli by right- and left-handed persons.' *Neuropsychologia,* **5,** 119–126.
Dalby, J.T., Gibson, D. (1981) 'Functional cerebral lateralization in subtypes of disabled readers.' *Brain and Language,* **14,** 34–48.
Damasio, H., Maurer, R.G., Damasio, A.R., Chui, H.C. (1980) 'Computerized tomographic scan findings in patients with autistic behavior.' *Archives of Neurology,* **37,** 504–510.
Daniels, E.M. (1940) 'An analysis of the relation between handedness and stuttering with special reference to the Orton–Travis theory of cerebral dominance.' *Journal of Speech Disorders,* **5,** 309–326.
Dart, C. (1938) 'Eye, hand, and foot preference of mentally subnormal subjects compared with individuals of normal or superior intelligence.' *Journal of Juvenile Research,* **22,** 119–122.
Dawson, G. (1988) 'Cerebral lateralization in autism: clues to its role in language and affective development.' *In:* Molfese, D., Segalowitz, S. (Eds.) *Brain Lateralization in Children: Developmental Implications.* New York: Guilford Press. (pp. 437–461)
—— Warrenburg, S., Fuller, P. (1982) 'Cerebral lateralization in individuals diagnosed as autistic in early childhood.' *Brain and Language,* **15,** 353–368.
—— Finley, C., Phillips, S., Galpert, L. (1986) 'Hemispheric specialization and the language abilities of autistic children.' *Child Development,* **57,** 1440–1453.
Dawson, J.L.M. (1972) 'Temne–Arunta hand–eye dominance and cognitive style.' *International Journal of Psychology,* **7,** 219–233.
—— (1974) 'Ecology, cultural pressures towards conformity and left-handedness: a bio-social approach.' *In:* Dawson, J.L.M., Lonner, W.J. (Eds.) *Readings in Cross-cultural Psychology.* Hong Kong: Hong Kong University Press. (pp. 424–447)
Delacato, C.H. (1963) *The Diagnosis and Treatment of Speech and Reading Problems.* Springfield, IL: C.C. Thomas.
Denckla, M.B. (1973) 'Development of speed in repetitive and successive finger-movements in normal children.' *Developmental Medicine and Child Neurology,* **15,** 635–645.
—— (1974) 'Development of motor co-ordination in normal children.' *Developmental Medicine and Child Neurology,* **16,** 729–741.
Denenberg, V.H. (1988) 'Laterality in animals: brain and behavioral asymmetries and the role of early experiences.' *In:* Molfese, D.L., Segalowitz, S.J. (Eds.) *Brain Lateralization in Children: Developmental Implications.* New York: Guilford Press. (pp. 59–71)
Dennis, M. (1976) 'Impaired sensory and motor differentiation with corpus callosum agenesis: a lack of

callosal inhibition during ontogeny?' *Neuropsychologia*, **14**, 455–469

Deuel, R.K., Moran, C.C. (1980) 'Cerebral dominance and cerebral asymmetries on computed tomogram in childhood.' *Neurology*, **30**, 934–938.

—— Schaffer, S.P. (1987) 'Patterns of hand preference in monkeys.' *Behavioral and Brain Sciences*, **10**, 270–271.

Dlugosz, L.J., Byers, T., Cooke, R.E., Lesswing, A., Marshall, J., Msall, M.E. (1988) 'Relationships between laterality of congenital upper limb reduction defects and school performance.' *Clinical Pediatrics*, **27**, 319–324.

Doehring, D.G. (1968) *Patterns of Impairment in Specific Reading Disability*. Bloomington, IN: Indiana University Press.

Douglas, J.W.B., Ross, J.M., Cooper, J.E. (1967) 'The relationship between handedness, attainment and adjustment in a national sample of school children.' *Educational Research*, **9**, 223–232.

Downey, J.E. (1927) 'Types of dextrality among North American Indians.' *Journal of Experimental Psychology*, **10**, 478–488.

—— (1933) 'Laterality of function.' *Psychological Bulletin*, **30**, 109–142.

Dunlop, D.B., Dunlop, P., Fenelon, B. (1973) 'Vision laterality analysis in children with reading disability.' *Cortex*, **9**, 227–236.

Dusek, C.D., Hicks, R.A. (1980) 'Multiple birth risk factors and handedness in elementary school children.' *Cortex*, **16**, 471–478.

Edly, L.M., Blood, G.W., Blood, I.M. (1986) 'Dichotic listening performance of articulatory-impaired children: divided attention, severity, and data analysis.' *Journal of Communication Disorders*, **19**, 405–425.

Ehrlichman, H., Zoccolotti, P., Owen, D. (1982) 'Perinatal factors in hand and eye preference: data from the Collaborative Perinatal Project.' *International Journal of Neuroscience*, **17**, 17–22.

Elliott, C.D., Murray, D.J., Pearson, L.S. (1978) *British Ability Scales*. Windsor: NFER–Nelson.

Elliott, D. (1985) 'Manual asymmetries in the performance of sequential movement by adolescents and adults with Down syndrome.' *American Journal of Mental Deficiency*, **90**, 90–97.

Ellis, S.J., Ellis, P.J., Marshall, E. (1988) 'Hand preference in a normal population.' *Cortex*, **24**, 157–163.

Eme, R.F. (1979) 'Sex differences in childhood psychopathology: a review.' *Psychological Review*, **86**, 574–595.

Ettlinger, G., Jackson, C.V., Zangwill, O.L. (1956) 'Cerebral dominance in sinistrals.' *Brain*, **79**, 569–588.

Evans-Pritchard, E.E. (1953) 'Nuer spear symbolism.' *Anthropological Quarterly*, **1**, 1–19. (Reprinted *in:* Needham, R. (1973) *Right and Left: Essays on Dual Symbolic Classification*. Chicago: University of Chicago Press.)

Fagan, L.B. (1931) 'The relation of dextral training to the onset of stuttering. A report of cases.' *Quarterly Journal of Speech*, **17**, 73–76.

Fagot, J., Vauclair, J. (1988) 'Handedness and bimanual coordination in the lowland gorilla.' *Brain, Behaviour and Evolution*, **32**, 89–95.

Falconer, D.S. (1965) 'The inheritance of liability to certain diseases, estimated from the incidence among relatives.' *Annals of Human Genetics*, **29**, 56–76.

Falk, D., Cheverud, J., Vannier, M.W., Conroy, C.G. (1986) 'Advanced computer graphics technology reveals cortical asymmetry in the endocasts of rhesus monkeys.' *Folia Primatologica*, **46**, 98–103.

Falzi, G., Perrone, P., Vignolo, L.A. (1982) 'Right–left asymmetry in anterior speech region.' *Archives of Neurology*, **39**, 239–240.

Fein, D., Humes, M., Kaplan, E., Lucci, D., Waterhouse, L. (1984) 'The question of left hemisphere dysfunction in infantile autism.' *Psychological Bulletin*, **95**, 258–281.

—— Waterhouse, L., Lucci, D., Pennington, B., Humes, M. (1985) 'Handedness and cognitive functions in pervasive developmental disorders.' *Journal of Autism and Developmental Disorders*, **15**, 323–334.

Felton, R.H., Wood, F.B., Brown, I.S., Campbell, S.K., Harter, M.R. (1987) 'Separate verbal memory and naming deficits in attention deficit disorder and reading disability.' *Brain and Language*, **31**, 171–184.

Fennell, E.B., Bowers, D., Satz, P. (1977) 'Within-modal and cross-modal reliabilities of two laterality tests among left-handers.' *Perceptual and Motor Skills*, **45**, 451–456.

—— Satz, P., van den Abell, T., Bowers, D., Thomas, R. (1978) 'Visuospatial competency, handedness, and cerebral dominance.' *Brain and Language*, **5**, 206–214.

—— —— Morris, R. (1983) 'The development of handedness and dichotic listening asymmetries in

relation to school achievement: a longitudinal study.' *Journal of Experimental Child Psychology*, **35**, 248–262.
Finlayson, A.J., Reitan, R.M. (1976) 'Handedness in relation to measures of motor and tactile-perceptual functions in normal children.' *Perceptual and Motor Skills*, **43**, 475–481.
Finucci, J.M., Childs, B. (1983) 'Dyslexia: family studies.' *In:* Ludlow, C.L. Cooper, J.A. (Eds.) *Genetic Aspects of Speech and Language Disorders*. New York: Academic Press. (pp. 157–167)
Fischer, R.B., Meunier, G.F., White, P.J. (1982) 'Evidence of laterality in the lowland gorilla.' *Perceptual and Motor Skills*, **54**, 1093–1094.
Fleminger, J.J., Bunce, L. (1975) 'Investigation of cerebral dominance in "left-handers" and "right-handers" using unilateral electroconvulsive therapy.' *Journal of Neurology, Neurosurgery and Psychiatry*, **38**, 541–545.
Flor-Henry, P. (1983) 'Hemisyndromes of temporal lobe epilepsy: review of evidence relating psychopathological manifestations in epilepsy to right- and left-sided epilepsy.' *In:* Myslobodsky, M.S. (Ed.) *Hemisyndromes: Psychobiology, Neurology, Psychiatry*. New York: Academic Press. (pp. 149–174)
Flowers, K. (1975) 'Handedness and controlled movement.' *British Journal of Psychology*, **66**, 39–52.
Fog, F., Fog, M. (1963) 'Cerebral inhibition examined by associated movements.' *In:* Bax, M., Mac Keith, R. (Eds.) *Minimal Cerebral Dysfunction. Clinics in Developmental Medicine, No. 10*. London: S.I.M.P. with Heinemann Medical.
Fox, N., Lewis, M. (1982) 'Motor asymmetries in preterm infants: effects of prematurity and illness.' *Developmental Psychobiology*, **15**, 19–23.
Freedman, R.J., Rovegno, L. (1981) 'Ocular dominance, cognitive strategy, and sex differences in spatial ability.' *Perceptual and Motor Skills*, **52**, 651–654.
Fryns, J.P., Kleczkowska, A., Dereymaeker, A., Hoefnagels, M., Heremans, G., Marien, J., van der Berghe, H. (1986). 'A genetic-diagnostic survey in an institutionalized population of 173 severely mentally retarded patients.' *Clinical Genetics*, **30**, 315–323.
Fundudis, T., Kolvin, I., Garside, R. (1979) *Speech Retarded and Deaf Children: their Psychological Development*. London: Academic Press.
Gaillard, F., Satz, P. (1989) 'Handedness and reading disability: a developmental study.' *Archives of Clinical Neuropsychology*, **4**, 63–69.
Galaburda, A.M. (1987) 'Handedness in children with systemic lupus erythematosus: reply.' *Arthritis and Rheumatism*, **30**, 355–356.
—— Kemper, T.L. (1979) 'Cytoarchitectonic abnormalities in developmental dyslexia: a case study.' *Annals of Neurology*, **6**, 94–100.
—— Sherman, G.F., Rosen, G.D., Aboitiz, F., Geschwind, N. (1985) 'Developmental dyslexia: four consecutive patients with cortical anomalies.' *Annals of Neurology*, **18**, 222–233
—— Corsiglia, J., Rosen, G.D., Sherman, G.F. (1987) 'Planum temporale asymmetry, reappraisal since Geschwind and Levitsky.' *Neuropsychologia*, **25**, 853–868.
Galliford, D., James, F.E., Woods, G.E. (1964) 'Laterality in athetoid cerebral palsied children.' *Developmental Medicine and Child Neurology*, **6**, 261–263.
Gardner, J., Lewkowicz, D., Turkewitz, G. (1977) 'Development of postural asymmetry in premature human infants.' *Developmental Psychobiology*, **10**, 471–480.
Gardner, R.A., Broman, M. (1979) 'The Purdue pegboard: normative data on 1334 school children.' *Journal of Clinical Child Psychology*, **1**, 156–162.
Gates, A.I., Bond, G.L. (1936) 'Relation of handedness, eye-sighting and acuity dominance to reading.' *Journal of Educational Psychology*, **27**, 450–456.
Geffen, G., Caudrey, D. (1981) 'Reliability and validity of the dichotic monitoring test for language laterality.' *Neuropsychologia*, **19**, 413–423.
Geschwind, N. (1975) 'The apraxias: neural mechanisms of disorders of learned movement.' *American Scientist*, **63**, 188–195.
—— Behan, P. (1982) 'Left-handedness: association with immune disease, migraine, and developmental learning disorder.' *Proceedings of the National Academy of Sciences*, **79**, 5097–5100.
—— —— (1984) 'Laterality, hormones and immunity.' *In:* Geschwind, N., Galaburda, A.M. (Eds.) *Cerebral Dominance: the Biological Foundations*. Cambridge, Mass.: Harvard University Press. (pp. 211–224)
—— Galaburda, A.M. (1985a) 'Cerebral lateralization. Biological mechanisms, associations and pathology. I. A hypothesis and a program for research.' *Archives of Neurology*, **42**, 428–459.
—— —— (1985b) 'Cerebral lateralization. Biological mechanisms, associations and pathology. II. A hypothesis and a program for research.' *Archives of Neurology*, **42**, 521–552.

—— —— (1985c) 'Cerebral lateralization. Biological mechanisms, associations and pathology. III. A hypothesis and a program for research.' *Archives of Neurology*, **42**, 634–654.
—— —— (1987) *Cerebral Lateralization: Biological Mechanisms, Associations and Pathology.* Cambridge, MA: MIT Press.
—— Levitsky, W. (1968) 'Left–right asymmetries in temporal speech region.' *Science*, **161**, 186–187.
Gesell, A., Ames, L.B. (1947) 'The development of handedness.' *Journal of Genetic Psychology*, **70**, 155–175.
Gibson, J.B. (1973) 'Intelligence and handedness.' *Nature*, **243**, 482.
Gillberg, C. (1983) 'Autistic children's hand preferences: results from an epidemiological study of infantile autism.' *Psychiatry Research*, **10**, 21–30.
—— Svendsen, P. (1983) 'Childhood psychosis and computed tomographic brain scan findings.' *Journal of Autism and Developmental Disorders*, **13**, 19–32.
—— Waldenstrom, E., Rasmussen, P. (1984) 'Handedness in Swedish 10-year-olds: some background and associated factors.' *Journal of Child Psychology and Psychiatry*, **25**, 421–432.
les, F.H., Leviton, A., Dooling, E.C. (1983) *The Developing Human Brain: Growth and Epidemiological Neuropathology*. Boston: John Wright.
Gloning, I., Gloning, K., Haub, G., Quatember, R. (1969) 'Comparison of verbal behavior in right-handed and non right-handed patients with anatomically verified lesion of one hemisphere.' *Cortex*, **5**, 43–52.
Gloning, K. (1977) 'Handedness and aphasia.' *Neuropsychologia*, **15**, 355–358.
Goldfield, E.C., Michel, G.F. (1986) 'The ontogeny of infant bimanual reaching during the first year.' *Infant Behavior and Development*, **9**, 81–89.
Goodall, J. (1965) 'Chimpanzees of the Gombe stream reserve.' *In:* Devore, I. (Ed.) *Primate Behavior.* New York: Holt, Rinehart & Winston.
—— (1986) *The Chimpanzees of Gombe.* Cambridge, MA: Belknap Press.
Goodglass, H., Quadfasel, F.A. (1954) 'Language laterality in left-handed aphasics.' *Brain*, **77**, 521–548.
Gordon, H. (1920) 'Left-handedness and mirror writing, especially among defective children.' *Brain*, **43**, 313–368.
Gordon, H.W. (1980) 'Cognitive asymmetry in dyslexic families.' *Neuropsychologia*, **18**, 645–656.
Gottfried, A.W., Bathurst, K. (1983) 'Hand preference across time is related to intelligence in young girls, not boys.' *Science*, **221**, 1074–1076.
Gross, K., Rothenberg, S., Schottenfeld, S. (1978) 'Duration thresholds for letter identification in left and right visual fields for normal and reading disabled children.' *Neuropsychologia*, **16**, 709–715.
Guilford, J.P., Fruchter, B. (1973) *Fundamental Statistics in Psychology and Education, 5th Edn.* Tokyo: McGraw–Hill Kogakusha.
Haefner, R. (1929) *The Educational Significance of Left-handedness.* New York: Teachers College, Columbia University Bureau of Publications.
Hallgren, B. (1950) 'Specific dyslexia ("congenital word-blindness").' *Acta Psychiatrica et Neurologica*, Suppl. 65.
Hansen, O., Nerup, J., Holbek, B. (1987) 'Further indication of a possible common genetic origin of specific dyslexia and insulin-dependent diabetes mellitus.' *Hereditas*, **107**, 257–258.
Harcherik, D.F., Cohen, D.J., Ort, S., Paul, R., Shaywitz, B.A., Volkmar, F.R., Rothman, S.L.G., Leckman, J.F. (1985) 'Computed tomographic brain scanning in four neuropsychiatric disorders of childhood.' *American Journal of Psychiatry*, **142**, 731–734.
Hardyck, C. (1977) 'Laterality and intellectual ability: a just not noticeable difference?' *British Journal of Educational Psychology*, **47**, 305–311.
—— Petrinovich, L.F. (1977) 'Left-handedness.' *Psychological Bulletin*, **84**, 385–404.
—— —— Goldman, R.D. (1976) 'Left-handedness and cognitive deficit.' *Cortex*, **12**, 266–279.
Harris, A.J. (1957) 'Lateral dominance, directional confusion, and reading disability.' *Journal of Psychology*, **44**, 283–294.
—— (1958) *Harris Tests of Lateral Dominance.* New York: Psychological Corporation.
Harris, L.J. (1980) 'Left-handedness: early theories, facts, and fancies.' *In:* Herron, J. (Ed.) *Neuropsychology of Left-handedness.* New York: Academic Press. (pp. 3–78)
—— (1983) 'Laterality of function in the infant: historical and contemporary trends in theory and research.' *In:* Young, G., Segalowitz, S.J., Corter, C.M., Trehub, S.E. (Eds.) *Manual Specialization and the Developing Brain.* New York: Academic Press. (pp. 177–247)
—— (1989) 'Footedness in parrots: three centuries of research, theory, and mere surmise.' *Canadian Journal of Psychology*, **43**, 369–396.
—— Carlson, D.F. (1988) 'Pathological left-handedness: an analysis of theories and evidence.' *In:*

Molfese, D.L., Segalowitz, S.J. (Eds.) *Brain Lateralization in Children: Developmental Implications.* New York: Guilford Press. (pp. 289–372)
Harshman, R.A., Hampson, E., Berenbaum, S. (1983) 'Individual differences in cognitive abilities and brain organization. Part 1: Sex and handedness differences in ability.' *Canadian Journal of Psychology,* **37**, 144–192.
Haslam, R.H.A., Dalby, J.T., Johns, R.D., Rademaker, A.W. (1981) 'Cerebral asymmetry in developmental dyslexia.' *Archives of Neurology,* **38**, 679–682.
Hauser, S.L., Delong, G.R., Rosman, N.P. (1975) 'Pneumoencephalographic findings in the infantile autism syndrome: a correlation with temporal lobe disease.' *Brain,* **98**, 667–688.
Hay, D.A., Howie, P.M. (1980) 'Handedness and differences in birthweight of twins.' *Perceptual and Motor Skills,* **51**, 666.
—— Prior, M., Collett, S., Williams, M. (1987) 'Speech and language development in preschool twins.' *Acta Geneticae Medicae et Gemellologiae,* **36**, 213–223.
Heffner, H.E., Heffner, R.S. (1984) 'Temporal lobe lesions and perception of species-specific vocalizations by macaques.' *Science,* **226**, 75–76.
Heilbroner, P.L., Holloway, R.L. (1988) 'Anatomical brain asymmetries in New World and Old World monkeys: stages of temporal lobe development in primate evolution.' *American Journal of Physical Anthropology,* **76**, 39–48.
Heilman, K.M. (1979) 'Apraxia.' *In:* Heilman, K.M., Valenstein, E. (Eds.) *Clinical Neuropsychology.* New York: Oxford University Press. (pp. 159–185)
Heim, A.W., Watts, K.P. (1976) 'Handedness and cognitive bias.' *Quarterly Journal of Experimental Psychology,* **28**, 355–360.
Hemenway, D. (1983) 'Bimanual dexterity in baseball players.' *New England Journal of Medicine,* **309**, 1587–1588. (*Letter.*)
Herrmann, D.J., van Dyke, K.A. (1978) 'Handedness and the mental rotation of perceived patterns.' *Cortex,* **14**, 521–529.
Hicks, R.E., Barton, A.K. (1975) 'A note on left-handedness and severity of mental retardation.' *Journal of Genetic Psychology,* **127**, 323–324.
—— Kinsbourne, M. (1976) 'Human handedness: a partial cross-fostering study.' *Science,* **192**, 908–910.
—— Evans, E.A., Pellegrini, R.J. (1978a) 'Correlations between handedness and birth order: compilation of five studies.' *Perceptual and Motor Skills,* **46**, 53–54.
—— Pellegrini, R.J., Evans, E.A. (1978b) 'Handedness and birth risk.' *Neuropsychologia,* **16**, 243–245.
Hier, D.B., LeMay, M., Rosenberger, P.B., Perlo, V.P. (1978) 'Developmental dyslexia: evidence for a subgroup with reversal of cerebral asymmetry.' *Archives of Neurology,* **35**, 90–92.
—— —— —— (1979) 'Autism and unfavorable left-right asymmetries of the brain.' *Journal of Autism and Developmental Disorders,* **9**, 153–159.
Hildreth, G. (1948) 'Manual dominance in nursery school children.' *Journal of Genetic Psychology,* **72**, 29–45.
—— (1949a) 'The development and training of hand dominance. I. Characteristics of handedness.' *Journal of Genetic Psychology,* **75**, 197–220.
—— (1949b) 'The development and training of hand dominance. II. Developmental tendencies in handedness.' *Journal of Genetic Psychology,* **75**, 221–254.
—— (1949c) 'The development and training of hand dominance. III. Origins of handedness and lateral dominance.' *Journal of Genetic Psychology,* **75**, 255–275.
Hinshelwood, J. (1917) *Congenital Word-blindness.* London: H.K. Lewis.
Hiscock, M. (1988) 'Behavioral asymmetries in normal children.' *In:* Molfese, D.L., Segalowitz, S.J. (Eds.) *Brain Lateralization in Children: Developmental Implications.* New York: Guilford Press. (pp. 85–169)
Homzie, M.J., Lindsay, J.S. (1984) 'Language and the young stutterer: a new look at old theories and findings.' *Brain and Language,* **22**, 232–252.
Hopkins, B., Lems, W., Janssen, B., Butterworth, G. (1987) 'Postural and motor asymmetries in newlyborns.' *Human Neurobiology,* **6**, 153–156.
Hudson, P.T.W. (1975) 'The genetics of handedness—a reply to Levy and Nagylaki.' *Neuropsychologia,* **13**, 331–339.
Hull, C.J. (1936) 'A study of laterality test items.' *Journal of Experimental Education,* **4**, 287–290.
Humphrey, D.E., Humphrey, G.K. (1987) 'Sex differences in infant reaching.' *Neuropsychologia,* **25**, 971–975.
Humphrey, M.E. (1951) 'Consistency of hand usage.' *British Journal of Educational Psychology,* **22**, 214–225.

Hunter, J.E., Schmidt, F.L., Jackson, G.B. (1982) *Meta-analysis: Cumulating Research Findings Across Studies.* Beverly Hills: Sage.

Ingram, T.T.S. (1959) 'Specific developmental disorders of speech in childhood.' *Brain*, **82**, 450–467.

Isaacs, L.D., Haynes, W.O. (1984) 'Linguistic processing and performance in articulation-disordered subgroups of language-impaired children.' *Journal of Communication Disorders*, **17**, 109–120.

Jennekens-Schinkel, A., Linschooten-Duikersloot, E.M., Bouma, P.A.D., Peters, A.C.B., Stijnen, T. (1987) 'Spelling errors made by children with mild epilepsy: writing-to-dictation.' *Epilepsia*, **28**, 555–563.

Johnson, W., House, E. (1937) 'Certain laterality characteristics of children with articulatory disorders.' *Elementary School Journal*, **38**, 52–58.

—— King, A. (1942) 'An angle board and hand usage study of stutterers and non-stutterers.' *Journal of Experimental Psychology*, **31**, 293–311.

—— et al. (1942) 'A study of the onset and development of stuttering.' *Journal of Speech Disorders*, **7**, 251–257.

Johnston, R.B., Stark, R.E., Mellits, E.D., Tallal, P. (1981) 'Neurological status of language-impaired and normal children.' *Annals of Neurology*, **10**, 159–163.

Jones, B., Bell, J. (1980) 'Handedness in engineering and psychology students.' *Cortex*, **16**, 621–625.

Jones, H.E. (1931) 'Dextrality as a function of age.' *Journal of Experimental Psychology*, **14**, 125–143.

Jones, R.K. (1966) 'Observations on stammering after localized cerebral injury.' *Journal of Neurology, Neurosurgery and Psychiatry*, **29**, 192–195.

Kaufmann, A.S., Zalma, R., Kaufmann, N.L. (1978) 'The relationship of hand dominance to the motor coordination, mental ability, and right–left awareness of young normal children.' *Child Development*, **49**, 885–888.

Kaufmann, W.E., Galaburda, A.M. (1989) 'Cerebrocortical microdysgenesis in neurologically normal subjects.' *Neurology*, **39**, 238–244.

Keele, S.W. (1982) 'Learning and control of coordinated motor patterns: the programming perspective.' In: Kelso, J.A.S. (Ed.) *Human Motor Behavior: an Introduction.* Hillsdale, NJ: Erlbaum. (pp. 161–186)

Kertesz, A., Geschwind, N. (1971) 'Patterns of pyramidal decussation and their relationship to handedness.' *Archives of Neurology*, **24**, 326–332.

Kidd, D. (1906) *Savage Childhood: A Study of Kaffir Children.* London: A. & C. Black.

Kilshaw, D., Annett, M. (1983) 'Right and left hand skill. I: Effects of age, sex and hand preference showing superior skill in left handers.' *British Journal of Psychology*, **74**, 253–268.

Kimura, D. (1961a) 'Some effects of temporal-lobe damage on auditory perception.' *Canadian Journal of Psychology*, **15**, 156–165.

—— (1961b) 'Cerebral dominance and the perception of verbal stimuli.' *Canadian Journal of Psychology*, **15**, 166–171.

—— (1964) 'Left–right differences in the perception of melodies.' *Quarterly Journal of Experimental Psychology*, **16**, 355–358.

—— (1966) 'Dual functional asymmetry of the brain in visual perception.' *Neuropsychologia*, **4**, 275–285.

—— (1973a) 'Manual activity during speaking. I. Right-handers.' *Neuropsychologia*, **11**, 45–50.

—— (1973b) 'Manual activity during speaking. II. Left-handers.' *Neuropsychologia*, **11**, 51–55.

—— (1983) 'Speech representation in an unbiased sample of left-handers.' *Human Neurobiology*, **2**, 147–154.

—— Archibald, Y. (1974) 'Motor functions of the left hemisphere.' *Brain*, **97**, 337–350.

Kinsbourne, M., Hiscock, M. (1977) 'Does cerebral dominance develop?' In: Segalowitz, S., Gruber, F.A. (Eds.) *Language Development and Neurological Theory.* New York: Academic Press. (pp. 171–191)

Knox, A.W., Boone, D.R. (1970) 'Auditory laterality and tested handedness.' *Cortex*, **6**, 164–173

—— Kimura, D. (1970) 'Cerebral processing of nonverbal sounds in boys and girls.' *Neuropsychologia*, **8**, 227–237.

Komai, J., Fukuoka, G. (1934) 'A study on the frequency of left-handedness and left-footedness among Japanese school children.' *Human Biology*, **6**, 33–42.

Konishi, Y., Mikawa, H., Suzuki, J. (1986) 'Asymmetrical head-turning of preterm infants: some effects on later postural and functional lateralities.' *Developmental Medicine and Child Neurology*, **28**, 450–457.

—— Kuriyama, M., Mikawa, H., Suzuki, J. (1987) 'Effect of body position on later postural and functional lateralities of preterm infants.' *Developmental Medicine and Child Neurology*, **29**, 751–757.

Korczyn, A.D., Sage, J.I., Karplus, M. (1978) 'Lack of limb motor asymmetry in the neonate.' *Journal of Neurobiology*, **9**, 483–488.

Kurtzberg, D., Vaughan, H.G., Daum, C., Grellong, B.S., Albin, S., Rotkin, L. (1979) 'Neurobehavioral performance of low-birthweight infants at 40 weeks conceptual age: comparison with normal fullterm infants.' *Developmental Medicine and Child Neurology*, **21**, 590–607.

Kutas, M., McCarthy, G., Donchin, E. (1975) 'Differences between sinistrals' and dextrals' ability to infer a whole from its parts: a failure to replicate.' *Neuropsychologia*, **13**, 455–464.

Lazarus, J.C., Todor, J.I. (1987) 'Age differences in the magnitude of associated movement.' *Developmental Medicine and Child Neurology*, **29**, 726–733.

Le Gros Clark, W.E. (1927) 'Description of the cerebral hemispheres of the brain of a gorilla (John Daniels II).' *Journal of Anatomy*, **61**, 467–475.

Lehman, R.A.W. (1987) 'On the other hand . .' *Behavioral and Brain Sciences*, **10**, 280–281.

LeMay, M. (1977) 'Asymmetries of the skull and handedness.' *Journal of the Neurological Sciences*, **32**, 243–253.

—— (1982) 'Morphological aspects of human brain asymmetry: an evolutionary perspective.' *Trends in the Neurological Sciences*, **5**, 273–275.

—— Geschwind, N. (1975) 'Hemispheric differences in the brains of great apes.' *Brain, Behavior and Evolution*, **11**, 48–52.

—— Billig, M.S., Geschwind, N. (1982) 'Asymmetries of the brains and skulls of nonhuman primates.' In: Armstrong, E., Falk, D. (Eds.) *Primate Brain Evolution: Methods and Concepts*. New York: Plenum.

Lenneberg, E.H. (1967) *Biological Foundations of Language*. New York: Wiley.

Leviton, A., Kilty, T. (1976) 'Birth order and left-handedness.' *Archives of Neurology*, **33**, 664.

Levy, J. (1969) 'Possible basis for the evolution of lateral specialization of the human brain.' *Nature*, **224**, 614–615.

—— (1976) 'Cerebral lateralization and spatial ability.' *Behaviour Genetics*, **6**, 171–188.

—— (1977*a*) 'A reply to Hudson regarding the Levy–Nagylaki model for the genetics of handedness.' *Neuropsychologia*, **15**, 187–190.

—— (1977*b*) 'The origins of lateral asymmetry.' In: Harnad, S., Doty, R., Goldstein, L., Jaynes, J., Krauthamer, G. (Eds.) *Lateralization in the Nervous System*. New York: Academic Press. (pp. 195–209)

—— Nagylaki, T. (1972) 'A model for the genetics of handedness.' *Genetics*, **72**, 117–128.

—— Reid, M. (1976) 'Variations in writing posture and cerebral organization.' *Science*, **194**, 337–339.

—— —— (1978) 'Variations in cerebral organization as a function of handedness, hand posture in writing, and sex.' *Journal of Experimental Psychology (General)*, **107**, 119–144.

Lewkowicz, D., Gardner, J., Turkewitz, G. (1979) 'Lateral differences and head-turning responses to somesthetic stimulation in premature human infants.' *Developmental Psychobiology*, **12**, 607–614.

Liederman, J. (1983) 'Mechanisms underlying instability in the development of hand preference.' In: Young, G., Segalowitz, S.J., Corter, C.M., Trehub, S.E. (Eds.) *Manual Specialization and the Developing Brain*. New York: Academic Press. (pp. 71–92)

—— (1987) 'Neonates show an asymmetric degree of head rotation but lack an asymmetric tonic neck reflex asymmetry: neuropsychological implications.' *Developmental Neuropsychology*, **3**, 101–112.

—— Coryell, J. (1981) 'Right-hand preference facilitated by rightward turning biases in infancy.' *Developmental Psychobiology*, **14**, 439–450.

—— —— (1982) 'The origin of left hand preference: pathological and non-pathological influences.' *Neuropsychologia*, **20**, 721–725.

—— Kinsbourne, M. (1980*a*) 'Rightward motor bias in newborns depends on parental right-handedness.' *Neuropsychologia*, **18**, 579–584.

—— —— (1980*b*) 'Rightward turning biases in neonates reflect a single neural asymmetry in motor programming.' *Infant Behavior and Development*, **3**, 245–251.

Lippman, H.S. (1927) 'Certain behavior responses in early infancy.' *Journal of Genetic Psychology*, **34**, 424–440.

Longoni, A.M., Orsini, L. (1988) 'Lateral preferences in preschool children.' *Journal of Child Psychology and Psychiatry*, **29**, 533–539.

Longstreth, L.E. (1980) 'Human handedness: more evidence for genetic involvement.' *Journal of Genetic Psychology*, **137**, 275–283.

Lonton, A.P. (1976) 'Hand preference in children with myelomeningocele and hydrocephalus.' *Developmental Medicine and Child Neurology*, **18** (Suppl. 37), 143–149.

Lucas, J.A., Rosenstein, L.D., Bigler, E.D. (1989) 'Handedness and language among the mentally retarded: implications for the model of pathological left-handedness and gender differences in hemispheric specialization.' *Neuropsychologia*, **27**, 713–723.

Luessenhop, A.J., Boggs, J.S., LaBorwit, L.J., Walle, E.L. (1973) 'Cerebral dominance in stutterers determined by Wada testing.' *Neurology*, **23**, 1190–1192.

Luria, A.R. (1970) *Traumatic Aphasia: its Syndromes, Psychology and Treatment.* The Hague: Mouton.

MacNeilage, P.F., Studdert-Kennedy, M.G., Lindblom, B. (1987) 'Primate handedness reconsidered.' *Behavioral and Brain Sciences*, **10**, 247–303.

Malmquist, E. (1960) *Factors Related to Reading Disabilities in the First Grade of the Elementary School.* Stockholm: Almqvist & Wiksell.

Marrion, L. (1986) 'Writing-hand differences in Kwakiutls and Caucasians.' *Perceptual and Motor Skills*, **62**, 760–762.

Marshall, J.C. (1981) 'Lateral and focal organization in the human brain.' *In:* Lebrun, Y., Zangwill, O. (Eds.) *Lateralisation of Language in the Child.* Lisse: Swets & Zeitlinger. (pp. 71–81)

Martin, F., Friedrich, G., Mottier, C., Guignard, F. (1968) 'La latéralité chez l'épileptique.' *Annales Médico-Psychologiques*, **2**, 665–692.

Mascie-Taylor, C.G.N. (1980) 'Hand preference and components of IQ.' *Annals of Human Biology*, **7**, 235–248.

Mattis, S. (1978) 'Dyslexia syndromes: a working hypothesis that works.' *In:* Benton, A., Pearl, D. (Eds.) *Dyslexia: An Appraisal of Current Knowledge.* Oxford: Oxford University Press. (pp. 43–58)

McAllister, A.H. (1937) *Clinical Studies in Speech Therapy.* London: London University Press.

McCarthy, D. (1970) *McCarthy Scales of Children's Abilities.* New York: Psychological Corporation.

McFarland, D. (Ed.) (1981) *The Oxford Companion to Animal Behaviour.* Oxford: Oxford University Press.

McKeever, W.F., VanDeventer, A.D. (1977) 'Failure to confirm a spatial ability impairment in persons with evidence of right hemisphere speech capability.' *Cortex*, **13**, 321–326.

McLean, J.M., Ciurczak, F.M. (1982) 'Bimanual dexterity in major league baseball players: a statistical study.' *New England Journal of Medicine*, **307**, 1278–1279. (Letter.)

McManus, I.C. (1980a) 'Handedness in twins: a critical review.' *Neuropsychologia*, **18**, 347–355.

—— (1980b) 'Left-handedness and epilepsy.' *Cortex*, **16**, 487–491.

—— (1984) 'Genetics of handedness in relation to language disorder.' *Advances in Neurology*, **42**, 125–138.

—— (1985a) *Handedness, Language Dominance and Aphasia: A Genetic Model.* Psychological Medicine Monograph, Supplement 8. Cambridge: Cambridge University Press.

—— (1985b) 'Right- and left-hand skill: failure of the right shift model.' *British Journal of Psychology*, **76**, 1–16.

—— (1985c) 'On testing the right shift theory: a reply to Annett.' *British Journal of Psychology*, **76**, 31–34.

—— Sik, G., Cole, D.R., Mellon, A.F., Wong, J., Kloss, J. (1988) 'The development of handedness in children.' *British Journal of Developmental Psychology*, **6**, 257–273.

McMeekan, E.R.L., Lishman, W.A. (1975) 'Retest reliabilities and interrelationship of the Annett hand preference questionnaire and the Edinburgh handedness inventory.' *British Journal of Psychology*, **66**, 53–59.

Mebert, C.J. (1983) 'Laterality in manipulatory and cognitive-related activity in four- to ten-month-olds.' *In:* Young, G., Segalowitz, S.J., Corter, C.M., Trehub, S.E. (Eds.) *Manual Specialization and the Developing Brain.* New York: Academic Press. (pp. 349–365)

—— Michel, G.F. (1980) 'Handedness in artists.' *In:* Herron, J. (Ed.) *The Neuropsychology of Left-handedness.* New York: Academic Press. (pp. 273–279)

Melekian, B. (1981) 'Lateralization in the human newborn at birth: asymmetry of the stepping reflex.' *Neuropsychologia*, **19**, 707–711.

Meyer, B.C. (1945) 'Psychosomatic aspects of stuttering.' *Journal of Nervous and Mental Diseases*, **101**, 127–157.

Michel, G.F. (1981) 'Right-handedness: a consequence of infant supine head-orientation preference?' *Science*, **212**, 685–687.

—— (1983) 'Development of hand-use preference in infancy.' *In:* Young, G., Segalowitz, S.J., Corter, C.M., Trehub, S.E. (Eds.) *Manual Specialization and the Developing Brain.* New York: Academic Press. (pp. 33–70)

—— Goodwin, R. (1979) 'Intrauterine birth position predicts newborn supine head position preferences.' *Infant Behavior and Development*, **2**, 29–38.

—— Ovrut, M.R., Harkins, D.A. (1986) 'Hand-use preference for reaching and object manipulation in 6- through 13-month-old infants.' *Genetic, Social and General Psychology Monographs*, **111**, 409–427.

Miller, E. (1971) 'Handedness and the pattern of human ability.' *British Journal of Psychology*, **62**, 111–112.
Milner, B., Branch, C., Rasmussen, C. (1966) 'Evidence for bilateral speech representation in some non-right-handers.' *Transactions of the American Neurological Association*, **91**, 306–308.
Molfese, D.L., Betz, J.C. (1988) 'Electrophysiological indices of the early development of lateralization for language and cognition, and their implications for predicting later development.' *In:* Molfese, D.L., Segalowitz, S.J. (Eds.) *Brain Lateralization in Children: Developmental Implications.* New York: Guilford Press. (pp. 171–190)
Monroe, M. (1932) *Children Who Cannot Read.* Chicago: University of Chicago Press.
Morgan, M.J. (1977) 'Embryology and inheritance of asymmetry.' *In:* Harnad, S., Doty, R., Goldstein, L., Jaynes, J., Krauthamer, G. (Eds.) *Lateralization in the Nervous System.* New York: Academic Press. (pp. 173–194)
—— Corballis, M. (1978) 'On the biological basis of human laterality. II: The mechanisms of inheritance.' *Behavioral and Brain Sciences*, **1**, 270–277.
Morley, M. (1972) *The Development and Disorders of Speech in Childhood, 3rd Edn.* Edinburgh: Churchill Livingstone.
Moscovitch, M., Smith, L.C. (1979) 'Differences in neural organization between individuals with inverted and non-inverted handwriting postures.' *Science*, **205**, 71–713.
Naidoo, S. (1972) *Specific Dyslexia.* London: Pitman.
Napier, J. (1980) *Hands.* London: Allen & Unwin.
Nass, R. (1985) 'Mirror movement asymmetries in congenital hemiparesis: the inhibition hypothesis revisited.' *Neurology*, **35**, 1059–1062.
Neale, M.C. (1988) 'Handedness in a sample of volunteer twins.' *Behavior Genetics*, **18**, 69–79.
Nebes, R.D. (1971) 'Handedness and the perception of part-whole relationships.' *Cortex*, **7**, 350–356.
Needham, R. (1973) *Right and Left: Essays on Dual Symbolic Classification.* Chicago, IL: University of Chicago Press.
Neils, J.R., Aram, D.M. (1986) 'Handedness and sex of children with developmental language disorders.' *Brain and Language*, **28**, 53–65.
Netley, C., Rovet, J. (1982a) 'Verbal deficits in children with 47,XXY and 47,XXX karyotypes: a descriptive and experimental study.' *Brain and Language*, **17**, 58–72.
—— —— (1982b) 'Handedness in 47,XXY males.' *Lancet*, **2**, 267.
—— —— (1984) 'Hemispheric lateralization in 47,XXY Klinefelter's syndrome boys.' *Brain and Cognition*, **3**, 10–18.
—— —— (1988) 'The development of cognition and personality in X aneuploids and other subject groups.' *In:* Molfese, D.L., Segalowitz, S.J. (Eds.) *Brain Lateralization in Children: Developmental Implications.* New York: Guilford Press. (pp. 401–416)
Newcombe, F.G., Ratcliff, G.G., Carrivick, P.J., Hiorns, R.W., Harrison, G.A., Gibson, J.B. (1975) 'Hand preference and IQ in a group of Oxfordshire villages.' *Annals of Human Biology*, **2**, 235–242.
Newman, H.H. (1928) 'Asymmetry reversal or mirror imaging in identical twins.' *Biological Bulletin*, **55**, 298–315.
Newman, S.P., Karle, H., Wadsworth, J.F., Archer, R., Hockly, R., Rogers, P. (1985) 'Ocular dominance, reading and spelling: a reassessment of a measure associated with specific reading difficulties.' *Journal of Research in Reading*, **8**, 127–138.
Nomura, Y., Segawa, M., Hasegawa, M. (1984) 'Rett syndrome—clinical studies and pathophysiological consideration.' *Brain and Development*, **6**, 475–486.
Oates, D.W. (1929) 'Left-handedness in relation to speech defects, intelligence, and achievement.' *Forum of Education*, **7**, 91–103.
O'Callaghan, E.M., Tudehope, D.I., Dugdale, A.E., Mohay, H., Burns, Y., Cook, F. (1987) 'Handedness in children with birthweights below 1000 g.' *Lancet*, **1**, 1155. (Letter.)
Oldfield, R.C. (1971) 'The assessment and analysis of handedness: the Edinburgh inventory.' *Neuropsychologia*, **9**, 97–113.
Olsson, B., Rett, A. (1986) 'Shift to righthandedness in Rett syndrome around age 7.' *American Journal of Medical Genetics*, **24** (Suppl. 1), 133–141.
—— —— (1987) 'Autism and Rett syndrome: behavioural investigations and differential diagnosis.' *Developmental Medicine and Child Neurology*, **29**, 429–441.
Orsini, D.L., Satz, P. (1986) 'A syndrome of pathological left-handedness.' *Archives of Neurology*, **43**, 333–337.
Orton, S.T. (1925) '"Word-blindness" in school children.' *Archives of Neurology and Psychiatry*, **14**, 581–615.

—— (1927) 'Studies in stuttering.' *Archives of Neurology and Psychiatry*, **18**, 671–672.
—— (1937) *Reading, Writing and Speech Problems in Children.* London: Chapman & Hall.
Ounsted, C. (1955) 'The hyperkinetic syndrome in epileptic children.' *Lancet*, **2**, 303–311.
Overstreet, R. (1938) 'An investigation of prenatal position and handedness.' *Psychological Bulletin*, **35**, 520. (*Abstract.*)
Paine, R.S., Brazelton, T.B., Donovon, D.E., Drorbaugh, J.E., Hubbell, J.P., Sears, E.M. (1964) 'Evolution of postural reflexes in normal infants and in the presence of chronic brain syndromes.' *Neurology*, **14**, 1036–1048.
Palmer, R.D. (1964) 'Development of a differentiated handedness.' *Psychological Bulletin*, **62**, 257–272.
Penfield, W., Roberts, L. (1959) *Speech and Brain Mechanisms*. Princeton, NJ: Princeton University Press.
Pennington, B.F., Smith, S.D., Kimberling, W.J., Green, P.A., Haith, M.M. (1987). 'Left-handedness and immune disorders in familial dyslexics.' *Archives of Neurology*, **44**, 634–639.
Peters, M. (1976) 'Unilateral control of bilaterally symmetrical movement as a factor in lateralization of speech.' *Perceptual and Motor Skills*, **42**, 841–842.
—— (1980) 'Why the preferred hand taps more quickly than the non-preferred hand: three experiments on handedness.' *Canadian Journal of Psychology*, **34**, 62–71.
—— (1983a) 'Differentiation and lateral specialization in motor development.' *In:* Young, G., Segalowitz, S.J., Corter, C.M., Trehub, S.E. (Eds.) *Manual Specialization and the Developing Brain*. New York: Academic Press. (pp. 141–159)
—— (1983b) 'Lateral bias in reaching and holding at six and twelve months.' *In:* Young, G., Segalowitz, S.J., Corter, C.M., Trehub, S.E. (Eds.) *Manual Specialization and the Developing Brain*. New York: Academic Press. (pp. 367–374)
—— (1987) 'A nontrivial motor performance difference between right-handers and left-handers: attention as intervening variable in the expression of handedness.' *Canadian Journal of Psychology*, **41**, 91–99.
—— (1988) 'Footedness: asymmetries in foot preference and skill and neuropsychological assessment of foot movement.' *Psychological Bulletin*, **103**, 179–192.
—— Durding, B. (1978) 'Handedness measured by finger tapping: a continuous variable.' *Canadian Journal of Psychology*, **32**, 257–261.
—— McGrory, J. (1987) 'Dichotic listening performance and writing posture in right- and left-handers.' *Brain and Language*, **32**, 253–264.
—— Petrie, B.F. (1979) 'Functional asymmetries in the stepping reflex of human neonates.' *Canadian Journal of Psychology*, **33**, 198–200.
—— Servos, P. (1990) 'Performance of subgroups of lefthanders, and righthanders.' *Canadian Journal of Psychology.* (*In press.*)
Petersen, M.R., Beecher, M.D., Zoloth, S.R., Green, S., Marler, P.R., Moody, D.B., Stebbins, W.C. (1984) 'Neural lateralization of vocalizations by Japanese macaques: communicative significance is more important than acoustic structure.' *Behavioral Neuroscience*, **98**, 779–790.
Peterson, J.M. (1979) 'Left-handedness: differences between student artists and scientists.' *Perceptual and Motor Skills*, **48**, 961–962.
—— Lansky, L.M. (1974) 'Left-handedness among architects: some facts and speculation.' *Perceptual and Motor Skills*, **38**, 547–550.
Petrie, B.F., Peters, M. (1980) 'Handedness: left–right differences in intensity of grasp response and duration of rattle holding in infants.' *Infant Behavior and Development*, **3**, 215–221.
Pickersgill, M.J., Pank, P. (1970) 'Relation of age and mongolism to lateral preferences in severely subnormal subjects.' *Nature*, **228**, 1342–1344.
Pipe, M. (1987) 'Pathological left-handedness: is it familial?' *Neuropsychologia*, **25**, 571–577.
Porac, C., Coren, S. (1981) *Lateral Preferences and Human Behavior*. New York: Springer Verlag.
—— —— Steiger, J.H., Duncan, P. (1980) 'Human laterality: a multidimensional approach.' *Canadian Journal of Psychology*, **34**, 91–96.
—— —— Searleman, A. (1986) 'Environmental factors in hand preference formation: evidence from attempts to switch the preferred hand.' *Behavior Genetics*, **16**, 251–261.
Porfert, A.R., Rosenfield, D.B. (1978) 'Prevalence of stuttering.' *Journal of Neurology, Neurosurgery and Psychiatry*, **41**, 954–956.
Prechtl, H.F.R. (1977) *The Neurological Examination of the Full-term Newborn Infant. Clinics in Developmental Medicine, No. 63.* London: S.I.M.P. with Heinemann Medical; Philadelphia: Lippincott.
Prior, M.R., Bradshaw, J.L. (1979) 'Hemisphere functioning in autistic children.' *Cortex*, **15**, 73–81.

—— Frolley, M., Sanson, A. (1983) 'Language lateralization in specific reading retarded children and in backward readers.' *Cortex*, **19**, 149–163.
—— Tress, B., Hoffman, W.L., Boldt, D. (1984) 'Computed tomographic study of children with classic autism.' *Archives of Neurology*, **41**, 482–484.
Provins, K.A. (1956) 'Handedness and skill.' *Quarterly Journal of Experimental Psychology*, **8**, 79–95.
—— (1967) 'Motor skills, handedness and behaviour.' *Australian Journal of Psychology*, **19**, 137–150.
—— Milner, A.D., Kerr, P. (1982) 'Asymmetry of manual preference and performance.' *Perceptual and Motor Skills*, **54**, 179–194.
Pye-Smith, P.H. (1871) 'Left-handedness.' *Guy's Hospital Reports (3rd series)*, **16**, 141–146. (*Cited in* Harris 1980.)
Quinn, P.T. (1972) 'Stuttering: cerebral dominance and the dichotic word test.' *Medical Journal of Australia*, **2**, 639–643.
Raczkowski, D., Kalat, J.W., Nebes, R. (1974) 'Reliability and validity of some handedness questionnaire items.' *Neuropsychologia*, **12**, 43–47.
Ramaley, F. (1913) 'Inheritance of left-handedness.' *American Naturalist*, **47**, 730–738.
Ramsay, D.S. (1983) 'Unimanual hand preference and duplicated syllable babbling in infants.' *In:* Young, G., Segalowitz, S.J., Corter, C.M., Trehub, S.E. (Eds.) *Manual Specialization and the Developing Brain*. New York: Academic Press. (pp. 161–176)
—— (1984) 'Onset of duplicated syllable babbling and unimanual handedness in infancy. Evidence for developmental change in hemispheric specialization?' *Developmental Psychology*, **20**, 64–71.
—— Campos, J.J., Fenson, L. (1979) 'Onset of bimanual handedness in infants.' *Infant Behavior and Development*, **2**, 69–76.
Rasmussen, T., Milner, B. (1977) 'The role of early left-brain injury in determining lateralization of cerebral speech functions.' *Annals of the New York Academy of Sciences*, **299**, 355–369.
Ratcliff, G., Dila, C., Taylor, L., Milner, B. (1980) 'The morphological asymmetry of the hemispheres and cerebral dominance for speech: a possible relationship.' *Brain and Language*, **11**, 87–98.
Records, M.A., Heimbuch, R.C., Kidd, K.K. (1977) 'Handedness and stuttering: a dead horse?' *Journal of Fluency Disorders*, **2**, 271–282.
Rey, M., Dellatolas, G., Bancaud, J., Talairach, J. (1988) 'Hemispheric lateralization of motor and speech functions after early brain lesion: study of 73 epileptic patients with intracarotid amytal test.' *Neuropsychologia*, **26**, 167–172.
Rice, T., Plomin, R., DeFries, J.C. (1984) 'Development of hand preference in the Colorado adoption project.' *Perceptual and Motor Skills*, **58**, 683–689.
Riess, B.F., Ross, S., Lyerly, S.B., Birch, H.G. (1949) 'The behavior of two captive specimens of the Lowland Gorilla, *Gorilla gorilla gorilla*.' *Zoologica*, **34**, 111–118.
Rife, D.C. (1939) 'Handedness of twins.' *Science*, **89**, 178–179.
—— (1940) 'Handedness, with special reference to twins.' *Genetics*, **25**, 178–186.
Risch, N., Pringle, G. (1985) 'Segregation analysis of human hand preference.' *Behavior Genetics*, **15**, 385–400.
Roberts, F.H.H. (1937) 'In the empire of the Aztecs.' *National Geographic Magazine*, **71**, 725–750.
Robinson, R.J. (1987) 'The causes of language disorder: introduction and overview.' *In: Proceedings of the First International Symposium on Specific Speech and Language Disorders in Children*. London: AFASIC. (pp. 1–19)
Rogers, L.J. (1980) 'Lateralization in the avian brain.' *Bird Behavior*, **2**, 1–12.
Rosenberger, P.B., Hier, D.B. (1980) 'Cerebral asymmetry and verbal intellectual deficits.' *Annals of Neurology*, **8**, 300–304.
Rosenbloom, S., Campbell, M., George, A., Krichoff, I., Taleporos, E., Anderson, L., Reuben, R., Korein, J. (1984) 'High resolution CT scanning in infantile autism: a quantitative approach.' *Journal of the American Academy of Child Psychiatry*, **23**, 72–77.
Rosenfield, D.B., Goodglass, H. (1980) 'Dichotic testing of cerebral dominance in stutterers.' *Brain and Language*, **11**, 170–180.
Ross, G., Lipper, E.G., Auld, P.A.M. (1987) 'Hand preference of four-year-old children: its relationship to premature birth and neurodevelopmental outcome.' *Developmental Medicine and Child Neurology*, **29**, 615–622.
Rubens, A.B. (1977) 'Anatomical asymmetries of human cerebral cortex.' *In:* Harnad, S., Doty, R., Goldstein, L., Jaynes, J., Krauthamer, G. (Eds.) *Lateralization in the Nervous System*. New York: Academic Press. (pp. 503–516)
Rudel, R.G., Healey, J., Denckla, M.B. (1984) 'Development of motor co-ordination by normal left-handed children.' *Developmental Medicine and Child Neurology*, **26**, 104–111.
Rumsey, J.M., Berman, K.F., Denckla, M.B., Hamburger, S.D., Kruesi, M.J., Weinberger, D.R.

—— (1987) 'Regional cerebral blood flow in severe developmental dyslexia.' *Archives of Neurology*, **44**, 1144–1150.
—— Dorwart, R., Vermess, M., Denckla, M.B., Kruesi, M.J.P., Rapoport, J.L. (1986) 'Magnetic resonance imaging of brain anatomy in severe developmental dyslexia.' *Archives of Neurology*, **43**, 1045–1046.
Rutter, M. (1969) 'The concept of dyslexia.' *In:* Wolff, P., Mac Keith, R. (Eds.) *Planning for Better Learning. Clinics in Developmental Medicine, No. 33.* London: S.I.M.P. with Heinemann Medical; Philadelphia: Lippincott. (pp. 129–139)
—— Graham, P., Yule, W. (1970a). *A Neuropsychiatric Study in Childhood. Clinics in Developmental Medicine, No. 35/36.* London: S.I.M.P. with Heinemann Medical; Philadelphia: Lippincott.
—— Tizard, J., Whitmore, K. (1970b). *Education, Health and Behaviour.* London: Longman.
Saint-Anne Dargassies, S. (1977) *Neurological Development in the Full-term and Premature Neonate.* Amsterdam: Excerpta Medica.
Salcedo, J.R., Spiegler, B.J., Gibson, E., Magilavy, D.B. (1985) 'The autoimmune disease systemic lupus erythematosus is not associated with left-handedness.' *Cortex*, **21**, 645–647.
Saling, M. (1979) 'Lateral differentiation of the neonatal head turning response: a replication.' *Journal of Genetic Psychology*, **135**, 307–308.
Salk, L. (1973) 'The role of the heartbeat in the relations between mother and infant.' *Scientific American*, **228** (5), 24–29.
Sanders, B., Wilson, J.R., Vandenburg, S.G. (1982) 'Handedness and spatial ability.' *Cortex*, **18**, 79–90.
Satz, P. (1972) 'Pathological left-handedness: an explanatory model.' *Cortex*, **8**, 121–135.
—— (1973) 'Left-handedness and early brain insult: an explanation.' *Neuropsychologia*, **11**, 115–117.
—— (1977) 'Laterality tests: an inferential problem.' *Cortex*, **13**, 208–212.
—— (1979) 'A test of some models of hemispheric speech organization in the left- and right-handed.' *Science*, **203**, 1131–1133.
—— Fletcher, J.M. (1987) 'Left-handedness and dyslexia: an old myth revisited.' *Journal of Pediatric Psychology*, **12**, 291–298.
—— Soper, H.V. (1986) 'Left-handedness, dyslexia, and autoimmune disorder: a critique.' *Journal of Clinical and Experimental Neuropsychology*, **8**, 453–458.
—— Achenbach, K., Pattishall, E., Fennell, E. (1965) 'Order of report, ear asymmetry and handedness in dichotic listening.' *Cortex*, **1**, 377–396.
—— —— Fennell, E. (1967) 'Correlations between assessed manual laterality and predicted speech laterality in a normal population.' *Neuropsychologia*, **5**, 295–310.
—— Baymur, L., van der Vlugt, H. (1979) 'Pathological left-handedness: cross-cultural tests of a model.' *Neuropsychologia*, **17**, 77–81.
—— Yanowitz, J., Wilmore, J. (1984) 'Early brain damage and lateral development.' *In:* Bell, R., Elias, J., Green, R., Harvey, J. (Eds.) *Developmental Psychobiology and Clinical Neuropsychology. Interfaces in Psychology Series, No. 1.* Lubbock, TX: Texas Technical Press. (pp. 87–107)
—— Morris, R., Fletcher, J. (1985a) 'Hypotheses, subtypes, and individual differences in dyslexia: some reflections.' *In:* Gray, D.B., Kavanagh, J.F. (Eds.) *Biobehavioral Measures of Dyslexia.* Parkton, MD: York Press. (pp. 25–40)
—— Orsini, D.L., Saslow, E., Henry, R. (1985b) 'The pathological left-handedness syndrome.' *Brain and Cognition*, **4**, 27–46.
Schachter, S.C., Ransil, B.J., Geschwind, N. (1987) 'Associations of handedness with hair color and learning disabilities.' *Neuropsychologia*, 25, 269–276.
Schaller, G.B. (1963) *The Mountain Gorilla: Ecology and Behavior.* Chicago, IL: Chicago University Press.
Schettel-Neuber, T., O'Reilly, J. (1983) 'Handedness and career choice: another look at supposed left–right differences.' *Perceptual and Motor Skills*, **57**, 391–397.
Schevill, H.S. (1980) 'Tactile learning, handedness and reading disability.' *In:* Herron, J. (Ed.) *The Neuropsychology of Left-handedness.* New York: Academic Press. (pp. 331–351)
Schlichting, C.L. (1982) 'Handedness in Navy and student populations.' *Perceptual and Motor Skills*, **55**, 699–702.
Schonell, F.J. (1941) 'The relation of reading disability to handedness and certain ocular factors. Part II.' *British Journal of Educational Psychology*, **11**, 20–27.
Schur, P.H. (1986) 'Handedness in systemic lupus erythematosus.' *Arthritis and Rheumatism*, **29**, 419–420.
Schwartz, M. (1988) 'Handedness, prenatal stress and pregnancy complications.' *Neuropsychologia*, **26**, 925–929.

Searleman, A., Fugagli, A.K. (1987) 'Suspected autoimmune disorders and left-handedness: evidence from individuals with diabetes, Crohn's disease and ulcerative colitis.' *Neuropsychologia*, **25**, 367–374.
—— Cunningham, T.F., Goodwin, W. (1988) 'Association between familial sinistrality and pathological left-handedness: a comparison of mentally retarded and nonretarded subjects.' *Journal of Clinical and Experimental Neuropsychology*, **10**, 132–138.
—— Porac, C., Coren, S. (1989) 'Relationship between birth order, birth stress, and lateral preferences: a critical review.' *Psychological Bulletin*, **105**, 397–408.
Silva, D.A., Satz, P. (1979) 'Pathological left-handedness: evaluation of a model.' *Brain and Language*, **7**, 8–16.
Simon, C.W. (1948) 'Proactive inhibition as an effect of handedness in mirror drawing.' *Journal of Experimental Psychology*, **38**, 697–707.
Slorach, N., Noehr, B. (1973) 'Dichotic listening in stuttering and dyslalic children.' *Cortex*, **9**, 295–300.
Smart, J.L., Jeffery, C., Richards, B. (1980) 'A retrospective study of the relationship between birth history and handedness at six years.' *Early Human Development*, **4**, 79–88.
Smith, J. (1987) 'Left-handedness: its association with allergic disease.' *Neuropsychologia*, **25**, 665–674.
Smith, L. (1950) 'A study of the laterality characteristics of retarded readers and reading achievers.' *Journal of Experimental Education*, **18**, 321–329.
Sommers, R.K., Moore, W.H., Brady, W., Jackson, P. (1976) 'Performances of articulatory defective, minimal brain dysfunctioning, and normal children on dichotic ear preference, laterality, and fine-motor skills tasks.' *Journal of Special Education*, **10**, 5–14.
Soper, H.V., Satz, P. (1984) 'Pathological left-handedness and ambiguous handedness: a new explanatory model.' *Neuropsychologia*, **22**, 511–515.
—— —— Orsini, D.L., Henry, R.R., Zvi, J.C., Schulman, M. (1986) 'Handedness patterns in autism suggest subtypes.' *Journal of Autism and Developmental Disorders*, **16**, 155–167.
—— —— —— Van Gorp, W.G., Green, M.F. (1987) 'Handedness distribution in a residential population with severe or profound mental retardation.' *American Journal of Mental Deficiency*, **92**, 94–102.
—— Cicchetti, D.V., Satz, P., Light, R., Orsini, D.L. (1988) 'Null hypothesis disrespect in neuropsychology: dangers of alpha and beta errors.' *Journal of Clinical and Experimental Neuropsychology*, **10**, 255–270.
Spadino, E.J. (1941) *Writing and Laterality Characteristics of Stuttering Children.* New York: Teachers College, Columbia University Bureau of Publications.
Sparrow, S.S., Satz, P. (1970) 'Dyslexia, laterality, and neuropsychological development.' *In:* Bakker, D.J., Satz, P. (Eds.) *Specific Reading Disability.* Rotterdam: Rotterdam University Press. (pp. 41–60)
Spennemann, D.R. (1984) 'Handedness data on the European Neolithic.' *Neuropsychologia*, **22**, 613–615.
Springer, S.P., Deutsch, G. (1981) *Left Brain, Right Brain.* San Francisco, CA: W.H. Freeman.
—— Eisenson, J. (1977) 'Hemispheric specialization for speech in language-disordered children.' *Neuropsychologia*, **15**, 287–293.
—— Searleman, A. (1980) 'Left-handedness in twins: implications for the mechanisms underlying cerebral asymmetry of function.' *In:* Herron, J. (Ed.) *Neuropsychology of Left-handedness.* New York: Academic Press. (pp. 139–158)
Steenhuis, R.E., Bryden, M.P. (1989) 'Different dimensions of hand preference that relate to skilled and unskilled activities.' *Cortex*, **25**, 289–304.
Stein, J.F., Fowler, M.S. (1981) 'Visual dyslexia.' *Trends in the Neurological Sciences*, **4**, 77–80.
—— Riddell, P.M., Fowler, M.S. (1986) 'The Dunlop test and reading in primary school children.' *British Journal of Ophthalmology*, **70**, 317–320.
Steingrueber, H.J. (1975) 'Handedness as a function of task complexity.' *Perceptual and Motor Skills*, **40**, 263–266.
Steklis, H.D., Marchant, L.F. (1987) 'Primate handedness: reaching and grasping for straws?' *Behavioral and Brain Sciences*, **10**, 284–286.
Stott, D.H., Moyes, F.A., Henderson, S.E. (1984) *Test of Motor Impairment: Henderson Revision.* New York: Psychological Corporation.
Strauss, E. (1982) 'Manual persistence in infancy.' *Cortex*, **18**, 319–322.
Subirana, A. (1958) 'The prognosis in aphasia in relation to cerebral dominance and handedness.' *Brain*, **81**, 415–425.
—— (1969) 'Handedness and cerebral dominance.' *In:* Vinken, P.J., Bruyn, G.W. (Eds.) *Handbook of*

Clinical Neurology, Vol. 4: Disorders of Speech, Perception and Visual Behaviour. Amsterdam: North Holland. (pp. 248–272)
Sussman, H.M., MacNeilage, P.F. (1975) 'Hemispheric specialization for speech production and perception in stutterers.' *Neuropsychologia*, **13**, 19–26.
Swanson, H.L., Mullen, R.C. (1983) 'Hemispheric specialization in learning disabled readers' recall as a function of age and level of processing.' *Journal of Experimental Child Psychology*, **35**, 457–477.
Tallal, P., Katz, W. (1989) 'Neuropsychological and neuroanatomical studies of developmental language/reading disorders: recent advances.' *In:* von Euler, C., Lundberg, I., Lennerstrand, G. (Eds.) *Brain and Reading.* New York: Stockton Press. (pp. 183–196)
Tambs, K., Magnus, P., Berg, K. (1986) 'Left handedness in twin families: support of an environmental hypothesis.' *Perceptual and Motor Skills*, **63**, 155–170.
Tan, L.E. (1983) 'Handedness in two generations.' *Perceptual and Motor Skills*, **56**, 867–874.
—— (1985) 'Laterality and motor skills in four-year-olds.' *Child Development*, **56**, 119–124.
—— Nettleton, N.C. (1980) 'Left handedness, birth order and birth stress.' *Cortex*, **16**, 363–373.
Tapley, S.M., Bryden, M.P. (1985) 'A group test for the assessment of performance between the hands.' *Neuropsychologia*, **23**, 215–221.
Taylor, D.C. (1969) 'Differential rates of cerebral maturation between sexes and between hemispheres.' *Lancet*, **2**, 140–142.
—— Falconer, M.A., Bruton, C.J., Corsellis, J.A.N. (1971) 'Focal dysplasia of the cerebral cortex in epilepsy.' *Journal of Neurology, Neurosurgery and Psychiatry*, **34**, 369–387.
Teleki, G. (1974) 'Chimpanzee subsistence technology: materials and skills.' *Journal of Human Evolution*, **3**, 575–594.
Teng, E.L., Lee, P., Yang, K., Chang, P.C. (1976) 'Handedness in a Chinese population: biological, social, and pathological factors.' *Science*, **193**, 1148–1150.
Thielgaard, A. (1981) 'The personalities of XYY and XXY men.' *In:* Schmid, W., Nielsen, J. (Eds.) *Human Behavior and Genetics.* Amsterdam: Elsevier. (pp. 75–84)
Tierney, I., Smith, L., Axworthy, D., Ratcliffe, S.G. (1984) 'The McCarthy Scales of Children's Abilities—sex and handedness effects in 128 Scottish five-year-olds.' *British Journal of Educational Psychology*, **54**, 101–105.
Todor, J.I., Doane, T. (1977) 'Handedness classification: preference versus proficiency.' *Perceptual and Motor Skills*, **45**, 1041–1042.
Trankell, A. (1955). 'Aspects of genetics in psychology.' *American Journal of Human Genetics*, **7**, 264–276.
Travis, L.E. (1978) 'The cerebral dominance theory of stuttering: 1931–1978.' *Journal of Speech and Hearing Disorders*, **43**, 278–281.
—— (1986) 'Postscript: emotional factors.' *In:* Shames, G.H., Rubin, H. (Eds.) *Stuttering Then and Now.* Columbus: Charles E. Merrill. (pp. 117–122)
—— Johnson, W. (1934) 'Stuttering and the concept of handedness.' *Psychological Review*, **41**, 534–562.
Trehub, S.E., Corter, C.M., Shosenberg, N. (1983) 'Neonatal reflexes: a search for lateral asymmetries.' *In:* Young, G., Segalowitz, S.J., Corter, C.M., Trehub, S.E. (Eds.) *Manual Specialization and the Developing Brain.* New York: Academic Press. (pp. 257–274)
Tsai, L.Y. (1982) 'Brief report: Handedness in autistic children and their families.' *Journal of Autism and Developmental Disorders*, **12**, 421–423.
—— (1983) 'The relationship of handedness to the cognitive, language, and visuo-spatial skills of autistic patients.' *British Journal of Psychiatry*, **142**, 156–162.
—— Stewart, M.A. (1982) 'Handedness and EEG correlation in autistic children.' *Biological Psychiatry*, **17**, 595–597.
—— Jacoby, C.G., Stewart, M.A., Beisler, J.M. (1982) 'Unfavorable left–right asymmetries of the brain and autism: a question of methodology.' *British Journal of Psychiatry*, **140**, 312–319.
Turkewitz, G. (1977) 'The development of lateral differences in the human infant.' *In:* Harnad, S., Doty, R., Goldstein, L., Jaynes, J., Krauthamer, G. (Eds.) *Lateralization in the Nervous System.* New York: Academic Press. (pp. 251–259)
—— Birch, H. (1971) 'Neurobehavioral organization of the human newborn.' *In:* Hellmuth, J. (Ed.) *Exceptional Infant, 2: Studies in Abnormalities.* New York: Brunner/Mazel. (pp 24–40.)
—— Creighton, S. (1974) 'Changes in lateral differentiation of head posture in the human neonate.' *Developmental Psychobiology*, **8**, 85–89.
—— Gordon, E.W., Birch, H.G. (1965) 'Head turning in the human neonate: spontaneous patterns.' *Journal of Genetic Psychology*, **107**, 143–158.
—— Moreau, T., Birch, H.G. (1968) 'Relation between birth condition and neuro-behavioral

organization in the neonate.' *Pediatric Research*, **2**, 243–249.
Ullman, D.G. (1977) 'Children's lateral preference patterns: frequency and relationships with achievement and intelligence.' *Journal of School Psychology*, 15, 36–43.
Urion, D.K. (1988) 'Nondextrality and autoimmune disorders among the relatives of language-disabled boys.' *Annals of Neurology*, **24**, 267–269.
Vandenberg, S.G., Kuse, A.R. (1978) 'Mental rotations: a group test of three-dimensional spatial visualization.' *Perceptual and Motor Skills*, **47**, 599–604.
Van Dusen, C.R. (1939) 'A laterality study of non-stutterers and stutterers.' *Journal of Speech Disorders*, **4**, 261–265.
Van Riper, C. (1982) *The Nature of Stuttering, 2nd Edn.* Englewood Cliffs, NJ: Prentice Hall.
Van Strien, J.W., Bouma, A., Bakker, D. (1987) 'Birth stress, autoimmune diseases and handedness.' *Journal of Clinical and Experimental Neuropsychology*, **9**, 775–780.
Vargha-Khadem, F., O'Gorman, A.M., Watters, G.V. (1985) 'Aphasia and handedness in relation to hemispheric side, age at injury, and severity of cerebral lesion during childhood.' *Brain*, **108**, 677–696.
Vauclair, J., Fagot, J. (1987) 'Visually guided reaching in adult baboons.' *Behavioral and Brain Sciences*, **10**, 287.
Vellutino, F.R. (1979) *Dyslexia: Theory and Research.* Cambridge, MA: MIT Press.
Verhaegen, P., Ntumba, A. (1964) 'A note on the frequency of left-handedness in African children.' *Journal of Educational Psychology*, **55**, 89–90.
Volpe, B.T., Sidtis, J.J., Gazzaniga, M.S. (1981) 'Can left-handed writing posture predict cerebral language laterality?' *Archives of Neurology*, **38**, 637–638.
Wada, J.A., Rasmussen, T. (1960) 'Intracarotid injection of sodium amytal for the lateralization of cerebral speech dominance.' *Journal of Neurosurgery*, **17**, 266–282.
Warren, J.M. (1977) 'Handedness and cerebral dominance in monkeys.' *In:* Harnad, S., Doty, R., Goldstein, L., Jaynes, J., Krauthamer, G. (Eds.) *Lateralization in the Nervous System.* New York: Academic Press. (pp. 151–172)
—— (1980) 'Handedness and laterality in humans and other animals.' *Physiological Psychology*, **8**, 351–359.
Warrington, E.K., Pratt, R.T.C. (1973) 'Language laterality in left-handers assessed by unilateral E.C.T.' *Neuropsychologia*, **11**, 423–428.
Webster, W.G., Poulos, M. (1987) 'Handedness distributions among adults who stutter.' *Cortex*, **23**, 705–708.
Wilson, M.O., Dolan, L.B. (1931) 'Handedness and ability.' *American Journal of Psychology*, **43**, 261–268.
Witelson, S.F. (1980) 'Neuroanatomical asymmetry in left-handers: a review and implications for functional asymmetry.' *In:* Herron, J. (Ed.) *Neuropsychology of Left-handedness.* New York: Academic Press. (pp. 79–113)
—— (1987) 'Neurobiological aspects of language in children.' *Child Development*, **58**, 653–658.
Wofsy, D. (1984) 'Hormones, handedness, and autoimmunity.' *Immunology Today*, **5**, 169–170.
Wolf, M., Goodglass, H. (1986) 'Dyslexia, dysnomia, and lexical retrieval: a longitudinal investigation.' *Brain and Language*, **28**, 154–168.
Wolfe, L.S. (1941) 'Differential factors in specific reading disability. 1. Laterality of function.' *Journal of Genetic Psychology*, **58**, 45–56.
Wolff, P.H., Cohen, C., Drake, C. (1984) 'Impaired motor timing control in specific reading retardation.' *Neuropsychologia*, **22**, 587–600.
Wolpert, L. (1978) 'The problem of directed left-right asymmetry in development.' *Behavioral and Brain Sciences*, **1**, 324–325.
Woods, R.P., Dodrill, C.B., Ojemann, G.A. (1988) 'Brain injury, handedness and speech lateralization in a series of amobarbital studies.' *Annals of Neurology*, **23**, 510–518.
Wussler, M., Barclay, A. (1970) 'Cerebral dominance, psycholinguistic skills and reading disability.' *Perceptual and Motor Skills*, **31**, 419–425.
Yanowitz, J., Satz, P., Heilman, K. (1981) 'Hemispheric laterality and body asymmetries.' *Science*, **212**, 1418.
Yen, W.M. (1975) 'Independence of hand preference and sex-linked genetic effects on spatial performance.' *Perceptual and Motor Skills*, **41**, 311–318.
Yeni-Komshian, G.H., Benson, D.A. (1976) 'Anatomical study of cerebral asymmetry in the temporal lobe of humans, chimpanzees, and rhesus monkeys.' *Science*, **192**, 387–389.
Yerkes, R.M. (1928) 'The mind of a gorilla. Part III. Memory.' *Comparative Psychology Monographs*, **5** (2), 1–92.

Young, A.W., Lock, A.J., Service, V. (1985) 'Infants' hand preferences for actions or gestures.' *Developmental Neuropsychology*, **1**, 17–27.

Young, G., Segalowitz, S.J., Misek, P., Alp, I.E., Boulet, R. (1983) 'Is early reaching left-handed? Review of manual specialization research.' *In:* Young, G., Segalowitz, S.J. Corter, C.M., Trehub, S.E. (Eds.) *Manual Specialization and the Developing Brain.* New York: Academic Press. (pp. 13–32)

Yule, W. (1973) 'Differential prognosis of reading backwardness and specific reading retardation.' *British Journal of Educational Psychology*, **43**, 244–248.

Yu-Yan, M., Cun-Ren, F., Over, R. (1983) 'Lateral symmetry in duration of grasp by infants.' *Australian Journal of Psychology*, **35**, 81–84.

Zangwill, O.L. (1960) *Cerebral Dominance and its Relation to Psychological Function.* Edinburgh: Oliver & Boyd.

—— (1962) 'Dyslexia in relation to cerebral dominance.' *In:* Money, J. (Ed.) *Reading Disability: Progress and Research Needs in Dyslexia.* Baltimore: Johns Hopkins Press. (pp. 103–113)

Zeman, S.S. (1967) 'A summary of research concerning laterality and reading.' *Journal of the Reading Specialist*, **6**, 116–123.

Zoloth, S.R., Petersen, M.R., Beecher, M.D., Green, S., Marler, P., Moody, D.B., Stebbins, W. (1979) 'Species-specific perceptual processing of vocal sounds by monkeys.' *Science*, **204**, 870–873.

Zurif E.B., Bryden, M.P. (1969) 'Familial handedness and left–right difference in auditory and visual perception.' *Neuropsychologia*, **7**, 179–187.

AUTHOR INDEX

A
Adams, C., 118, 131
Ajersch, M.K., 40
Albrecht, H., 9, 9 *(fig.)*
Alekoumbides, A., 18–19, 19 *(table)*
Ames, L.B., 53, 54, 57, 58, 62
Anderson, E.M., 107
Andrews, G., 142, 143
Annett, M., 17, 36, 37, 40–49 *passim*, 43 *(fig.)*, 44 *(fig.)*, 46 *(table)*, 52, 63, 64, 70, 70 *(fig.)*, 71, 71 *(fig.)*, 73, 74, 78, 80, 80 *(fig.)*, 88, 90, 95, 122, 125 *(table)*, 127–128, 131, 133, 139, 146, 148, 150, 151, 156, 157–160 *passim*, 159 *(table)*, 163, 171 *(fig.)*, 176–178, 177 *(fig.)*, 178 *(table)*
Aram, D.M., 96, 133, 134
Archibald, Y., 27
Ardila, A., 27
Auzias, M., 65, 169
Aylward, E.H., 126

B
Baddeley, A.D., 118
Bailey, R.E., 37 *(fig.)*
Baird, H.W., 57 *(fig.)*
Bakan, P., 90, 92
Bakare, C.G.M., 12, 13
Ballard, P.B., 59, 140, 144
Balow, I.H., 82
Barclay, A., 124 *(table)*
Barnsley, R.H., 81
Barry, R.J., 110, 111, 111 *(table)*
Barton, A.K., 104
Bates, E., 62
Batheja, M., 106
Bathurst, K., 67, 107
Beale, I.L., 2, 11
Beckman, L., 73
Beecher, M.D., 31
Behan, P., 147, 153, 154, 155, 162, 163
Bell, J., 158
Belmont, L., 63, 123
Benbow, C.P., 160–161
Benson, D.A., 30
Benson, R.C., 14 *(fig.)*
Bergström, K., 137
Berker, E.A., 18
Berlin, C.I., 24, 26
Best, C.T., 68, 148, 150
Bettman, J.W., 124 *(table)*
Betz, J.C., 68
Bingley-Wennström, T., 95, 101
Birch, H., 55
Birch, H.G., 63, 123
Bishop, D.V.M., 68, 74, 76 *(fig.)*, 77, 83, 87, 88, 95, 96–100 *passim*, 97 *(figs.)*, 104, 106, 107, 118, 119, 119 *(fig.)*, 121, 122, 123, 125 *(table)*, 128, 130, 131, 133, 134, 136, 137, 139, 142, 150, 154, 155, 160, 164, 167
Blau, A., 11
Blood, G.W., 142–143
Blood, I.M., 142–143
Bloodstein, O., 140, 142, 143
Blumstein, S., 25
Boder, E., 118
Boklage, C.E., 34, 36, 38, 77, 78
Bolin, B.J., 145
Bolser, L.A., 9
Bond, G.L., 124 *(table)*
Boone, D.R., 24
Boucher, J., 110, 111, 111 *(table)*
Brackenridge, C.J., 13
Bradshaw, J.L., 112, 114
Bradshaw-McAnulty, G., 104, 108
Brain, W.R., 27, 145
Briggs, G.G., 95
Broca, P., 12, 148
Broman, M., 176, 177 *(table)*
Broman, S., 104
Brooker, R.J., 8
Bruml, H., 4 *(table)*, 64, 73, 169, 173 *(table)*
Bryant, P., 118
Bryden, M.P., 6, 20 *(table)*, 21, 24, 25, 50 *(fig.)*, 64, 71, 77, 83, 126, 161, 178
Bryngleson, B., 141
Bryson, S., 68
Bunce, L., 22
Burt, C., 3 *(fig.)*, 16, 69, 104, 141
Butterworth, G.E., 53, 118, 150
Buxton, C.E., 4, 79

C
Calnan, M., 88
Caparulo, B.K., 112
Caplan, P.J., 53, 61
Cappa, S.F., 151
Carlson, D.F., 92, 145
Carter-Saltzman, L., 34, 35 *(table)*, 36, 37, 52
Caudrey, D., 24, 26
Chamberlain, H.D., 32–33, 33 *(table)*
Chi, J.G., 148, 150
Childs, B., 118
Christian, J.C., 36
Chrysanthis, K., 142
Chui, H.C., 30
Churchill, J.A., 15, 15 *(table)*
Ciurczak, F.M., 156–157
Clymer, P.E., 82
Cobb, K., 53, 57
Cohen, A.I., 67

Cohen, J., 165
Colbourn, C., 26
Colby, K.M., 110
Coleman, M., 112
Collins, R.L., 35, 50
Comings, B.G., 147
Comings, D.E., 147
Connolly, K., 2, 64
Conrad, K., 19
Corballis, M.C., 2, 11, 50–51, 148
Coren, S., 12, 63, 71, 72, 73, 74, 121, 152
Coryell, J.F., 58, 59, 91
Creighton, S., 56
Critchley, E.A., 78
Critchley, M., 78, 117
Crovitz, H.F., 70, 78, 170 *(fig.)*
Curry, F.K.W., 24, 142

D
Dalby, J.T., 123
Damasio, A.R., 30
Damasio, H., 113
Daniels, E.M., 141
Dart, C., 104, 106
Dawson, G., 114–115, 115 *(fig.)*
Dawson, J.L.M., 12, 13
Delacato, C.H., 122
Denckla, M.B., 173–175, 174–175 *(tables)*, 178
Denenberg, V.H., 31
Dennis, M., 2
Deuel, R.K., 7, 30
Deutsch, G., 23 *(fig.)*, 25 *(fig.)*
Dlugosz, L.J., 138
Doane, T., 71, 74
Doehring, D.G., 124 *(table)*
Dolan, L.B., 104
Douglas, J.W.B., 88, 101, 104, 121, 158
Downey, J.E., 12, 48
Dunlop, D.B., 121
Dunnett, S.C., 9, 9 *(fig.)*
Durding, B., 41 *(fig.)*, 74
Dusek, C.D., 90

E
Edly, L.M., 135
Edmundson, A., 139
Ehrlichman, H., 15, 16, 91
Eisenson, J., 135
Elliott, C.D., 119
Elliott, D., 106, 107
Elliott, J., 64
Ellis, S.J., 35
Elston, R., 73
Eme, R.F., 146
Ettlinger, G., 18
Evans-Pritchard, E.E., 13

F
Fagan, L.B., 140
Fagot, J., 7, 10–11

Falconer, D.S., 46
Falk, D., 30
Falzi, G., 29
Fein, D., 111, 112
Felton, R.H., 125 *(table)*
Fennell, E.B., 26, 63, 84
Finlayson, A.J., 79
Finucci, J.M., 118
Fischer, R.B., 10
Fleminger, J.J., 22
Fletcher, J.M., 82
Flor-Henry, P., 103
Flowers, K., 79
Fog, E., 67
Fog, M., 67
Fowler, M.S., 121
Fox, N., 55, 56
Freedman, R.J., 84
Fruchter, B., 72
Fryns, J.P., 106
Fugagli, A.K., 155
Fukuoka, G., 12
Fundudis, T., 133

G
Gaillard, F., 63
Galaburda, A.M., 28 *(fig.)*, 102–103, 111, 122, 138, 139, 146–162 *passim*, 165
Galliford, D., 92
Gardner, J., 55, 56, 67
Gardner, R.A., 176, 177 *(table)*
Gates, A.I., 124 *(table)*
Geffen, G., 24, 26
Geschwind, N., 16, 26, 27, 28 *(fig.)*, 30, 31, 102–103, 111, 122, 138, 139, 146–162 *passim*, 163
Gesell, A., 53, 54, 57, 58, 62
Gibson, D., 123
Gibson, J.B., 83
Gillberg, C., 98, 110, 111 *(table)*, 112, 113
Gilles, F.H., 38
Gloning, I., 20–21
Gloning, K., 20–21
Goldfield, E.C., 59
Goodall, J., 8, 9
Goodglass, H., 18, 125 *(table)*, 142
Goodwin, R., 16, 16 *(table)*
Gordon, E.C., 57 *(fig.)*
Gordon, H., 36, 104, 145
Gordon, H.W., 150
Gottfried, A.W., 67, 107
Gregory, H.H., 142
Gross, K., 124 *(table)*
Guilford, J.P., 72

H
Haefner, R., 82, 143
Hallgren, B., 117, 123, 124 *(table)*
Hansen, O., 156
Harcherik, D.F., 114

Hardyck, C., 78, 82, 84, 87, 89, 163
Harris, A.J., 123, 124 *(table)*, 128, 129, 163, 169
Harris, L.J., 10, 11, 15, 16, 32, 59, 92, 145
Harris, M., 142
Harshman, R.A., 85–86
Haslam, R.H.A., 126
Hauser, S.L., 112
Hay, D.A., 36, 37, 151
Haynes, W.O., 135
Heffner, H.E., 31
Heffner, R.S., 31
Heilbroner, P.L., 30
Heilman, K.M., 26
Heim, A.W., 84
Hemenway, D., 157
Herrmann, D.J., 84
Hicks, R.A., 34, 90, 104
Hier, D.B., 113, 126, 136
Hildreth, G., 1, 12, 15, 32, 53, 54 *(fig.)*, 64
Hinshelwood, J., 117
Hiscock, M., 24, 68
Holloway, R.L., 30
Homzie, M.J., 140
Hopkins, B., 53, 55, 55 *(fig.)*
House, E., 132, 134
Howie, P.M., 36–37
Hudson, P.T.W., 40
Hull, C.J., 71
Humphrey, D.E., 67
Humphrey, G.K., 67
Humphrey, M.E., 48
Hunter, J.E., 123

I
Impey, L., 118
Ingram, T.T.S., 132, 134
Isaacs, L.D., 135

J
James, A.L., 110, 111 *(table)*
Jennekens-Schinkel, A., 103
Johnson, W., 132, 134, 141, 142
Johnston, R.B., 133, 138, 167
Jones, B., 158
Jones, H.E., 63
Jones, R.K., 143

K
Katz, W., 130, 136
Kaufmann, A.S., 67
Kaufmann, W.E., 153
Keele, S.W., 1
Kemper, T.L., 103
Kertesz, A., 16
Kidd, D., 13
Kilshaw, D., 42, 49, 71 *(fig.)*, 90, 125 *(table)*, 127, 128, 131, 148, 156, 158–160, 159 *(table)*, 163
Kilty, T., 90
Kimura, D., 20, 21, 23, 24, 26

King, A., 141, 142
Kinsbourne, M., 33, 34, 52, 53, 56, 61, 68
Knox, A.W., 24
Komai, J., 12
Konishi, Y., 56, 58
Korczyn, A.D., 54
Kurtzberg, D., 92
Kuse, A.R., 85 *(fig.)*
Kutas, M., 84

L
Lansky, L.M., 158
Lazarus, J.C., 2
Le Gros Clark, W.E., 10
Lehman, R.A.W., 7, 8
LeMay, M., 28 *(fig.)*, 30, 31
Lenneberg, E.H., 67–68
Leviton, A., 90
Levitsky, W., 27, 150
Levy, J., 32, 35, 38–40, 39 *(table)*, 40 *(table)*, 44, 51, 83, 84, 149, 156, 163
Lewis, M., 55, 56
Lewkowicz, D., 92
Liederman, J., 33, 53, 56, 58, 66, 91, 92
Lindsay, J.S., 140
Lippman, H.S., 59
Lishman, W.A., 71
Longoni, A.M., 63
Longstreth, L.E., 34
Lonton, A.P., 107
Lucas, J.A., 105
Luessenhop, A.J., 143
Luria, A.R., 19, 20

M
MacNeilage, P.F., 6, 7, 142, 145
Malmquist, E., 124 *(table)*
Manning, M., 128
Marchant, L.F., 7
Marrion, L., 12
Marshall, J.C., 87
Martin, F., 101
Mascie-Taylor, C.G.N., 84
Mattis, S., 118
McAllister, A.H., 132, 134, 141
McCarthy, D., 63–64, 63 *(fig.)*
McFarland, D., 7 *(fig.)*
McGrory, J., 40
McKeever, W.F., 84
McLean, J.M., 156–157
McManus, I.C., 35, 47–49, 49 *(fig.)*, 64, 69, 72–74, 101, 106
McMeekan, E.R.L., 71
Mebert, C.J., 59, 157
Melekian, B., 54
Meyer, B.C., 141, 142
Michel, G.F., 16, 16 *(table)*, 54, 57–61 *passim*, 60 *(fig.)*, 61 *(table)*, 68, 157
Miller, E., 83
Milner, B., 21–22, 22 *(table)*, 40, 93

Molfese, D.L., 68
Monroe, M., 124 *(table)*
Moran, C.C., 30
Morgan, M.J., 50–51, 148
Morley, M., 132, 133–134
Moscovitch, M., 39
Mullen, R.C., 123

N
Nagylaki, T., 32, 35, 38–40, 39 *(table)*, 44, 51
Naidoo, S., 124 *(table)*, 129
Napier, J., 8
Nass, R., 2
Neale, M.C., 35, 47
Nebes, R.D., 84
Needham, R., 13
Neils, J.R., 133, 134
Netley, C., 152
Nettleton, N.C., 90
Newcombe, F.G., 84
Newman, H.H., 36
Newman, S.P., 121
Noehr, B., 135, 142
Nomura, Y., 115–116
Ntumba, A., 12

O
Oates, D.W., 140
O'Callaghan, E.M., 90
Oldfield, R.C., 70, 78, 172 *(fig.)*
Olsson, B., 115–116
O'Reilly, J., 157
Orsini, D.L., 93
Orsini, L., 63
Orton, S.T., 68, 117, 120, 141, 163, 165
Ounsted, C., 101, 103
Overstreet, R., 15

P
Paine, R.S., 58
Palmer, R.D., 104
Pank, P., 106
Parkison, C., 110
Penfield, W., 101–102
Pennington, B.F., 125 *(table)*, 151, 155
Peters, M., 40, 41 *(fig.)*, 48, 49, 53, 54, 56, 59, 61, 64, 74, 79, 81, 145, 167
Petersen, M.R., 31
Peterson, J.M., 157, 158
Petrie, B.F., 53, 54, 56
Petrinovich, L.F., 87
Pickersgill, M.J., 106
Pipe, M., 106, 108
Porac, C., 12, 15, 71, 72, 73, 74, 79, 106, 121, 147
Porfert, A.R., 142
Poulos, M., 142
Pratt, R.T.C., 22
Prechtl, H.F.R., 56
Pringle, G., 46, 47

Prior, M.R., 112, 113, 114, 124 *(table)*
Provins, K.A., 4, 5 *(fig.)*, 66, 79
Pye-Smith, P.H., 11

Q
Quadfasel, F.A., 18
Quinn, P.T., 142

R
Rabinovitch, M.S., 81
Raczkowski, D., 71
Ramaley, F., 32, 33
Ramsay, D.S., 60, 62
Rasmussen, T., 21, 22 *(table)*, 93
Ratcliff, G., 29, 29 *(fig.)*, 30 *(fig.)*
Records, M.A., 142
Reid, M., 39, 40 *(table)*
Reitan, R.M., 79
Rett, A., 115–116
Rey, M., 22
Rice, T., 63
Richardson, K., 88
Riess, B.F., 10
Rife, D.C., 33, 37, 38, 40
Risch, N., 46, 47
Roberts, F.H.H., 157
Roberts, L., 101, 102
Robinson, R.J., 138
Rogers, L.J., 10
Rosenberger, P.B., 136
Rosenbloom, L., 130
Rosenbloom, S., 113
Rosenfield, D.B., 142
Ross, G., 91
Rovegno, L., 84
Rovet, J., 152
Rubens, A.B., 27
Rudel, R.G., 90, 173
Rumsey, J.M., 126
Rutherford, B., 141
Rutherford, D.R., 24
Rutter, M., 92, 101, 117, 123, 124 *(table)*, 125, 129

S
Saint-Anne Dargassies, S., 56, 57, 58
Salcedo, J.R., 155
Saling, M., 54
Salk, L., 16
Sanders, B., 84, 85, 86
Satz, P., 19, 24, 25, 48, 48 *(fig.)*, 63, 73, 82, 92, 93, 96, 101, 102, 102 *(fig.)*, 105, 107, 112, 118, 123, 136–137, 154
Schachter, S.C., 148, 162, 163
Schaffer, S.P., 7
Schaller, G.B., 8, 10
Schettel-Neuber, T., 157
Schevill, H.S., 124 *(table)*
Schlichting, C.L., 158
Schonell, F.J., 124 *(table)*

Schur, P.H., 155
Schwartz, M., 91
Searleman, A., 35, 36, 90, 108, 155
Servos, P., 64
Silva, D.A., 105
Silva, P.A., 82
Simon, C.W., 78
Slorach, N., 135, 142
Smart, J.L., 90, 91
Smith, J., 155
Smith, L., 124 *(table)*
Smith, L.C., 39
Sommers, R.K., 135
Soper, H.V., 83, 106, 107, 113, 154, 163–164, 166, 173
Spadino, E.J., 141, 142
Spain, B., 107
Sparrow, S.S., 123
Spennemann, D.R., 12
Springer, S.P., 23 *(fig.)*, 25 *(fig.)*, 35, 36, 135
Steenhuis, R.E., 6, 64
Stein, J.F., 121
Steingrueber, H.J., 79
Steklis, H.D., 7
Stewart, M.A., 112
Stott, D.H., 167
Stratton, P., 2
Strauss, E., 61
Subirana, A., 18, 19, 96
Sussman, H.M., 142, 145
Svendsen, P., 113
Swanson, H.L., 123

T
Tallal, P., 130, 136
Tambs, K., 35
Tan, L.E., 67, 78, 90
Tapley, S.M., 50 *(fig.)*, 71, 178
Taylor, D.C., 103, 151
Teleki, G., 8
Teng, E.L., 13, 144
Thielgaard, A., 152
Tierney, I., 67
Todor, J.I., 2, 71, 74
Trankell, A., 33
Travis, L.E., 141, 142
Trehub, S.E., 56
Tsai, L.Y., 111, 112, 113
Turkewitz, G., 16, 32, 54–55, 56, 58, 91
Turner, A., 88

U
Ullman, D.G., 82
Urion, D.K., 155

V
Vandenberg, S.G., 85 *(fig.)*
Van Deventer, A.D., 84
Van Dusen, C.R., 78, 141
Van Dyke, K.A., 84
Van Riper, C., 142, 144
Van Strien, J.W., 147, 155
Vargha-Khadem, F., 92, 93, 137
Vauclair, J., 7, 10–11
Vellutino, F.R., 122, 130
Verhaegen, P., 12
Volpe, B.T., 40

W
Wada, J.A., 21
Warren, J.M., 6, 8, 10
Warrington, E.K., 22
Watts, K.P., 84
Webster, W.G., 142
Wilson, M.O., 104
Witelson, S.F., 29, 68
Wofsy, D., 153
Wolf, M., 125 *(table)*
Wolfe, L.S., 124 *(table)*
Wolff, P.H., 129
Wolpert, L., 51
Woods, R.P., 93
Wussler, M., 124 *(table)*

Y
Yanowitz, J., 96
Yen, W.M., 84
Yeni-Komshian, G.H., 30
Yerkes, R.M., 10
Young, A.W., 59
Young, G., 54
Yule, W., 118
Yu-Yan, M., 53

Z
Zangwill, O.L., 122, 163
Zeman, S.S., 117, 163, 168
Zener, K., 70, 78, 170 *(fig.)*
Zoloth, S.R., 31
Zurif, E.B., 25

SUBJECT INDEX

A
Aborigines, Australian, 12, 13
Adoption studies, 34, 35 *(table)*
Allergies, 154–155
Ambidexterity, 1, 32
  in Klinefelter syndrome, 152
  vs. 'mixed handedness', 69 *(footnote)*
  in primitive man, 11–12
  in stutterers, 141
Ambiguous handedness, 107–108, 166, 169
  in autism, 112–113
  in learning disability, 147
Amytal, *see* Wada test
Animals, laterality in, 6–10, 41
  Chimpanzee, 8–10, 9 *(fig.)*
  Gorilla, 8, 10, 31
  Mice, 50
  Monkey, 6, 7, 8, 30–31
  Parrot, 10
Anomalous dominance, 147
Apgar score, 91
Aphasia, 18–21, 39
  in children, 68, 133
Apraxia, 26
Architecture students, 158
Arm pronation–supination testing, 175
  normative data, 175 *(table)*
Artists, 157–158
Assessment, 69–81, 166–168, 169–178
  see also Inventories
Asymmmetries
  biological, 16–17
  cerebral, 27–31
    in dyslexia, 126–127
    in left-handers, 48
  development, 50–51
  functional, 68
  morphological, *see* Brain, physical asymmetries
  spontaneous vs. elicited, 57–58
  tonic neck reflex, 57 *(fig.)*, 57–59.
Autism, 110–115, 111 *(table)*, 116, 146
Autoimmune disorders, *see* Immune disorders

B
Baseball players, 156–157
Betz cells, 90
Bilateral coordination, 4, 6, 107
  in chimpanzees, 9, 9 *(fig.)*
  in infants, 60–61, 60 *(fig.)*, 61 *(table)*
Birth position, 14 *(fig.)*, 15 *(table)*, 15–16
  See also Intrauterine environment; Perinatal factors
Birth rank, 90

Birthweight, low, 90–91
Brain
  damage
    aphasia following, 18–22, 68
    and autism, 110
    early, 22, 90–100, 107
    in epilepsy, 101–102
  physical asymmetries in, 27–31, 150
    in autism, 113–114
    in dyslexia, 126–127
    in left-handers, 48
    in speech/language disorders, 136
  See also Cerebral lateralization

C
Caesarian delivery, 90
Cerebral lateralization, 18–31, 83, 149–150, 169
  assessment of (Wada test), 21–22
  in autism, 110, 113, 114–115
  and cognitive function, 83
  development of, 67–68
  in dyslexia, 120–121, 125–126
  and learning disabilities, 147
  and neurosurgery, 166, 169
  for speech/language, 17, 23, 38–40, 67–68
    disordered, 131, 135–136
    and right shift theory, 45, 131
  and stuttering, 141, 144
  and writing hand, 72–73
Cerebral palsy, 91, 92–93
Chimpanzee, 8–10, 9 *(fig.)*
Chinese peoples, 12, 36
Clumsiness
  in language-impaired children, 139
  of non-preferred hand, 96–98, 99 *(figs.)*, 137
  in twins, 36
Coeliac disease, 154
Cognitive correlates, *see* Intellectual function; IQ
Comparative studies (human vs. non-human), *see* Animals, laterality in
Congolese children, 12
Consistency of hand use, 4–6, 4 *(table)*, 5 *(fig.)*, 64–66, 65 *(fig.)*, 96, 169, 173 *(table)*
Corpus callosum, 23–24, 66–67, 107
Cricketers, 156
Crohn's disease, 154
Crossed dominance, 121
Cultural pressures, 11–15, 36, 42, 69, 70, 78

D
Darwin, Charles, 11
da Vinci, Leonardo, 157
Definitions, 19 *(footnote)*, 45, 69–81

Development of handedness, 53–68, 54 *(fig.)*
 <6 months, 53–59
 6–18 months, 59–62
 >18 months, 62–68
Diabetes, 155, 156
Dichotic listening, 23 *(fig.)*, 23–26, 40, 46, 68, 93
 and autism, 114
 and dyslexia, 125–126
 and speech/language disorder, 135
 and stuttering, 142
Down syndrome, 106, 107, 108
Drawing, 3–4
 consistency of hand use in, 4 *(table)*, 5 *(fig.)*, 67, 173, 173 *(table)*
Dunlop test, 121
Dyslalia, 133, 135
Dyslexia, 117–129, 150, 152–153, 163
 and diabetes, 156
 and immune disorders, 146
 and left-handedness, 87, 147–148, 162
 and speech/language disorder, 130

E
Ear preference, 73, 78–79
Eating, hand use in, 13
 consistency of, 4 *(table)*, 5 *(fig.)*, 173, 173 *(table)*
Edinburgh Handedness Inventory, 172 *(fig.)*
EEG abnormality, 105 *(table)*, 105–106, 112
Electroconvulsive therapy, 22
Environmental influences, 33, 51
 See also Cultural pressures
Epilepsy, 21, 23, 101–103
 and stuttering, 145
 temporal lobe, 151
Escher, M.C., 157
Eskimos, Alaskan, 12, 13
Ethnicity
 and sex, 85
 See also Cultural pressures
Eye–hand coordination, 59
Eye preference, 73, 78–79, 120, 121
 measurement, 121
 and speech/language disorder, 132–133

F
Familial sinistrality, *see under* Left-handedness
Fencing champions, 156
Fetal maturation in twins, 37–38
Fetal position, 15, 37
 of twins, 37, 37 *(fig.)*
 See also Intrauterine environment
Fine motor control, 59
 See also Precision grip
Finger movements
 normative data, 174 *(table)*
 repetitive, 174
 successive, 175
 tapping, 49, 74
Fisting, in newborns, 53, 57

Foot preference, 48, 73, 78–79, 167
 in left-handers, 48
 and speech/language disorder, 132–133

G
Gender, *see* Sex differences
Genetics, 32–52
 polygenic models, 46–47
 right shift theory (Annett), 40–46, 48–52 *passim*, 64, 83
 and dyslexia, 127–128
 and familial sinistrality, 95
 and language delay, 152
 and learning disabilities, 122
 single gene model (McManus), 47–50
 two gene model (Levy and Nagylaki), 38–40, 39 *(table)*
 and writing hand, 72–73
 See also Left handedness, familial
Geographical variation, 12
Gogo peoples (Tanzania), 13
Gorilla, 8, 10, 31

H
Hand clasping, 73
Handedness questionnaires, *see* Inventories
Hand–face/hand–mouth contacts in newborns, 53, 55 *(fig.)*
Handwriting, *see* Writing
Head-turning in newborns, 16, 33, 53, 54–56, 58–59
 and low Apgar score, 91–92
Hearing, *see* Ear preference
Heel–toe alternating movements, 176
 normative data, 175 *(table)*
Heschl's gyrus, 149
Hormones, 122, 146–162
Hydrocephalus, 107

I
Illiteracy, 27
Immune disorders, 146, 153
Increased randomness hypothesis, 104, 106–107, 112
 and speech/language disorder, 131, 138–139
Infancy, handedness in, *see under* Development of handedness
Inheritance
 genetic, *see* Genetics
 non-genetic biological, 50–51
Instantaneous action, 4, 6
Intellectual function, 82–89
 in twins, 36
 See also IQ; Mental impairment
Interference hypothesis, 2–4
Intrauterine environment, 15, 32, 34, 52, 138
 See also Fetal position
Inventories, 5 *(fig.)*, 70–71, 77–81, 129, 166, 169, 170–172 *(figs.)*
 scores, J-shaped distribution of, 70 *(fig.)*

205

IQ, 82, 84, 91
  and dyslexia, 118

J
Japanese schoolchildren, 12

K
Kafir peoples (South Africa), 13
Klinefelter syndrome, 152
Kwakiutl Indians (British Columbia), 12

L
Landseer, 157
Language function, 18–21, 22–31 *passim*, 38–40, 42, 46 *(table)*, 47
  in autism, 114–115
  and brain damage, 93
  development, 61–62, 68
    in twins, delayed, 38, 151
  and dyslexia, 121–122
  and mental impairment, 105
  See also under Cerebral lateralization
Laterality quotient, 41 *(fig.)*, 70, 71, 77, 81
  J-shaped distribution, 78
Left-handedness
  and allergies, 154
  in architecture students, 158
  and birth rank, 90
  and cerebral palsy, 92
  and coeliac disease, 154
  and Crohn's disease, 154, 155
  cultural attitudes to, 13, 69
  definition of, 45
  and diabetes, 155
  and dyslexia, 87, 124–125 *(table)*
  and early brain damage, 90–100
  and ethnicity, 85
  familial, 83, 95, 98
    and autism, 111
    and mental impairment, 108–109
  and immune disorders, 154–156
  and intellectual function, 83–87
  in Kwakiutl Indians, 12
  and mathematical skill, 148, 158–161, 159 *(table)*
  and mental impairment, 88
  and migraine, 154
  pathological
    and autism, 112
    frequency of, 98–100
    indicators of, 95–98
    and mental impairment, 104–109
    and Rett syndrome, 116
    and speech/language disorder, 131, 136–137
    and stuttering, 144–145
    in twins, 35–36
  and predisposition to produce twin offspring, 38
  and right hemisphere skills, 156–161
  secular increase in, during this century, 45

  and skeletal malformations, 154
  in sports champions, 156–157
  and thyroid disorders, 154
  in twins, 35–38
  and ulcerative colitis, 154, 155
Left hemisphere, *see* Cerebral lateralization

M
Manipulation, in infants, 60 *(fig.)*, 61 *(table)*
  See also Precision grip
Maternal carrying, 16, 17 *(fig.)*, 34
  See also Parental hand preference
Mathematical ability, 82, 148, 158–161, 159 *(table)*
Maturation, brain, 148–149
  delayed, 128–129, 151–152
  as determinant of handedness, 66–67
McCarthy Scales of Children's Abilities, 63 *(fig.)*
Measurement, *see* Assessment
Mental impairment, 88, 104–109
  and stuttering, 140–141
  in twins, 36
Mental rotation task, 84, 85 *(fig.)*
Methodological issues, 163–165
Mice, selective breeding, 50
Michaelangelo, 157
Migraine, 154
Mirror-image movements, 2–4, 6, 66–67, 107
Mirror writing, 2–4, 3 *(fig.)*
  by Leonardo da Vinci, 157
Mixed handedness, 69, 166
  vs. age, 63
  in autism, 112–113
  in children, 68
  in dyslexia, 124–125 *(table)*
  and low birthweight, 91
  See also Ambidexterity
Models, genetic, *see* Genetics
Monkeys, 6, 7, 8, 30–31
Moro reflex, 57
Morphological asymmetry, *see* Brain, physical asymmetries in
Motor coordination tests, 173–176
Motor learning hypothesis, 1–2
Myasthenia gravis, 154

N
Neuromotor maturation, 66–67
Neurosurgery, 166, 169
Newborns, *see* Development of handedness
Nigerian children, 12, 13
North American Indians, 12
Nuer peoples (Upper Nile), 13

P
Parental handedness, 15, 44–45, 52, 91
  and cerebral lateralization, 47
  See also Maternal carrying
Parrots, left-footedness in, 10

206

Pathological left-handedness, *see* Left-handedness, pathological
Pawedness, *see* Animals, laterality in
Peg-moving tasks, 80, 80 *(fig.)*, 176, 177 *(fig.)*
  consistency of hand use, 4
  distribution of L-R difference, 71 *(fig.)*, 74
  and language impairment, 139
  normative data, 177 *(table)*, 178, 178 *(table)*
  procedure, 176, 177–178
  relative hand skill, 42, 176–178
  sex differences, 146
Perinatal factors, 32, 55–56, 90–92
  in twins, 35–36
Petalia, 27–29
Pincer grip, 80, 107
Planum temporale, 27, 28 *(fig.)*, 148, 149, 150
Pointing, 4 *(fig.)*, 62
Population vs. clinical studies, 87–89
Power grip, 6, 7 *(fig.)*
Practice, 66, 80, 81
Precision
  grip, 6, 7 *(fig.)*
    development of, 59–60
  in hand use, 4, 6
Primitive man, 11–12, 27
Proficiency, 74–78, 75–76 *(figs.)*
Psychosis, 103
Publication bias, 163–164

Q
Questionnaires, *see* Inventories

R
Random hand preference, *see* Increased randomness hypothesis
Reading ability, 82, 117
Relative hand skill, 42–44, 43 *(fig.)*
  measurement of, 71–80, 176–178
Restricted growth, 96
Rett syndrome, 115–116
Right-handedness
  enforced, 140–141
    See also Cultural pressures
  population bias to, 10–17
Right hemisphere, *see* Cerebral lateralization; Speech, right hemisphere
Right shift theory, *see under* Genetics

S
School attainment, 82
Self-report, 77–78
Sex differences, 67
  in brain maturation, 150–151
  and conformity, 15
  and ethnicity, 85
  and learning disabilities, 146–148
  in mathematical skill, 160
  in responses to questionnaire items, 77–78
Sinistrality, *see* Left-handedness
Skeletal malformations, 154

Social learning, *see* Cultural pressures
Spatial ability, *see* Visuospatial ability
Specific reading retardation, *see* Dyslexia
Speech
  bilateral, 19, 22, 47
  and dyslexia, 120, 122, 125–127
  and speech/language disorders, 131
  right hemisphere, 19, 22–23, 25, 30, 37
Speech/language function, 23, 130–139
  See also under Cerebral lateralization
Speed of hand in manual activity, 4
Spelling, 82, 103
Spina bifida, 107
Sports, 156–157
Spurious associations with small samples, 164–165
Square tracing task, 96–98, 97 *(figs.)*, 167
Stability of hand preference, 4–6, 4 *(table)*, 5 *(fig.)*, 64–66, 65 *(fig.)*, 77, 166
  measures of, 169, 173 *(table)*
Stepping reflex, 54, 56
Strength, 4
Stuttering, 140–145, 146, 147
Swaddling, 56
Sylvian arch asymmetry, 27–30, 28–29 *(figs.)*
  distribution vs. language lateralization, 30 *(fig.)*
Symbolic vs. non-symbolic actions, in infancy, 62

T
Tapping task, *see* Finger tapping
Temne peoples (Sierra Leone), 12, 13
Temporal lobes, 27, 31
  epilepsy, 151
Tennis professionals, 156
Test of Motor Impairment (Henderson Revision), 167
Testosterone, fetal, 146, 150–151, 153, 162
Thymus, development of, 153
Thyroid disorders, 154
Tonic neck reflex, asymmetrical, 57 *(fig.)*, 57–59
Toradja peoples (Indonesia), 13
Tourette syndrome, 147
Twins
  fetal position, 37, 37 *(fig.)*
  fetofetal transfusion syndrome, 36
  left-handedness in, 151
    pathological, 35–36
  mirror-imaging, 36–37
  MZ, discordant handedness in, 44
  studies, 34–38

U
Ulcerative colitis, 154
Unclean activities, 13
Upper limb reduction defects, 138

V
Verbal ability, 82–86

Visual cortex, neural pathways, 25 *(fig.)*
Visual half-field test of lateralization, 24
Visuospatial ability, 82–86, 150, 156–158

W

Wada test, 21–22, 166
   studies using, 23, 29, 40, 46, 47, 93, 143
Warfare shield theory, 11
Wernicke's area, 149, 150
Writing, 2, 3, 78, 80
   and activities performed with non-preferred hand, 48, 48 *(fig.)*
   consistency of hand use in, 5 *(fig.)*
   cultural pressures, 13, 69, 78
   definition of handedness by, 69, 72–73
   posture, inverted, 39–40, 40 *(fig.)*
   See also Mirror writing

X

XXY and XYY syndromes, 152